AF600478

IMAGINING THE BRITISH ATLANTIC AFTER THE AMERICAN REVOLUTION

THE UCLA CLARK MEMORIAL LIBRARY SERIES

General Editor: Barbara Fuchs

IMAGINING THE BRITISH ATLANTIC AFTER THE AMERICAN REVOLUTION

Edited by Michael Meranze and Saree Makdisi

Published by the University of Toronto Press in association with the UCLA Center for Seventeenth- and Eighteenth-Century Studies and the William Andrews Clark Memorial Library

www.utppublishing.com

ISBN 978-1-4426-5069-5

Library and Archives Canada Cataloguing in Publication

Imagining the British Atlantic after the American revolution / edited by Michael Meranze and Saree Makdisi.

(UCLA Clark Memorial Library series)
Includes bibliographical references and index.
ISBN 978-1-4426-5069-5 (bound)

1. British – Atlantic Ocean Region – Historiography. 2. Revolutions – Atlantic Ocean Region – Historiography. 3. Great Britain – Colonies – Atlantic Ocean Region – Historiography. 4. Atlantic Ocean Region – Historiography. I. Meranze, Michael, editor II. Makdisi, Saree, editor III. Series: UCLA Clark Memorial Library series

E18.82.143.2015 970 C2015-904154-6

This book has been published with the help of a grant from the UCLA Center for Seventeenth- and Eighteenth-Century Studies.

University of Toronto Press acknowledges the financial assistance to its publishing program of the Canada Council for the Arts and the Ontario Arts Council, an agency of the Government of Ontario.

Canada Council for the Arts
Conseil des Arts du Canada

ONTARIO ARTS COUNCIL
CONSEIL DES ARTS DE L'ONTARIO
an Ontario government agency
un organisme du gouvernement de l'Ontario

Funded by the Government of Canada
Financé par le gouvernement du Canada

For
Helen and Theodore
and
Christina, Samir, and Maissa

Contents

Illustrations

Acknowledgments

Any volume that emerges from the UCLA Center for Seventeenth- and Eighteenth-Century Studies is truly a collective effort, and this one is no exception. We would like to thank Peter Reill, then Director of the Center, for his support, encouragement, and participation in the year-long program that we organized; as anyone knows who attended Clark Library conferences when Peter was Director, he displayed a unique grace and curiosity about the ideas and issues discussed and debated. We would also like to thank the Center and Clark staff; especially Candis Snoddy, Fritze Rodic, Suzanne Tatian, and Camie Howard-Rock, who made the conferences actually function. The conferences and this volume were immeasurably improved by everyone who participated in them – both the presenters and the audiences. At the University of Toronto Press, Richard Ratzlaff, John St James, and Wayne Herrington were models of patience and professionalism. Cailey Hall did a wonderful job with the index. Finally we want to thank Helen Deutsch and Christina Makdisi for putting up with this project for as long as they did.

IMAGINING THE BRITISH ATLANTIC AFTER THE AMERICAN REVOLUTION

introduction

Division, Renewal, and Repetition – Imagining the British Atlantic after the American Revolution

MICHAEL MERANZE AND SAREE MAKDISI

The imperial conflicts, wars, and revolutions that cascaded across the Atlantic basin between 1750 and 1820 seemed to turn the world upside down, overturning both some of the anciens régimes in Europe and newly established governments in the Americas. From the backwoods of Virginia to the "untilled field" of Peterloo, decades of violence were unleashed, in which politicians and thinkers – radicals and conservatives alike – sought either to altogether re-imagine the basis of society or to reform the existing order to preserve the traditional structures of life and authority more or less intact: neither wholly new, nor wholly obsolete, as Edmund Burke would put it in *Reflections on the Revolution in France.* The great battles over transformation traversed the realms of politics, of thought, and of war. Few areas of the world were spared the implications of these struggles – if not in the immediate moment then in the ongoing aftermath, as the legacies of the British Empire, the French Revolution, and the expansion of the United States would trouble the world's nations for two centuries, and as various enslaved or colonized populations and nations, around the world, sought to resist first European and then American encroachment.

Most of the populations of the northern Atlantic were affected intermittently in this period. They sought to survive the upheavals, to maintain their own hopes and dreams, or, at least, to prevent the more powerful from reducing their lives even further. But the transformations of the late eighteenth and early nineteenth centuries were not limited to the realms of high politics and bloody warfare. They also reached deep into everyday life and beyond: into culture and law, the imagination and the psyche, into literature, art, science, and medicine as well as the intimate realms of sexuality, consciousness, and the body. As they reached deep into everyday life they also extended outward into the ways that people experienced history and imagined the course of time; indeed, these revolutions – and the reactions to them – transformed the ways that men and women imagined the place of their moment in the larger and longer sweep of their own civilization and the civilizations of others.

Even within this general picture, however, questions remain. One, perhaps most fundamental, question concerns the sites of truly revolutionary activity. Before 1989 and the collapse of the Soviet system and its dependencies, at least, Western political thinking had long structured itself around the apparent dichotomy between the American and French Revolutions. According to this traditional understanding, the American Revolution was a revolution mostly in name: its fundamental impulses were simply to ratify already existing social and political conditions and to secure a modern national independence. It was only in France, according to this logic, that true revolutionary activity occurred – either as heroic step into the future (for the Left) or catastrophic madness (for the Right). R.R. Palmer's great *Age of the Democratic Revolution* (1959), which emphasized the connections between the American and French revolutionary movements, did so in terms of an accelerating and deepening logic. For Eric Hobsbawm in his *Age of Revolution* (1962), although the American Revolution might have functioned as a trigger, it was only in the core of political France and industrializing England that true revolutionary transformation occurred; the Atlantic was an afterthought. If we extended our vision to Saint-Domingue, following the lead of C.L.R. James's classic *The Black Jacobins* (1938), the contrast between French and American Revolutions seemed even sharper – after all, the logic of the French Revolution led to the only successful slave revolution in history, while that of the American Revolution led to the consolidation of what remained for many decades the modern world's most powerful slave regime. Indeed, if David Brion Davis's *The Problem of Slavery in the Age of Revolution* (1975) established the centrality of the Age of Revolution for the history of slavery and the problem of slavery for the Age of Revolution, his emphasis lay on wars, the French Revolution, and the dynamics of British industrial capital – not the American Revolution itself.[1]

More recently, however, scholars have reopened the question of the transformative nature of the American Revolution. Whether in the form of Gordon Wood's reclamation of a Whig view of the Revolution or Gary Nash's arguments for the power of contestation within the Revolution, the transformative power of the Revolution for American society has been powerfully reasserted.[2] At the same time, younger historians and literary critics have begun remapping the social and cultural reimaginings that grew up out of war and nation building. In their hands, it has been clear that the Revolution itself was simultaneously a transatlantic phenomenon and a powerful, often violent, struggle to redefine society and the individual.[3] It is no longer possible to view the American Revolution as the consensual and polite alternative to the French.

Although to some extent downplaying older claims for the world importance of American Revolutionary ideology,[4] scholars have also shown how the American upheaval fundamentally altered the systems of Atlantic states and empires in concrete and ongoing ways. Christopher Brown, for one, has demonstrated that the loss of the North American colonies changed the political context within Britain itself. In his particular accounting, the defeat in the American War opened up space for the spread of anti-slave-trade politics as one effort to reclaim a moral basis for Empire lost in the revolutionary struggle. Emma Christopher and Maya Jasanoff have demonstrated that the American Revolution created new forms of diaspora – both loyalist and criminal – that reshaped both the Atlantic and Pacific worlds while promoting new visions of Empire in their wake. Alan Taylor and David Waldstreicher have, albeit from different vantage points, taken up the notion that the American Revolution was crucial for consolidating slavery in the wake of the Somerset Case of 1772. Or, to take a more legal and state-centred approach, Eliga Gould has shown that the emergence of the United States forced a reconfiguration of the transatlantic system of nation states.[5]

To this we must add the proliferation of recent scholarship on the revolutionary tensions that bubbled and simmered and frothed though – for all the efforts of activists like Thomas Spence or Colonel Despard or the ill-fated Cato Street conspirators – they didn't quite take off on a large scale in England and its immediate colonial dependencies (above all Ireland); but nevertheless had huge significance for the ways that the British state articulated its strategies of surveillance, repression, and containment, both locally and globally. The actual revolutions of America and France played an enormous role in the almost-revolution of Britain, at both a political level and an aesthetic one. Take, for example, the role in all three events of transatlantic commuters like Joel Barlow or Tom Paine, who wrote pamphlets like *Common Sense* and *The American Crisis* to help propel the American Revolution, and *Rights of Man* to draw on the inspiration of the French Revolution to inspire his native England on its own revolutionary course, only to end up sentenced to death in absentia by the government in Westminster, and in a Paris jail cell following the overthrow of his allies the Girondins at the hands of Robespierre.

Consider also the immense though often underrated role of America, not to mention France, in British Romanticism, from Samuel Coleridge's and Robert Southey's letters on Pantisocracy – a utopian scheme whose American setting was absolutely vital to its conception – to such works as William Blake's *America: A Prophecy* and Thomas Campbell's *Gertrude of Wyoming*, which is set, like Southey's and Coleridge's fleeting images of Pantisocracy, on the banks of the Susquehanna River. All these works opened the space for British writers and artists to re-interrogate their own revolutionary moment through a reconsideration or reimagination of the American and French Revolutions, and indeed to participate in the reimagining of the space that was seen to either tie together or separate Europe from America. It was not a coincidence that Blake would, in *America*, fill in this void, conceiving of the Atlantic precisely as a space capable both of linking and of separating peoples and continents to and from one another, in his depiction of "those vast shady hills between America & Albions shore; / Now barr'd out by the Atlantic sea: call'd Atlantean hills," from the tops of which "you may pass to the Golden world."[6] Revolution is, in this depiction anyway, tied to a golden world that one can access from the visionary hills only when the Atlantic itself lines up in the right kind of way.

And indeed, much of the newer scholarship to which we are here referring has developed from the growing attention to the specificity of the Atlantic context. To be sure, the Atlantic was present in the earlier scholarship touched on above. But there the Atlantic functioned primarily as a given background or horizon. In recent decades, by contrast, the Atlantic has emerged as a governing frame through which to address the interconnections that bound together individuals around the modern Atlantic basin. To take only two of the more forceful manifestos of the new Atlantic history, David Armitage's "Three Concepts of Atlantic History" and Susan Manning and Francis D. Cogliano's "The Enlightenment and the Atlantic," the Atlantic has been proposed as an essential (if multiple) context for understanding late eighteenth- and early nineteenth-century history and culture.[7] We should be careful not to overlook the differences in these two essays. Armitage's essay is prescription masquerading as description: he offers a typology of approaches to the study of the British Atlantic while arguing for an emphasis on what he calls a "cis-Atlantic" approach. He argues that this latter perspective – in which the Atlantic is approached through local or regional sites and where the scholar's project is to map and understand the interconnections between those local sites and the larger Atlantic basin – will prove the most productive for understanding the early modern British Atlantic. Manning and Cogliano, by contrast, are concerned to deconstruct notions of a unitary and abstract Enlightenment without falling into the opposite trap of multiple self-contained regional or national Enlightenments. From their perspective, the Atlantic stands in for the larger process of communication, transfer, and travel that made Enlightenment discourses possible. Indeed, central to their vision is the notion of the Atlantic world as a self-conscious system of motion and the idea that scholars need to track both the self-consciousness and the motion to understand how people produced a shared Atlantic world. But despite the differences between these two approaches, they each propose some notion of the Atlantic as a unifying – dare we say master – category in which to place their more detailed inquiries.

There is no question that the Atlantic turn has been productive for the study of the modern world in general and the Age of Revolution in particular. On the broader early modern canvas, scholars have opened new vistas in the history of slavery,[8] colonization,[9] the circulation of ideas and cultures, and religious beliefs,[10] and the evolution of imperial structures.[11] On the Revolutionary age itself, the works we discussed earlier alone indicate that range of new ideas generated out of the intersection between Revolutionary and Atlantic histories.

Viewed in the light of recent work in both Atlantic and Revolutionary history, it becomes difficult to identify exactly where the "revolutionary British Atlantic" was. One way to approach the problem, of course, is as a story of Revolution and Reaction. In this telling, a systematic reshaping of the Atlantic world occurred as first the North Americans, then the French, and finally the enslaved of Saint-Domingue engaged in democratic and anti-colonial revolutions, revolutions that – in turn – helped transform and modernize the British empire as it struggled to maintain its position of hegemony and contain the new national, democratic orders. From this perspective, late eighteenth- and early nineteenth-century British Atlantic history can be conceptualized as a set of relays: first of dramatically intensifying revolution crisscrossing the Atlantic and then of a massive and remarkable reassertion of power by the imperial and counter-revolutionary British state. From its moment of apparent defeat in 1783 to its triumph in the wake of Waterloo in 1815, the British imperium not only defeated and contained the revolutionary drives of the North Atlantic (though it could not, to be sure, prevent the assertion of nationalism in Latin America), but also severely crippled domestic resistance to empire, all the while transferring the heart of its empire from West to East. In all, the period's simultaneous assertion of democratic nationalism and imperial outreach set the foundations for the modern period of world history that follows.

The essays in the present volume take up the intersection between these Atlantic and Revolutionary historiographies, albeit with a critical twist. Although the essays engage with the larger narrative of Revolution and Reaction, far more central is the notion of dispersion. That is to say, the essays document a period of Atlantic upheaval that was always internally contested and locally inflected, in which the contradictions of moment and the social order of particular spaces assumed greater urgency than the larger narratives that might have enveloped them. The papers establish that it mattered deeply where you were (and where you came from) during the period; although moving across space could reshape a person, an experience, a text in profound ways. In addition, it not only mattered profoundly *when* you were but how you understood the past that led to your present. The chapters in the volume are not micro-histories in any conventional sense, but they trace histories of fragments, indeed of the process of fragmentation itself. The Revolutionary British Atlantic became many times and many spaces. The chapters point to efforts – cross-crossing the Atlantic and moving backwards and forwards in time – of those who lived in the British Atlantic to imagine what a "Revolutionary" British Atlantic might be. It is not just scholars today but contemporaries of the great period of Revolution who sought to understand a revolutionary British Atlantic of the imagination.

This dual emphasis on dispersal and imagination, we think, suggests an important caution for the history of the Revolutionary British Atlantic. Importantly, the essays stress the importance of temporality and periodization for our understanding. Throughout the volume we are reminded that although there were ways in which the Atlantic made possible new forms of connection and communication, the American Revolution is one singular moment in an ongoing process of division. Insofar as we treat the Atlantic as a coherent and shared realm (even allowing for class and racial struggles), we overlook the fact that there was never a single Atlantic that was not marked spatially and temporally by various forms of splitting and fragmentation. In this way, one implicit support for the essays in the volume can be found in the work of Benedict Anderson, whose *Imagined Communities*, while it did set the stage for notions of the unifying force of print, also told the stories of nations withdrawing from larger imperial (and Atlantic) structures. The Atlantic we present cannot be a master figure. Instead, it can only stand in for the gap between coherence and division, renewal and repetition.

It is no coincidence, then, that our volume opens with an essay that tracks the themes of coherence, renewal, and repetition as it traces the transatlantic journey of a set of anatomical paintings – a journey that captures part of the nature of the material movement of objects and people across revolutionary time and space. The immediate concern of Aris Sarafianos's essay is a group of anatomical paintings produced in London but shipped to Pennsylvania, drawn by the Dutch artist Jan van Rymsdyk under the auspices of the Scottish anatomist William Hunter, organized within a popular anatomical theatre but displayed in a borderlands hospital. As even this brief description of the international dimensions of anatomic painting reveals, the story that Sarafianos tells is imperial and diasporic to the core. Its condition of possibility was the cosmopolitan scope of London and the existence of British imperial connections and commercial connections in a revolutionary age – and, of course, the extension of those networks and connections across the Revolutionary Atlantic.

Yet within these more general imperial conditions were more specific and local sets of connections: especially concerning the interplay between science and religious affiliation. As Sarafianos reveals, the paintings moved according to a particular Quaker axis (tying together London and Philadelphia) and were enmeshed in a colonial project of scientific legitimacy. The anatomical paintings sent by Hunter enabled Philadelphia's elite to demonstrate their participation within the Atlantic world of letters while providing needed material support for their charitable institutions. As material objects, the paintings functioned to produce both actual capital and cultural capital for colonial Quakers and Philadelphia's merchant and professional classes: a striking example of the kind of self-legitimizing Anglophilia that other scholars (including Elisa Tamarkin and Leonard Tennenhouse) have traced in post-colonial America.[12]

Yet alongside this contextualization within a specific moment of metropolitan/colonial relations within medicine, there is a second layer to the story recounted by Sarafianos. As he argues, the anatomical paintings were more than realistic; they were painted to provide a form of access to the body that exceeded both the conventional notions of representation and also the visual impact of actual bodies. They were drawn to produce certain affective intensities, to make death more than life and to create an investment in the possibility of medical knowledge and representation. Jan van Rymsdyk's paintings helped make possible – in their joining together of the aesthetic and the scientific – the very conditions of possibility of bringing the body under the regulation of biopolitics. By imagining more than we can see, van Rymsdyk enabled a new structure to spread through the exchange patterns of the medical and imperial ancien régime.

For Sarafianos, then, the Age of Revolution exceeded its particular moment by reconfiguring the aesthetics (and the imagination) of past and future. While aesthetic agents remained profoundly embedded in, and responsive to, their particular situations, their creations broke free of their situations by deploying and redeploying techniques and figures that made time a set of open possibilities. In anticipating a form of hyperrealism, van Rymsdyk and his followers and circles made of the revolutionary crises multiple spaces of the imagination.

If the intersection of aesthetics, revolutionary crisis, and the body served to disrupt and reconfigure time, the revolutionary British Atlantic also fractured space. Interestingly, as the essays of Sarah Crabtree and Catherine O'Donnell make clear, the problem of the nation took on particular intensity in relationship to religious belief and form. The development of national churches that had been initiated with the Reformation moved into a new phase when they became reconfigured in the light of the emergent democratic nation states that asserted their collective identities in the Age of Revolution. The complex post-Reformation efforts to manage the relationship of the particular and the universal within religious life placed religious groups in powerful tension with the demands of the nation.

As Sarah Crabtree demonstrates in the case of the Quakers, the age of national revolutions posed particular challenges and opportunities for religious groups that aimed at a truly cosmopolitan spirituality. In this context, the Society of Friends was particularly vulnerable. As Crabtree shows, there was a remarkable uniformity in anti-Quaker polemic – from the Seven Years' War through the struggles of the French Revolution; critics of the Friends were convinced of their disloyalty to the nation. That they could be accused of disloyalty to the same empire in the middle of the century and then accused – by Tom Paine – of excessive loyalty to the British Empire in the 1770s and 1780s only points to their paradoxical situation.

Or perhaps their situation was not so paradoxical after all. For the Quakers remained revolutionaries of a particular stripe. Contrary to conventional views of Quakerism as having lost its original, and deeply insurgent, character by the late seventeenth century, Crabtree's Quakers reach back to their seventeenth-century revolutionary heritage and challenge the closing down of the open space of the trans-national. As she shows in a telling series of individual stories, Quakers in the Revolutionary Age refused the demands of national militarization while seeking their own nation in an imagined Zion of the spirit. Maintaining ties across national and imperial boundaries, insisting on their right to refuse the demands of war, and embracing the egalitarianism of revolutionary politics, many Quakers stood as living examples that democracy need not be national – and that equality need not be asserted through the barrel of a gun. Because they constructed an actual trans-national community of shared belief and social ties, and not simply a cosmopolitanism of the imaginary citizen of the world, newly consolidating nation states treated them with great suspicion and sought to place bounds on their "Zion."

For the Catholic Church in the United States, as Catherine O'Donnell reveals, the problems were different. If the Quakers sought to refuse the nation in the name of a trans-national and revolutionary cosmopolitanism that in some sense sought to preserve a radical potential that the nation-state form would necessarily foreclose, the leaders of the American Catholic Church aimed to create a sufficiently national form for a universal faith. Focusing her attention on two reformers on either side of the revolutionary Atlantic (Joseph Berington in England and John Carroll in the United States), O'Donnell is able to demonstrate that the relationship of church and state provoked both deep reflection and institutional creativity within Catholicism in the face of revolutionary upheaval. Attempting to create a flourishing Catholic Church in cultures noted for their deep and visceral anti-Catholicism meant insisting on a particularistic form of universalism. Paradoxically, this challenge meant that Berington and Carroll had to define their visions against Rome as well as against London or Philadelphia. On both sides of the Anglo-Atlantic divide, then, Catholic leaders insisted on the separation of church and state and made the Catholic Church a reforming force in the relationship of the temporal and the spiritual.

Ironically, Berington and Carroll both assumed the mantle of Reason in order to reinforce the position of their faith. Contending against the traditional Anglo Protestant prejudice against Catholics as subordinate drones of Rome, the English and American Catholic Churches had to contend that they deserved to be treated as rational interlocutors of shared national history. Although maintaining ties to Rome and its tradition of wisdom and faith, Berington and Carroll, as O'Donnell skilfully shows, insisted that their Church was the true source of tolerance and an example of the continued richness of diverse religious traditions. Their authority, to put it another way, depended – in an age of increasing secular state power – precisely on their renunciation of the power of the state.

Viewed from the perspective of minority universalisms then, the relationship of the spiritual and the temporal in the Age of Revolution reveals less an expanding liberty of conscience than repressive national and revolutionary efforts to contain the religious imagination in the name of national loyalty. But as both the Catholic Church in England and America and the Society of Friends across the Revolutionary Atlantic demonstrated, the nation state could not, in fact, shut its borders to alternative imagined communities. The hope for a new age did not lie only within the democratic nation.

The Revolutionary British Atlantic, then, witnessed the articulation – in art, science, and religion – of new ways to imagine communities both within, and against, the stream of revolutionary struggle. But it also was the site of efforts to rethink social relationships on the terrain of everyday life. Interestingly, as the essays of Andrew Cayton, Jenna Gibbs, and Iain McCalman make clear, the effort to reimagine social life, although it was taking place in conjunction with a large transatlantic logic, repeatedly pushed actors back onto the local. If Catholics and Quakers sought to protect their particular universalisms against the demands of the nation state, efforts at universal emancipation could not help but be entwined with the particular limits of specific locales.

This theme of the local limits for generalized emancipation emerges most clearly in the essays of Cayton and Gibbs. Each (Cayton looking at the triangular relationship of William Godwin, Gilbert Imlay, and Mary Wollstonecraft, Gibbs at the trans-Atlantic career of Susanna Rowson) highlights both the centrality of personal commitments and the continuing, in some ways intensifying, power of place in the possible success of revolutionary projects. It mattered deeply where you were in the Revolutionary Atlantic when you pursued your dreams of freedom; the zone of upheaval was not an undifferentiated space.

In his retelling of the infamous love triangle of Godwin, Imlay, and Wollstonecraft, Cayton eschews both the almost customary moralizing condemnation of Imlay and the effort to see Godwin and Wollstonecraft as indicators or bearers of an emerging Romanticism. Instead, he resituates the three in a crisis of the professional and literary classes of both England and the United States and shows how their personal passions intersected with real and imagined social topographies to create an explosive mix. Imlay, for example, was too deeply rooted – both emotionally and imaginatively – in the American borderlands to effectively operate in the much more complex world of London literati, while Wollstonecraft took for granted a shared English set of mannered habits and understandings that Imlay simply did not possess. Godwin, finally, worked out a relationship of equality with Wollstonecraft due to their shared marginality and caution; but even he threw it away in his rendering of Wollstonecraft after her death – driving a stake into the heart of her literary reputation by allowing his own grief to lose sight of social conventions.

In Cayton's hands, the clash of conventions as much as the clash of personalities determined the outcome of their triangular effort to reimagine the family. But the larger meaning of his analysis points to the ultimately multiple nature of the Revolutionary Atlantic. London, after all, was the great cosmopolis of the age. If it was possible for the many Atlantics to come together it would have been there, mixed in with other global spaces from Africa and the Indian Ocean to the Mediterranean and south and east Asia, which also found due expression in London. But even there, and even among radicals committed to a project of the refashioning of society in terms of new enlightened norms, no such convergence was possible. Instead, proximity in the great city only threw into clearer relief the extreme differences that marked individuals by nation, place, and local setting.

Another way of grasping that multiplicity, as Jenna Gibbs demonstrates, is through the example of the individual career. As Gibbs reveals through her careful reconstruction of Rowson's essential transatlantic identity, it was possible for Rowson to transplant a formative experience (the England of the 1780s) in another space and moment (the United States of the 1790s) by moving with the currents of revolutionary change. Rowson's engagement with the British anti-slavery campaign consistently marked her literary and political activities no matter where she was or what other issues (e.g., feminism) she took up.

Just as importantly, however, Rowson's projects were constrained by the specific times and places she encountered. Gibbs, in one of her more provocative revisionist claims, takes on critics of Rowson's 1793 *Slaves of Algiers* (who accuse her of "using" the issue of slavery to make a point about the condition of women at home) by arguing that it is only by recognizing both Rowson's ongoing commitment to anti-slavery and the particular crises of 1790s Philadelphia that we can truly understand the play and its productions. For despite (or because of) its place as the capital of a revolutionary nation, Philadelphia was also the site of a large population of refugees from the Revolution in Saint-Domingue. Rowson may have toned down her explicit critique of slavery and the slave trade in the play, but in doing so she was able to link the problem of enslavement to a wide range of social issues at the limits of her audience's tolerance.

Put another way, if Cayton demonstrates the difficulty of provincials being thrown together in a cosmopolitan city, Gibbs shows the challenges facing the cosmopolitan reformer in a provincial – even if revolutionary – city. There was no single Atlantic through which ideas and social movements flowed. Nor was this problem limited to the relationship between England and the new United States.

As Iain McCalman's discussion of Philippe de Loutherbourg establishes, the tension among fantasy, emancipation, and place did not need the distance of the Atlantic to create tumultuous reaction. McCalman takes up the complex history of de Loutherbourg's efforts to dabble in mesmerism, the mystical arts, and libertinism and his opening of a clinic for the poor that promised to bring health to a greater portion of London's population to shed light on a crucial problem of the Revolutionary British Atlantic: the place of enthusiasm in politics and thought. The story he tells – of de Loutherbourg's descent from noted artistic figure to social outcast and then his redemption through an alliance with conservative political forces seeking to control 1790s England and finally his resurrection as a romantic artist – demonstrates the fracturing of politics and imagination that helped fuel Romanticism itself.

But this story is not yet another version of the conventional tale (first spawned by Robert Southey to excuse his older and conservative self from his youthful revolutionary indiscretion) of a Romantic poet emerging from the foolishness of youth, that is, a story about growing wisdom in politics leading to great art, but the reverse. For what McCalman indicates is that in the case of de Loutherbourg, enthusiasm did not disappear so much as go underground or get redirected, rechannelled; faced with the demands to conform in public, de Loutherbourg drew his mystical and religious impulses into his art. If his movement from France to England placed him at a certain sort of political risk at the end of the eighteenth century, his intellectual movement reveals another divided set of spaces, those of the categories (art, politics, intellect) through which we understand the relationship of culture and society.

We are left, then, with a paradoxical outcome. As Cayton, Gibbs, and McCalman reveal in different ways, the intensifying transatlantic revolutionary process deepened the importance of specific locales and places (either of society or the imagination). We may speak of the Revolutionary British Atlantic, but only if we recognize that the revolutions of the Atlantic splintered and fragmented the Atlantic basin in new ways – and that that fragmentation of the basin continues to the present.

Yet it still is possible to read all these essays in terms of some fundamental transition to a new space. If the revolutionary impulses disrupted and divided the organization of space and time, surely they established a threshold, a new world of possibilities (both exciting and dangerous) that marked the advent of modernity. The last three essays in the collection – by Anthony Galluzzo, Randall McGowen, and Edward Gray – all call that assurance into question. For the last theme of this volume (and it was one of the great surprises of the original conferences) is the development within the revolutionary period of nostalgia for the lost promise of revolutionary breakthrough. This nostalgia was not a conservative one; it haunted the desire for progress from within.

For Hugh Henry Brackenridge, as Anthony Galluzzo carefully reveals, the revolutionary republic represented a series of missed opportunities. Taking as his object Brackenridge's two-part *American Chivalry*, Galluzzo takes us from the first part's picaresque effort to capture the boisterous possibilities of an emergent democratic public sphere to the second part's incessant moralizing in the name of law. But rather than accepting the conventional critical judgment of the decline of Brackenridge's literary creativity from the transatlantic 1790s energy of part 1 to the relative restraint of part 2 (which Brackenridge started in 1804), Galluzzo reconfigures the trajectory undertaken by the two parts of the novel in terms of Brackenridge's own complicated relationship to the events of those politically formative decades. As Galluzzo argues, Brackenridge himself embodied the shifts undertaken in America's post-Revolutionary settlement, and in particular the then still unresolved tensions between the advocates of a more expansively democratic and egalitarian vision and, on the other hand, those who sought to restrain the nation's democratic energies – positions that Brackenridge himself moved along in the decades during which he composed *American Chivalry*. Galluzzo reads these tensions in the often strained relationship between the imaginative and dialogical and indeed polyvocal mode of part 1, with all its democratic impulses, and the increasingly monovocal part 2, with its frequent digressions and departures from the narrative. Galluzzo's intervention is to see, where others have seen aesthetic weakness, the novel's greatest innovation in its formal representation of the tensions between different interests and the ideological fiction of a disinterested public sphere. Brackenridge's work, as Galluzzo argues, "is *simultaneously* a powerful representation of the idealized early American public sphere and its failure to meet the ostensibly disinterested and formally egalitarian claims that underwrote it at the moment of its inception."

What makes this situation – and Galluzzo's reading – so striking is that Brackenridge's sense of the failed republican experiment took place within the framework normally taken as the establishment of a more democratic polity – the triumph of Jefferson and the Democratic-Republicans in 1800. For Brackenridge, the triumph of the Jeffersonians was no triumph at all; instead it was a defeat – through the force of numbers – of the actual intelligence needed for a democratic polity. On Galluzzo's reading, Brackenridge fell back on the law (he was a judge after all) as a way of sustaining order in a society that had missed its mark: instead of the rational republic, there was a triumph of political passions of the majority. Although Brackenridge was no Federalist, he was also committed to the notion of a cosmopolitan elite; faced with the triumph of the multitude, he fell back on the rule of the law and its expertise. But he did so from within a republican framework and with a continued longing for the vibrant public sphere he had imagined in the 1790s.

A related dynamic emerges in Randall McGowen's study of penal reform in 1810s England. As McGowen demonstrates, penal reform was one of the surprising success stories for reformers in the years of reaction after the wars with Revolutionary France. Focusing on Samuel Romilly's bill to revitalize the Penitentiary Act of 1779, McGowen reveals a rich series of debates over what a prison should be. Although Romilly's initial effort failed, it set in motion a process that led not only to the construction of a national penitentiary but to the establishment of the parameters of the meaning of imprisonment that lasts till this day. In papers, journals, and Parliament, debates over the appropriate form of the prison engaged the public sphere across the decade and into the 1820s. At a moment when reform in so many domains seemed shut down in England, the question of the prison moved forward.

Yet, strikingly, this massive institutionalization was fundamentally backward-looking. Romilly's initial effort aimed to reclaim the legacy of the 1779 act, not to break new ground. Rapidly – in both liberal and conservative circles – the debate about prisons became self-referential. In a development that has been repeated right up to the present day, prison discourse insisted that the only answer to the problems of imprisonment was the prison itself. As McGowen demonstrates, prison reformers recreated the prison over and over again; looking backwards as they moved into the future. The contingencies of English politics in the 1810s – the alliances between Whigs and Evangelicals, the shifting relationships between more conventional political groupings – served to help the prison take centre stage in the system of punishment at precisely the point when its more utopian trappings were limited. The prison succeeded because it was capable of transforming political and class struggles into technical problems. Romilly's return to the past was achieved through a technical march into the future.

The paradoxical creation of the old out of the bowels of the new assumes its sharpest form in the last essay of the volume: Edward Gray's exploration of the rediscovery of Pitcairn Island in the nineteenth century. As Gray reveals, Pitcairn – the island partially populated by the surviving mutineers from the H.M.S. *Bounty* and their Tahitian wives – captivated the reading public in both the United States and Britain across the nineteenth century from the era of the Wars of the French Revolution to the emergence of the United States as a world power. When Europeans returned to Pitcairn in the nineteenth century they found a society governed by a single patriarch (appropriately named John Adams), who ruled in a seemingly Christian way over his extended mixed-race family.

Pitcairn figured in the Anglo-American imagination as a site of social and political meaning, a testing ground for theories and fantasies of population growth, governance, patriarchal power, and utopian happiness. Yet, crucially, these stories of island paradise left out one central fact: the way that Pitcairn was intertwined with the history of Atlantic slavery. As Gray shows, slavery shaped the history of Pitcairn: it was, after all, in order to provide a cheap source of food for West Indian slaves that the *Bounty* had embarked on its journey into the Pacific, it was the reduction of the native population to slaves that shaped the society of the early settlement, and it was a slave rebellion that ultimately gave rise to the seeming paradise that Europeans rediscovered in the nineteenth century. To make the matter even more complex and disturbing for Anglo-America, the paradise they found was the offshoot of the brutal suppression of a slave rebellion, albeit one in which the victors died out. Adams, the last surviving member of the initial rebellion against Bly, was simply a survivor of a series of revolts. He reinstated a biblical patriarchy on the ruins of a slave system that was the logical outgrowth of Britain's desire to protect its Atlantic slave societies. That this desire took practical shape in the midst of the age of Atlantic Revolution only heightened the irony of the old forms reinvented from the efforts of the new.

The essays in this volume, then, chart not only the dynamic upheavals of the British Revolutionary Atlantic, but their inner blockages as well. No single story emerges from these essays; instead what we get are a renewed attention to and awareness of the multiplicity of the era and of its antinomies. In important ways, it is these multiplicities and antinomies that continue to haunt us the most: the revolutionary British Atlantic did not mark the political or social threshold of modernity in a clean way as a neat, even cauterized, cutting off of the past, but the articulation of a series of inconsistent and often contradictory projects. The real lesson that emerges from this collection, in fact, is that revolutionary modernity itself did not mark nearly as clean a break with the past and its social, political, and economic forms (religion, pre-nationalist forms of universalism, patriarchy, slavery, enthusiasm, irrationalism, and so on – as well as the literary and aesthetic forms associated with them in various ways), but rather represented the extension of those forms into a post-revolutionary future, and in many cases their surprising rehabilitation and recuperation. The collection allows us to see all the more clearly that modernity involves the re-articulation of what are often marked as pre-modern forms, putting them to new uses within a new context. Perhaps this helps us more adequately understand the extent to which the conventional sense we have inherited of a homogeneous Revolutionary Atlantic age marked by a clean break from the past really ought to yield now to a sense of heterogeneous fractured and multiple times and spaces mixing together revolution and reaction in unexpected ways. It also instituted a drive towards an understanding of its own failures; a self-reflection upon the moment of Revolution to which these essays make a signal contribution.

NOTES

1 R.R. Palmer, *The Age of the Democratic Revolution: A Political History of Europe and America, 1760–1800* (Princeton, NJ, 1959–64); Eric Hobsbawm, *The Age of Revolution, 1789–1848* (New York, 1962); C.L.R. James, *The Black Jacobins: Toussaint Louverture and the San Domingo Revolution* (London, 1938); David Brion Davis, *The Problem of Slavery in the Age of Revolution, 1776–1823* (Ithaca, 1975).

2 Gordon Wood, *The Radicalism of the American Revolution* (New York, 1992); Gary B. Nash, *The Unknown American Revolution: The Unruly Birth of Democracy and the Struggle to Create America* (New York, 2005).

3 Catherine O'Donnell Kaplan, *Men of Letters in the Early Republic: Cultivating Forms of Citizenship* (Chapel Hill, NC, 2007); Sarah Knott, *Sensibility and the American Revolution* (Chapel Hill, NC, 2009); Michael A. McDonnell, *The Politics of War: Race, Class, and Conflict in Revolutionary Virginia* (Chapel Hill, NC, 2007), Eric Slauter, *The State as a Work of Art: The Cultural Origins of the Constitution* (Chicago, 2009).

4 However, see David Armitage's *The Declaration of Independence: A Global History* (Cambridge, MA, 2007).

5 Christopher L. Brown, *Moral Capital: Foundations of British Abolitionism* (Chapel Hill, NC, 2006); Emma Christopher, *A Merciless Place: The Fate of Britain's Convicts after the American Revolution* (New York, 2011); Maya Jasanoff, *Liberty's Exiles: American Loyalists in the Revolutionary World* (New York, 2011); Alan Taylor, *The Internal Enemy: Slavery and War in Virginia, 1772–1832* (New York, 2013) ; David Waldstreicher, *Slavery's Constitution: From Revolution to Ratification* (New York, 2009); Eliga Gould, *Among the Powers of the Earth: The American Revolution and the Making of a New World Empire* (Cambridge, MA, 2012).

6 William Blake, *America: A Prophecy* (Lambeth, 1793), plate 12.

7 David Armitage, "Three Concepts of Atlantic History," in Armitage and Michael J. Braddick, eds, *The British Atlantic World: 1500–1800* (New York, 2002), 11–27; Susan Manning and Francis D. Cogliano, "Introduction: The Enlightenment and the Atlantic," in Manning and Cogliano, eds, *The Atlantic Enlightenment* (Aldershot, 2008), 1–18.

8 Ira Berlin, *Many Thousands Gone: The First Two Centuries of Slavery in North America* (Cambridge, MA, 1988) John K. Thornton, *Africa and Africans in the Making of the Atlantic World: 1400–1800* (New York, 1988); Stephanie Smallwood, *Saltwater Slavery: A Middle Passage from Africa to American Diaspora* (Cambridge, MA, 1988); Marcus Rediker, *The Slave Ship: A Human History* (New York, 2007); Vincent Brown, *The Reaper's Garden: Death and Power in the World of Atlantic Slavery* (Cambridge, MA, 2008).

9 Christopher L. Tomlins, *Freedom Bound: Law, Labor, and Civic Identity in Colonizing English America, 1580–1865* (New York, 2010): Daniel Richter, *Before the Revolution: America's Ancient Pasts* (Cambridge, MA, 2011).

10 Joseph Roach, *Cities of the Dead: Circum-Atlantic Performance* (New York, 1996); Jon Sensbach, *Rebecca's Revival: Creating Black Christianity in the Atlantic World* (Cambridge, MA, 2005).

11 J.H. Elliot: *Empires of the Atlantic World: Britain and Spain in America, 1492–1830* (New Haven, 2006).

12 Elisa Tamarkin, *Anglophilia: Deference, Devotion, and Antebellum America* (Chicago, 2008): Leonard Tennenhouse, *The Importance of Feeling English: American Literature and the British Diaspora, 1750–1850* (Princeton, NJ, 2007).

chapter one

Transoceanic Spectacles of Dissection: London's Anatomical Art in Eighteenth-Century Pennsylvania

ARIS SARAFIANOS

To the memory of John V. Pickstone, historian of medicine, generous friend and mentor

The transfer of John Fothergill's collection of anatomical drawings by the Dutch artist Jan van Rymsdyk (fl. 1750–88) to Philadelphia's Pennsylvania Hospital is a remarkable, yet largely unexplored affair. Rymsdyk, considered by many to be the "father of British medical illustration,"[1] was intimately connected with almost every ambitious anatomical program in eighteenth-century London, but his work still awaits comprehensive evaluation. His pictures for anatomists such as William Hunter (1718–83), the unquestioned leader of British anatomy, and Charles Nicholas Jenty (fl. 1745–67), an obscure migrant from France, adopted a veracity of style and subject matter that throws into relief a broad range of innovative practices in art, science, and society throughout the long eighteenth century.

This chapter explores the joint British and American history of Rymsdyk's Pennsylvania pictures, identifying the role of educational mobility, professional migration, and social networking in the production and transatlantic dissemination of scientific knowledge. As I will show in the first two parts of the chapter, the long journey of these pictures to Pennsylvania came as a result of failed careers and professional difficulties specific to the organization of anatomy in Britain. From their position in the sequestered premises of an immigrant anatomist struggling for upward mobility, these pictures were, in Pennsylvania, catapulted to the centre of public attention in a civic institution. Better still, they were placed firmly within an aspirational framework acquiring a vital new role in the first introduction of anatomy courses in British America, in the official organization of institutionalized medical education, and the promotion of closer links between anatomy, medicine and art.

The remaining part of the chapter looks into the uneven fate of Rymsdyk's anatomical pictures in Britain and North America. It argues that the precise identification of the visual rhetoric or pictorial style of these pictures offers a unique, yet largely neglected point of entry into the social, professional, and cultural ramifications that mark their production and reception. It also shows that the patent realness of Rymsdyk's work for Jenty and Hunter renegotiated a series of key concerns recurrent in contemporary aesthetic criticism, art theory, and the fine arts. This analysis demonstrates that such pictures participated in the defining conflict of the time between established styles of polite abstraction and scrupulously particularized renditions of perceptual data procured directly from the anatomical working place. Moreover, in adopting such a minutely detailed approach to the shocking imagery of the dissection theatre, Rymsdyk's works also raised thorny questions about the representation of violence and other extreme phenomena in art. In this way, Rymsdyk's anatomical realism engaged with highly divisive discussions about the role of the sublime in art and in nature – a topic extensively theorized by contemporaries. At the same time, Rymsdyk employed his sensational techniques of amplified imitation in order to carve for himself a heterodox niche in the rising market of anatomical illustration. Yet, as I would emphasize, this did not rule out a series of internal variations in Rymsdyk's style: compared to his later realism for William Hunter, the much softer style of his early works in Pennsylvania expresses a smart, yet ultimately aborted compromise, which was the result of intense social manoeuvring on the part of fringe professionals like Rymsdyk and his patron Jenty.

The approach adopted in this chapter, therefore, differs from usual interpretations in that it tests the limits of utilitarian perspectives on scientific illustration as well as facile aestheticizations of the genre by historians of science. The new "life" of these works in Pennsylvania was not a simple matter of conveying useful scientific information, nor does it express any vaguely defined fondness for "beauty," virtuosity, or bravura. Still more crucially, this essay argues that anatomical realism cannot be explained, as it has been suggested, through the convenient assumption that it was imported in the art world from the thriving cultures of science. Apart from the fact that such an assumption falsely implies an essential divide between natural philosophy and art practices in this period, a closer look at the historical record shows that scientific cultures were as fiercely divided as the art world itself over the issue of abstract versus realist representations of anatomy.

Rymsdyk's anatomical pictures have a much broader framework of reference, which is best retrieved once they are situated back into the nuanced debates of the period concerning visual culture, art practices, and styles most appropriate for the representation of the human figure as a whole. The discrepancies between the two lives of the collection in Britain and North America, and the diverging histories of anatomy and pictorial realism they encompass, offer a good place to start unravelling this intricate story.

London's "Taste for Anatomy" and Imperial Mobility

William Hunter's role was pivotal in introducing anatomy into British America through his many disciples who came to London to obtain a formal medical education unavailable at home. Above all, commentators praised Hunter's vital role in the establishment of a new "taste for anatomy," or rather "a rage for it," as one of his most distinguished students from North America, John C. Warren, put it.[2] This "rage" for anatomy was predicated upon visual effects and practices: in the hands of William Hunter and his brother John, the anatomical theatre became the site of numerous techniques that sought to enlarge the domain of the senses, including public dissections, preparations, injections, drawings, casts, atlases, and even paintings.[3] London offered unique advantages for the cultivation of anatomy, and Hunter had an acute sense of the city's excellent prospects in promoting a type of anatomical inquiry with an international reach. London was, for Hunter, the ideal place for the establishment of an "effectual school for this art," precisely because London was "a large city" and anatomy "requires a great number and a regular succession of bodies, which cannot be procured in smaller towns."[4] Anatomy was a manifestly metropolitan phenomenon, but, in Hunter's eyes, the great metropolis seemed more like a great necropolis for the benefit of the living. Characteristically, Hunter considered the plentiful supply of corpses of recently deceased pregnant women as yet another example of the various "fortunate circumstances" prevailing in a "great metropolis" like London.[5]

In spite of Hunter's complacency, the London necropolis in which anatomists operated was a dislocated fabric, where commercial interests had already corroded social ties and, in the case of these pregnant women, ties of parenthood and kinship. As Ruth Richardson's work has amply shown, the traffic of bodies was a commerce in the ungrieved dead – men and women from the lower classes – for the benefit of ambitious medical men and their affluent clienteles.[6] As such, this commerce in cadavers extended post-mortem the invidious social splits that brought the bodies of paupers to their miserable end on the surgeon's dissection table – not without, it is true, public resistance and frequent riots, based on a shared sense of apprehension and disapproval of dissection.[7] Yet, such practices persisted, and they recycled the dead back into an economy of health, knowledge, and professional respectability.[8] As bizarre compensation for the insensibility of cutting up corpses, surgeons and anatomists were particularly keen to engage in art practices and alternative notions of sensibility.

Furthermore, this lively commerce put London at the centre of a wave of mobilized diasporas of skilled individuals in the field of anatomy, attracting not just anatomical students from British America and elsewhere, but also anatomical specialists from other parts of the world in pursuit of professional aggrandizement. The new anatomy was largely a product of international migration: Hunter came from Scotland, Rymsdyk from Holland, and Jenty from Paris, all during the 1740s, aspiring to capitalize upon the lucrative opportunities offered by the centre of a growing empire, London. In turn, this immigrant anatomy, shaped partly by practitioners coming from outside of the empire, would soon "migrate" from the centre to the outer reaches of the empire's expanses. Encouraged by the presence of colonial students in his theatre, Hunter became well aware that his local success in reforming the teaching of anatomy in the capital would eventually "be felt, for some time, by the sick and the lame in all parts of the British Empire."[9] Better still, this rapid dissemination of medical ideas in the empire followed the trajectories of real people. In 1762, William Shippen, Hunter's disciple, went back to Philadelphia, bringing with him Rymsdyk's pictures as added ammunition for his plans to set up the first systematic course of anatomical lectures and public dissections in America, modelled on the example of his London tutor. And it was the same year that an imperial expedition brought Jenty to Portugal as surgeon's mate to the British expeditionary force, thus forcing him to sell his entire medical collection before he left: drawings, ideas, and men of science followed routes of mobility opened by the empire's global operations.

Rymsdyk's career in the history of British anatomy epitomizes the critical role of this specialized diaspora in the field of image making. His collaboration with Jenty reveals two aspirant individuals, keenly aware of the unique opportunities to be found in a city like London during 1740s. Above all, the city combined a fast-growing entrepreneurial medical environment with little competition from local anatomists and artists. Rymsdyk, in particular, had been attracted to Britain by the emerging markets for precise visual description. Jenty indeed was not exaggerating when he emphasized the extreme "difficulty" of finding "a proper artist in anatomical painting; such it is well known, being very scarce, especially in England." Coming from Holland, that powerhouse of verisimilitude, Rymsdyk, on his part, must have felt very confident, very quickly, in Britain's embryonic art world. Jenty frequently expressed his admiration for the fine quality of Rymsdyk's art,[10] calling the original works for his book "pictures" (which were "painted"), and not drawings (or illustrations). Likewise, for Jenty, Rymsdyk was an "artist" or a "painter," and not a simple draughtsman or a "mechanic."[11]

Jenty, for his part, had settled down in London in the mid-1740s, working as a practical anatomist and private lecturer with his own anatomical school. Jenty published various ambitious books, but only those in which Rymsdyk's anatomical pictures were used are so emphatically focused on. The *Essay on the Demonstration of the Human Structure* (1757) contained four anatomical tables in mezzotint, while *The Demonstrations of a Pregnant Uterus of a Woman at her Full Time* (1757) had six tables in the same medium (figure 1.1). Both of these publications share the same unusual format designed to highlight the importance of the visual supplement of broadsheets: the text, published in separate octavo editions, was limited to a brief introduction and an even briefer section of epigrammatic table descriptions. Such ventures verify Lorraine Daston and Peter Galison's remark that similar images cannot be appropriately described as "illustrations," since their content and uses far exceed the parameters set by the accompanying texts. Rather, such usage of visual culture allows images to assume an autonomous and powerful role, becoming "the alpha and omega" of the scientific projects in which they appear.[12] Accordingly, the French surgeon insisted on the independence of Rymsdyk's broadsheets, which, as he underlined, were designed to be hung up on walls or exhibited in the lecture theatre, or, even, folded or rolled like maps for "the greater conveniency of transporting [them] abroad."[13] Such innovations were well adjusted to the increased mobility of students and aspiring professionals, who "after completing their anatomical studies, are obliged either to retire into the country, or go abroad" without "the cost and inconveniency of transporting [their hefty folios] from place to place."[14] From this point of view, Jenty's images exemplify most perfectly Bruno Latour's notion of "immutable mobiles," optically stabilized but physically portable images, which Latour placed at the very centre of the international scientific revolution in the eighteenth century.[15] And the success of Jenty's illustrations in achieving their mission also explains the extreme rarity today: according to their maker's stated wishes, these images were extensively used as precious accompaniments of travelling students, and were thus dispersed, damaged or lost in the process.

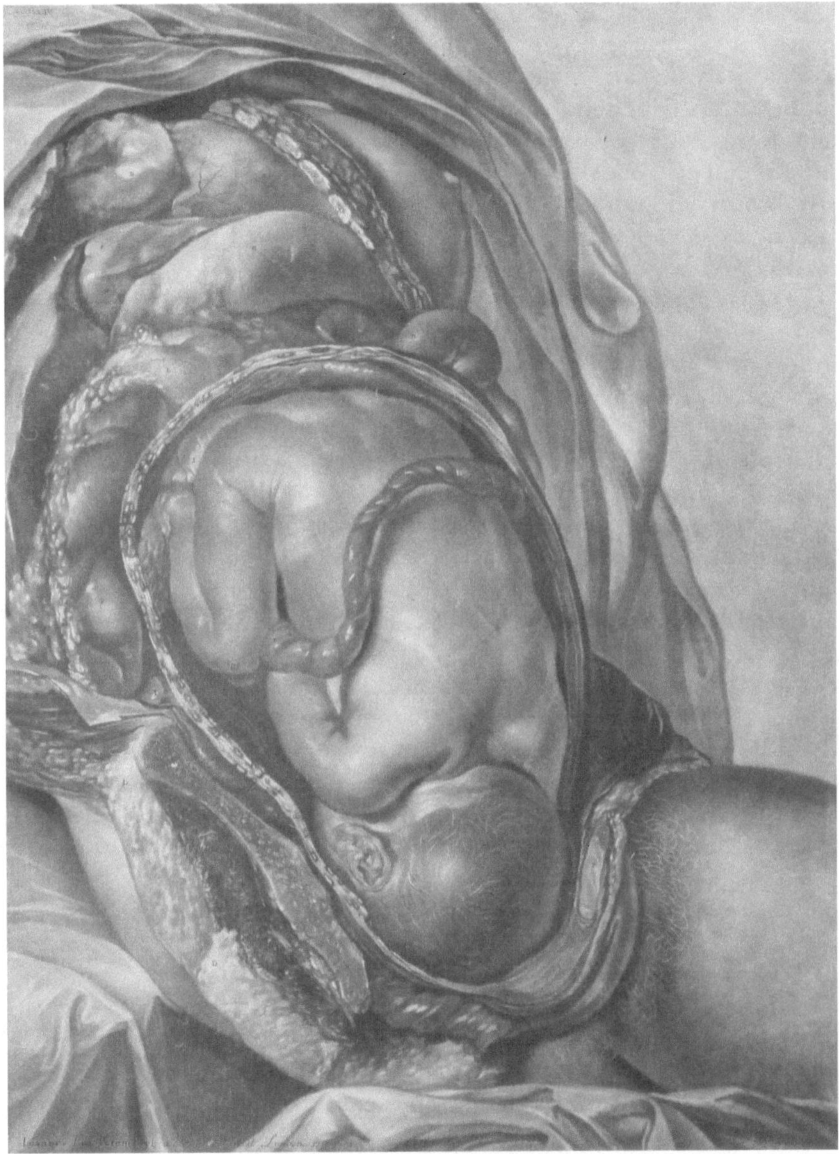

Figure 1.1 Jan Van Rymsdyk, Table 4, Jenty's *Demonstrations of a Pregnant Uterus*, mezzotint, 1757

Jenty's pragmatic focus on the mobility and practicality of his publications did not, however, distract him from the pursuit of artistic quality as well as stylistic and technical originality. Aware of Jenty's chosen technique of reproduction – mezzotint – as well as his projected but eventually aborted plan to use colour in the final plates, Rymsdyk employed in his original crayons a powerful colour scheme – a festive combination of red, brown, and yellow against sky-blue abstract backgrounds (figure 1.2 and figure 1.3) – which is absent from the monochromatic pink glow he used in his sets of original drawings for Hunter and William Smellie, kept today at Glasgow University Library. Yet, for all of Jenty's hard work and pioneering contributions, his professional fate in the exclusive and unforgiving markets of London medicine would be disappointing. After he suddenly left London for Portugal, in 1762, we know little about him apart from the fact that he would ultimately relocate in Madrid, where he probably lectured on anatomy and surgery, publishing in Spanish a book on amputations. His collection of Rymsdyk's paintings was finally acquired by John Fothergill, the famous Quaker physician, medical writer, and naturalist. Fothergill was a good friend of Hunter, with whom he collaborated on many occasions, not least in the formation of an informal but prolific medical society, as well as in attempts to make the system of government at the Royal College of Physicians more flexible. In his will, Fothergill left his extensive botanical collections of shells and corals to Hunter, while it was through him that Fothergill had first encountered Rymsdyk's as well as Jenty's work. Jenty may have designed the format of his illustrated publications so that they would be easily transported, but, ironically enough, it was Rymsdyk's originals that, through Fothergill's intervention, travelled the greatest distance – all the way to Pennsylvania.

The American Life of Rymsdyk's Pictures: The Arrival of a Gift

In 1762, immediately after the purchase of Jenty's collection of casts and drawings, Fothergill made arrangements to send it to Philadelphia as a gift to the newly founded Pennsylvania Hospital. The collection consisted of eighteen works, sixteen of which were painted by Rymsdyk and one by Thomas Burgess, three casts in Paris plaster representing pregnant women at different stages of dissection (figure 1.5), and two skeletons – of an adult and a foetus. These objects record dissections related to two separate branches of anatomical knowledge: the general anatomy of the human body and the anatomy of the pregnant uterus. Apart from the original drawings which were used for both of Jenty's publications, the collection also includes some bold, path-breaking, and, in many ways, superior examples of anatomical art, which were, in the end, not chosen for publication (figure 1.4).

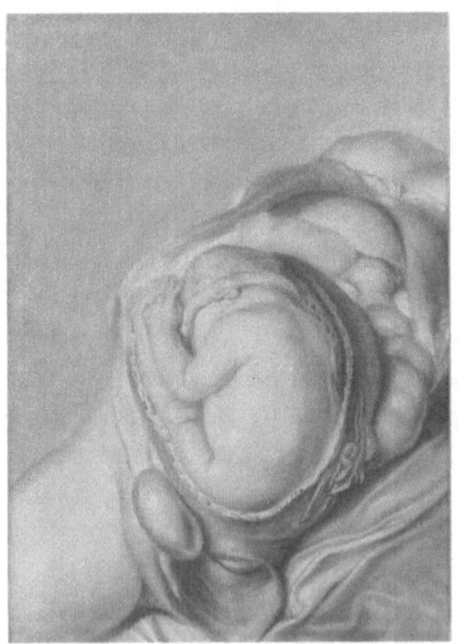

Figure 1.2 Jan Van Rymsdyk, Original drawing for table 3 of Jenty's *Demonstrations of a Pregnant Uterus*, c. 1755–7, Fothergill Collection, Pennsylvania Hospital

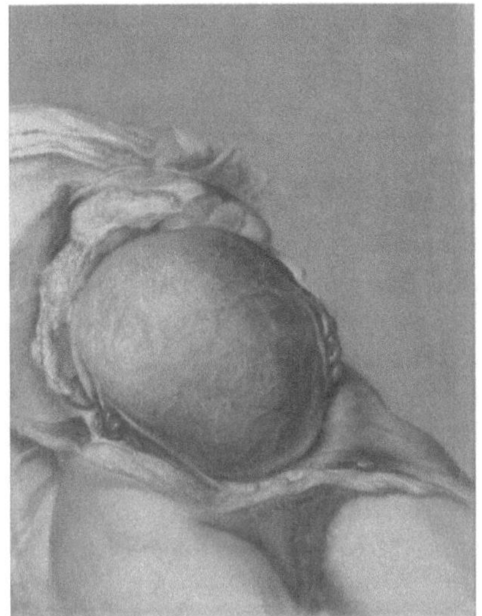

Figure 1.3 Jan Van Rymsdyk, Original drawing for table 2 of Jenty's *Demonstrations of a Pregnant Uterus*, c. 1755–7, Fothergill Collection, Pennsylvania Hospital

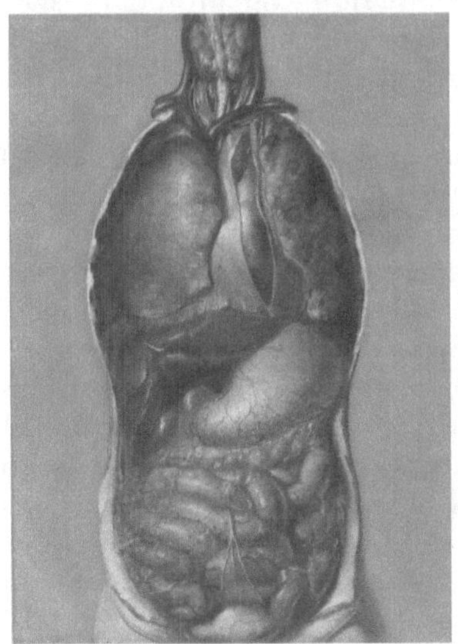

Figure 1.4 Jan Van Rymsdyk, Original drawing of the lungs and intestines, for Jenty's *Essay on the Demonstration of the Human Structure*, c. 1755–7, Fothergill Collection, Pennsylvania Hospital, unpublished

The dispatch of the collection to Philadelphia was situated within a tight yet extensive plexus of transactions. The role of the Quaker community of Philadelphia was essential in securing this consignment: the networks of transoceanic communication between metropolitan centre and colonial outpost were significantly lubricated by the international operations of this tightly knit religious community. By the time Fothergill bought Jenty's collection, he had already been involved in the politics and financial management of Pennsylvania, having become a respected political adviser to the Quaker members of the Pennsylvania assembly and trustee of the Pennsylvania Land Company (PLC). It was he who had also arranged for David Barclay, the banker, and Benjamin Franklin to become agents for the hospital fund, while promoting the use of unclaimed PLC shares for the benefit of the hospital. Moreover, as a charity institution modelled on the British Hospital movement,[16] the Pennsylvania Hospital relied on voluntary subscriptions by affluent supporters, as well as free specialist service by accomplished medical professionals.[17] In this context, the hospital, and especially the dominant Quaker element on its board, had been soliciting support from their Quaker contacts back at the colonial centre, London. The hospital's financial position, chronically precarious, had compelled the board to make frequent appeals for gifts and contributions from their medical suppliers in the United Kingdom, who were often Quakers.[18] James Pemberton – the brother of Israel Pemberton, called the "king of the Quakers" for the power he exerted over his Quaker friends and the Quaker city of Philadelphia – was the hospital's public-relations man with many regular contacts in Britain.[19] Such gifts as Fothergill's should, therefore, be understood in the context of a Quaker ethical code that operated on a transatlantic scale, bringing together business and religious charity, profit and utility.

The Fothergill present was not accompanied by an official letter of donation or an invoice. Fothergill had orally announced it to Shippen, assigning him to the duty of presenting it to the hospital board. Fothergill had also made a written reference to the impending gift in one of his letters to James Pemberton (dated April 1762), where he also expanded upon the various pressures, motivations, and aspirations involved in such charitable gestures.[20] The letter's apologetic tone indicates the sender's awareness of the hospital's high expectations, but, unfortunately, as Fothergill explained, the severe financial situation in the capital did not allow for much optimism about the possibility of raising any substantial amount of money. "The Hospital," as Fothergill explained, "must subsist itself till better times," but in the meantime, it could perhaps accept as

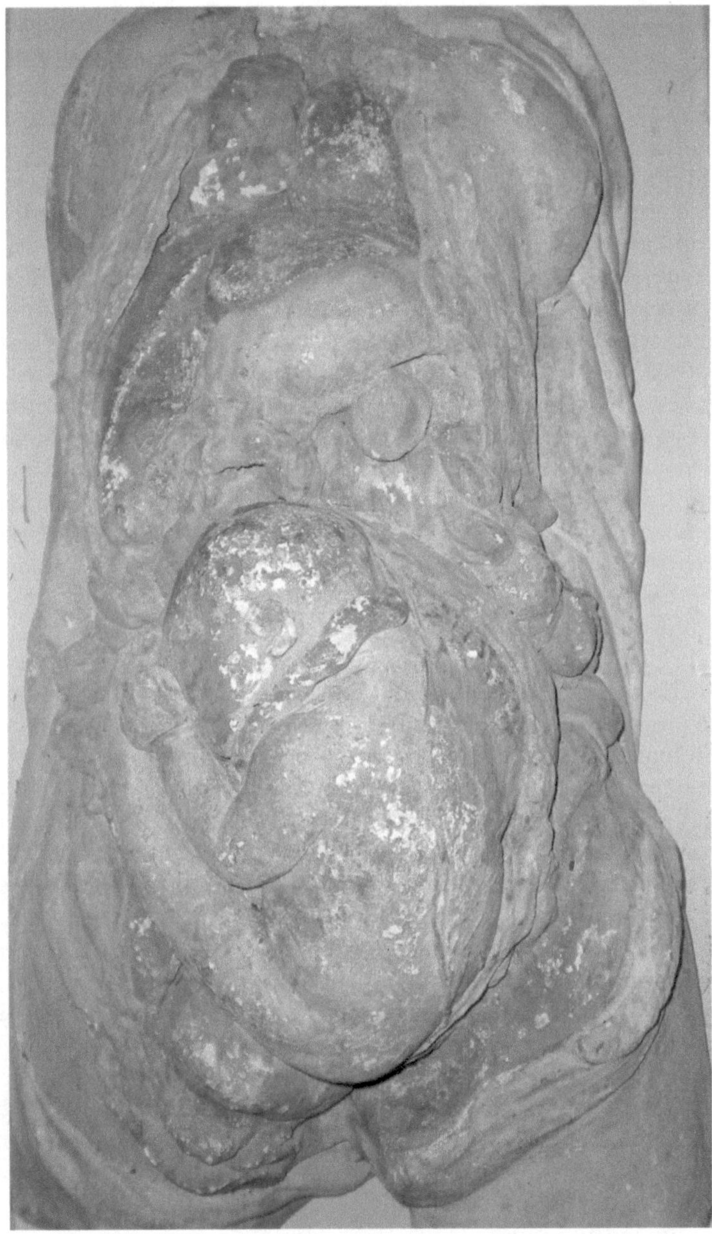

Figure 1.5 Plaster anatomical cast of a woman who died in childbirth, from Jenty's Anatomy Theatre, c. 1755–7, Fothergill Collection, Pennsylvania Hospital

compensation a present "of some intrinsic value," though "not probably of immediate benefit": the Fothergill collection of casts and drawings.

Fothergill devoted the rest of his letter to laying out all the reasons why his endowment may prove to be quite useful and significant. The donation had two very practical dimensions. First, "those pretty accurate anatomical drawings," "half as big as the life," could be used as a substitute for fresh corpses. Addressing his colleagues and friends in Philadelphia, Fothergill assumed, wrongly as I will show, that "the means of procuring [such] subjects with you are not easy." Moreover, he grounded the entire "use" of his drawings in the same argument of a supposed "want of real subjects," which was proving increasingly useful to London surgeons in promoting their calls to normalize the thriving, yet clandestine trade in corpses. The second practical use of the set, according to Fothergill, was a correlative of the first: the drawings could help promote in faraway America anatomical knowledge, and, what is more, medicine as a whole. Fothergill followed closely Hunter's passionate tone in underlining the then unconventional idea that "the knowledge of anatomy is of exceeding great use to practitioners in Physic and surgery," and was similarly certain that it would play an important role in the modernization of the medical profession.[21]

Fothergill also defined a number of more specific ways in which Rymsdyk's works could be put to optimal use. First, he advised that they should be explained to hospital students. Second, he noted that they could be used to make an independent display within the hospital, which would be visited and consulted by a broader audience – "not to be seen by every person," of course, but by those who may have the permission of a trustee and could pay "a small gratuity for the benefit of the house." Third, Fothergill linked his gift with the prospect of organizing much-needed anatomical courses in America. Anatomical lectures had only sporadically been organized in the past, but Fothergill suggested the need for a more permanent and systematic program of lectures in anatomy, and recommended Shippen as the most appropriate specialist to undertake this task. Even more strikingly, he also grabbed the same opportunity to urge the board "to erect a School of Physic." Such a school would be best placed to "draw many students from various parts of America and the West Indies and at least furnish them with a better idea of the rudiments of their profession than they have at present the means of acquiring on your side of the water." In this far-sighted manner, Fothergill actually articulated the rationale which would lead, three years later, to the creation of the first American school of medicine. With this significant difference, however: that Fothergill's and Shippen's plan envisaged a hospital-based medical school, in full accordance with medical education in London, whereas, in Pennsylvania, the Scottish model prevailed, according to which the first medical school was placed under the auspices of the College of Philadelphia, promoting medical education as a university discipline.[22]

Evidently, then, Fothergill saw his gift within a firmly aspirational, yet adverse framework of setting up medical training in colonial America. In this context, his choice of Shippen as his messenger reflects considerable care and calculation. Shippen was one of the many ambitious young Americans who in 1757, well before the appearance of organized teaching in America, had gone to Britain to study midwifery with Colin Mackenzie and anatomy with Hunter. In 1760 he moved to Edinburgh Medical School, from which he graduated in 1761 with an obstetrical thesis on the placenta. His surviving diary entries from the early period of his London stay detail his daily routine of hard work at the dissection theatre, immersion in metropolitan entertainment, and extensive liaising with useful contacts, including Benjamin Franklin, John Fothergill, and the Penn family – proprietors of Pennsylvania.[23] Though the evangelical youth was initially determined "to make pleasure give way to business," he soon endorsed the lively culture of playhouses, operas, coffee houses, and, ultimately, Garrick's performances at the Covent Garden theatre near Hunter's anatomical school. For Hunter's students, there seems to have existed an easy continuum between the absorbing life in the dissection theatre, where new spectacles and discoveries awaited every motion of the scalpel, and Garrick's sensational techniques and dramatic performances.[24] Shippen was a prominent member of this medical group of stage aficionados.[25]

Together with their solid anatomical and medical education, students from British America absorbed in London a whole range of high-brow assets central to social and professional ascendancy in the medical worlds of the eighteenth century: polite cultivation, cultural veneer, polished manners, as well as sensitivity to spectacle and an ability to attract influential patronage, were the most important among such assets. In these and various other respects, Hunter's school provided colonial men of medicine with the ideal foundations for meteoric professional success. As it has been already noted, "all [students] who are known to have attended [Hunter's] lectures are remembered in colonial medical history,"[26] and Shippen was no exception. Moreover, at Fothergill's instigation, Shippen had also acquired substantial hands-on experience in hospital observation and practical surgical work, before pursuing a one-year course on medical theory in Edinburgh.[27] It was this thorough training in the joint scientific and cultural aspects of contemporary medicine that placed Shippen at the centre of Fothergill's hopes to kick-start medical education in Pennsylvania. Rymsdyk's works were an inseparable part of this project.[28]

Fothergill's plan first became public knowledge in America on 8 November 1762, when the physician's collection of casts and drawings finally arrived in Philadelphia. At the initial meeting, where Fothergill's letter was read out, the Pennsylvania hospital board endorsed, in theory, all of Fothergill's suggestions; but, in practice, it accommodated only the most convenient ones. The board thus gave official permission to Shippen to "have recourse" to the drawings and casts for his private lectures of anatomy, and resolved to open the seven cases of the consignment the next day. The resolution on the day of the consignment's official inspection by the board shows that preparations had already been under way to address Fothergill's wish that his paintings "might be lodged in some … apartment of the hospital," preferably "low" and thus "not too dry" in order to preserve Rymsdyk's crayons.[29] The north room of the second floor was appropriately chosen. In the same meeting, the board referred to Shippen's intention to give guided tours of the Fothergill collection, made provisions for interested members of the public "who from curiosity may apply to view the said paintings," and fixed fees and other conditions of display for students or gentlemen. During this second meeting, the board decided that due to the fragility and conditions of preservation of Rymsdyk's works, Shippen could, actually, only use them in situ, after appropriate arrangements with the keeper. Undeterred by this setback,[30] Shippen moved to make a public announcement of his private scheme for anatomical courses. In his first advertisement for the courses, issued in the local press only two days after the official receipt of Fothergill's gift, Shippen did not fail to make a proud reference to the collection and its role in advancing his private initiative:

> The managers and physicians of the Pennsylvania Hospital, at a special Meeting, have generously consented to countenance and encourage this undertaking; and to make it the more entertaining and profitable, have granted [Shippen] the use of some curious anatomical casts and drawings … presented by the judicious and benevolent Doctor Fothergill.[31]

Despite the quick incorporation of the paintings in medical teaching – albeit on a small, private scale – there was no practical action regarding the guided tours for the wider public as envisioned by Fothergill. On 17 May 1763, however, a meeting at Philadelphia's London Coffee House occurred between Shippen and the managers of the hospital, where it was, finally, decided that Shippen would "attend twice a month to give some general explanation" of the collection to members of the public, who may be "desirous to gain some general knowledge of the structure of the human body."[32] The first public announcement of the commencement of these tours was made in the press two days later and similar notices were repeated regularly after that.[33]

Apparently, the board's ambition was to use the collection to attract an informed, influential, and cultivated public from which they could then conceivably recruit future financial support for the charity institution as a whole. However, the projected benefits from the collection extended far wider than this. The letter of acknowledgment that the hospital board finally sent to Fothergill many months after the reception of his gift is in this regard very eloquent. This is where the first evaluation of the collection as an epistemic and monetary asset was made by the special committee appointed to prepare the letter.[34] Acting in accordance with Fothergill's wishes, the hospital reassured their London patron that they had applied admission fees as a way of filtering visitors and boosting the hospital's revenue. They also, proudly, emphasized that the audiences attracted by the collection – both students in surgery and others – had exceeded their hopes: in consequence, the board boasted that "the Premium paid for this Privilege" – that of viewing the collection – "hath produced more than we expected."[35] Indeed, an earlier supposition of the board that "there may be many persons besides students of Physic" who would delight in anatomical painting and general knowledge of anatomy was now fully confirmed. Soon thereafter, in April 1764, the collection appeared for the first time in the capital stock of the Pennsylvania hospital, assessed at £350, considerably more than the price Fothergill had supposedly paid. Historians of the hospital usually divide the institution's assets into donations in cash, in notes or credit, and real estate.[36] The inclusion of a collection of visual objects adds a new, fourth category of assets in the hospital's capital stock: the fact that they figure, so prominently, among the hospital's investments and sources of income, may, at first, seem surprising. In fact, though, it fits well into the larger picture of Quaker notions of business and utilitarianism through which the group frequently negotiated its chronically fraught relations to visual culture.[37]

One of the most significant aspects of the board's letter to Fothergill, however, is that it echoes the physician's vision about the collection's role in introducing a school of medicine in the American colonies. It is clear that the board did not see the Rymsdyk group of pictures only as a stimulus to the public's interest in medicine, but also associated this interest closely with the larger aspiration of organized medical teaching. Turning to the future, therefore, the hospital board expressed the hope that eventually "such gentlemen of the faculty, who are duly qualified" would "devote their time and attention" to establish "such compleat courses of lectures given to the various branches of physical knowledge, as to render [the] service [of these pictures] very extensive." But, again, despite the board's vague assurances that such a public prospect would afford them "much satisfaction and pleasure to promote," it was Shippen's private initiative that was, in the meantime, exploiting the collection's practical value for medical teaching.[38]

Medical Education, Anatomical Drawings, and Cultural Polish in Pennsylvania

Shippen's advertisements demonstrate that his private lectures profited substantially from a steady engagement with the pictorial material at hand. His public announcements indeed show him to be a shrewd entrepreneur, a businessman with advanced understanding of the professional subtleties of eighteenth-century medicine – no doubt capitalizing on the practical knowledge he acquired in Britain near Hunter.[39] In the first place, Shippen's private lectures were designed to target the largest possible audiences. This involved addressing a prospective clientele from within the city, but also from "the neighboring provinces," and, even more broadly, from those "who live at a distance from Philadelphia." Moreover, Shippen broadened the spectrum of his potential professional clientele by introducing independent courses and lectures on a variety of medical subjects.[40] Still further, he designed his lectures in ways that showed serious consideration for "the entertainment of any gentlemen, who may have the curiosity to understand the anatomy of the human frame."[41] Shippen employed numerous strategies for attracting and amusing this particularly sensitive audience: a public event (an open and ceremoniously organized "Introductory Course" at the State House) to announce the inception of his courses to various "branches of civil society";[42] a pay-as-you-go approach to the main courses of instruction; and flexible deals for those who did not think it necessary to attend every technical lecture of the course, but still wished to "gratify their curiosity" by attending independent lectures.[43] For this civil audience, the gloss and polish of artworks, such as Rymsdyk's paintings, was a crucial point of attraction, intended by Shippen to make his courses all "the more entertaining and profitable."[44]

It is important that the Fothergill collection would remain a constant asset throughout Shippen's expanding medical courses. When, for example, in January 1765, he announced another pioneering enterprise, the beginning of the first independent lecture course on midwifery – which was combined with the first Lying-in-Hospital for pregnant women in North America – the collection was again mentioned with emphasis. The organization of such a course was a delicate matter, and Shippen took great care to present it as an emergency service to the community. But even here, Shippen did not fail to turn to the Fothergill collection, in particular to the items that dealt with gestational anatomy, promising "to explain and apply those curious anatomical plates and casts to the gravid uterus."[45] Rymsdyk's works continued to be valued highly, even after Shippen's lectures were integrated in the curriculum of the College of Philadelphia. The college's foundation triggered bitter tensions between institutions and personal careers, which persisted for years to come and peaked during the Revolutionary period.[46] Nevertheless, the collection's continuity of use in Pennsylvanian medical education was not afflicted by such conflicts: as the public announcements for the institution of the first American Medical School in Pennsylvania reveal, Rymsdyk's paintings and casts were again proudly listed among its teaching assets.[47]

Most significantly, the collection also survived a range of critical turns in Shippen's career, not least during the public scandals that erupted over his use of fresh corpses for public dissections. As we learn from explicit references in Shippen's advertisements for the second year of his lectures in 1763, the surgeon was already performing real-time dissections on a "fresh subject."[48] In the same vein, he had devised an autonomous course on "the arts of injecting and dissecting," also demonstrated on a "fresh subject." Clearly enough, the scarcity of corpses from among the recently deceased was not as dramatic as Fothergill's letter had supposed it to be. In fact, Shippen's name was closely associated with the first public "resurrection" scandals in America,[49] and, faced with public outrage, he frequently felt obliged to make passionate but firm declarations of innocence in the Pennsylvanian press.[50] Shippen denied categorically that he ever used corpses "from the church, or any other private burial place," and asserted that his subjects came from legitimate sources, that is, those "who had wilfully murdered themselves or were publicly executed."[51] Except, "now and then," as he admitted, when "death was owing to some particular disease," in which case, he procured bodies from the convenient pool of the unknown poor in "the Potters Field," the city's burial yard for vagrants.[52] But even as he had solved the difficult problem of the procurement of actual dead bodies, Shippen still continued to call attention to the unique benefits of pictures and artefacts such as those "curious and improving anatomical casts and drawings" held at the Pennsylvania Hospital.[53] Manifestly, therefore, Rymsdyk's pictures maintained their considerable use value for reasons that differ from Fothergill's initial concern that the supply of dead bodies in the American colonies had been insufficient.

The collection's use thus exceeded any simple notion of scientific utility. This also indicates that Shippen's mixed audiences found in Rymsdyk's pictures additional forms of satisfaction that need to be further specified. For gentlemen, the paintings offered another opportunity for tasteful delectation, as well as much-needed veneer for their "offbeat" anatomical interests. For medical students in Pennsylvania, they supplied a unique chance to come into contact with artworks, and cultivate more "enlarged views" of their vocation, which Shippen, following again his teacher's example, was teaching them to take seriously.[54] Shippen himself manifested a considerable desire to acquire lofty academic and cultural credentials, such as honorary degrees that served as "proper testimony of [his] literary merit," and he multiplied his symbolic cache by participating in the boards of enlightened societies, such as the American Philosophical Society. Such distinctions were all duly advertised in the local press.[55] Similarly civil practices provided colleagues and students with a model for professional success in medicine,[56] already tested in Britain's highly competitive environment of medical entrepreneurship. As Susan Lawrence has shown, the efforts of anatomists and surgeons to gain respectability in an otherwise hostile environment involved, on the one hand, evidence of social climbing, and, on the other, the persuasive presentation of dissection as vital in the progress of knowledge.[57] As important, however, for the social gentrification of surgeons were systematic invocations of gentility through language, address, manners;[58] or, as Shippen's teacher Hunter preferred, through engagements with the art and literary worlds, including such trappings of civilization as collections of "paintings, or anatomy dignified in art," art patronage and memberships in literary, artistic, or other societies.[59] Next to his other liberal and polite credentials, Shippen's close involvement with a collection of curious and original pictures served this precise purpose.

Crucially, however, I would argue that the enduring appeal of Rymsdyk's pictures was a more complex issue than simply being a matter of general association with the cultural sphere – or the "refined" arts and the advantages of social distinction that customarily accrued from them. Nor can the appeal of these pictures be measured solely according to their scientific or utilitarian value. As I suggest in the next sections, the specific visual choices (the content, style, and texture of these pictures), the visual experiences they represent, as well as their particular place within the history of picture making in this period are also key to the public attraction they generated, first in Britain and, then, in North America.

Anatomical Sympathy, Extreme Sensations, and British Criticism

The subject matter of Rymsdyk's anatomical art is the scientific experience of the anatomical theatre, namely, the dissection of cadavers and related practices. Proceedings of dissection in this period took the form of a public spectacle within a culture of scientific inquiry increasingly oriented towards showmanship.[60] Such spectacles had their own visual techniques and qualities, dictating meaningful choices between competing trends. In this environment of showmanship Philadelphia held a prominent place, and Shippen's public dissections or Rymsdyk's pictures provided further opportunities for visual stimulation.[61] Shippen, in fact, seems to have built on the example of a local predecessor, the illustrious Rev. Ebenezer Kinnersley, who represented the kind of "rational sensationalism" that became the distinguishing mark of Philadelphia's scientific scene.[62]

When Shippen, therefore, invited the "curious" to attend the dissections in his anatomical theatre, he was aware that a broad range of excessive affects, including shock and marvel, were essential elements in their curiosity. Though student notes from his anatomical lectures convey a certain dryness and matter-of-fact approach to anatomical description,[63] his famous "Introductory Lecture" in Philadelphia's State House, delivered in 1762, is embellished with strong expressions of fascination designed to inflame the imaginations of his audience. Drawing on the increasingly popular vocabularies of the sublime, Shippen underscored the capacity of human anatomy to trigger powerful sensations. In particular, he gave prominence to anatomy's ability to bring to light the "surprising order," "expensive structure," and "wonderful" or even "extraordinary apparatus" of the human body.[64] This rhetoric reflected the terms through which Shippen's teacher had articulated his bold "taste" for anatomy. Indeed, Hunter's writings are full of superlative expressions of "astonishment" and amazement at the indefinite complexity of anatomy which he deservedly called an "awful subject" – that is, an "awe-inspiring" or "sublimely majestic" subject.[65] However, Shippen and Hunter also favoured an uncensored approach to anatomical presentation emphasizing the various specular advantages of the raw dissection of corpses. Shippen was, in the same period, widely associated in the public imagination with the terrifying details of "resurrectionism,"[66] while his adopted hands-on approach to dissection increased the gruesome frisson of his shows.

The affective horizon of Shippen's dissections differed radically from the other much "gentler" economies of anatomical taste cultivated by his rivals. To be sure, there was more than one way of staging in public the realities of the anatomical theatre, and there was no shortage of practitioners who followed a much less realistic approach to anatomical showmanship. Abraham Chovet, another Philadelphian, was one of them. When he advertised his anatomical museum of "elegant Anatomical Wax-Work Figures" as the very foil to "the disagreeable sights or smells of recent disease and putrid carcasses, which often disgust even the students in Physick, as well as the curious," it was Shippen's theatre of raw experiences that he had in mind.[67] By thus appealing to the sensibilities of the polite, Chovet's civil handling was trying to lure away from Shippen the most polished and hard-won sector of his prospective audience.

By contrast, Shippen's anatomical performances promoted the opposite spectrum of sensations, accentuating the importance of immediate, concrete, and multi-sensorial contacts with the actual details of dead bodies. In this way, Shippen's teaching had a clear pedagogical rationale in that it familiarized students with the specificity of the dissection room. Such specificity was, undoubtedly, a messy affair compounded of experiences that were at once disagreeable and astounding, painful and ecstatic. Darker types of pleasure abounded in the anatomical theatre: as scholars have noted, these included the sadistic pleasures of moral punishment, the erotic pleasures of voyeurism and sensuality, or, even more perversely, the "malicious satisfaction" drawn from vicarious torture or from violations of sexual and funerary taboos.[68] Such extreme experiences frequently rendered anatomical theatres sites of "mayhem" where fear, disorder and excessive behaviour prevailed.[69] But such transgressions did not exclude the colder pleasures of mastery, of clinical detachment and discipline; rather, they reinforced them. The terror, astonishment, and repulsion of opened-up corpses went hand in hand with increasing demands for composure, emotional control and a steady hand to subdue the overwhelming reality of a dead body. Quite understandably, anatomy's "majestic" secrets had to be extorted and controlled by a like force, "a force majeure." And this extortion was a job for those surgeons and practical anatomists whom Michael Sappol has aptly called the "technicians of the sublime."[70]

The word "sublime" is aptly employed in this case; especially as its use seems to draw on landmark redefinitions of the term during this period. Such reinterpretations fleshed out relations between the sublime and extreme emotional tensions that were nowhere better described than in Edmund Burke's *Philosophical Enquiry into the Origins of Our Ideas of the Sublime and Beautiful* (1757/9).[71] The violent, dark, even "misanthropic" and "disturbing" aspects of this "shocking book" are increasingly attracting attention from different scholarly quarters.[72] Burke's ardent descriptions of the singular delights accompanying situations of physical pain, unnatural tensions, or extreme sensations alienated his contemporaries as a distinctly perverse and subversive stance. Especially his analysis of sympathy as a non-moral, non-rational, and instinctual emotion that compels men to take delight in the suffering of others broke open a whole new and previously forbidden realm of aesthetic gratifications that bore close resemblance to those drawn from anatomical spectacles.[73] All of Burke's examples illustrating the sublime force of sympathy come from "striking and affecting incidents," such as "violent death," "tragedy,"[74] and scenes of suffering at large. Moreover, in Burke's *Enquiry*, anatomy itself featured more than once as a powerful example through which the spirals of knowledge/pleasure intrinsic to the operation of taste could be best illuminated.[75] Besides, in a move that his contemporaries frequently described as "absurd" or "debasing and humiliating to the pride of human nature,"[76] Burke included such trademark experiences of the dissection theatre as "intolerable stenches" and "excessive bitters" in his list of sources of "grand sensations" associated with the sublime.[77]

Arguably, therefore, anatomy belonged to those "real calamities" or "natural objects" which inspired the extreme type of contrasting emotions that were placed at the root of Burke's definition of the sublime. To the extent that the sublime was described as a "relative pleasure" which "cannot exist without a relation, and that too a relation to pain,"[78] the spectacle of anatomy was a perfect tie to it. Such explosive mixtures of pain and pleasure or attraction and repulsion obsessed contemporaries, attracting the attention of no less a figure than Denis Diderot.[79] Anatomists themselves were frequently subject to the same emotional ambivalences, swinging between opposite affects of delight and disgust, exertion and powerlessness at the sight of the body's interior.[80]

The sublimity of anatomical spectacles is thus a historical phenomenon of which contemporaries had an advanced awareness, and the appropriate psychological and aesthetic vocabulary to describe. Yet, even more strikingly, such approaches to real spectacles of dissection were also applicable to the analysis of representations of anatomy in art. As Burke had put it, the pleasure of anatomical representations was tied up with the "pleasure arising from a natural object."[81] Rymsdyk's representations of anatomy relied for their impact on the powerful effects associated with the real events they represented, that is, extraordinary spectacles of dissection. In a nutshell, the sublime in Rymsdyk's art would seem to be the result of the sublime in nature. And yet, as Burke had also emphasized, the pleasure arising from a natural object was inseparable from the degree to which each viewer "perceives it justly imitated." This is an important addition to the argument in that it refocuses attention to the fact that the actual style, the means and the media of the representation were the most important factors in the production of those effects necessitated by the sublime. Such pictorial qualities and the powerful sensations they ignite soon became another critical and fiercely debated subject of inquiry linked to the nature of sublimity *in art.*

Sublime Simulations and Rymsdyk's Anatomical Realism

The scientific community was, as shown above, split around the issue of real anatomical demonstrations and their proper mode of public presentation. But it was even more fiercely divided over the *way*, the specific visual style, in which anatomical spectacles ought to be reproduced in scientific illustrations. To be sure, next to their epistemic content, such anatomical pictures as Rymsdyk's record meaningful choices from a pool of conflicting visual styles available for anatomical illustrations. And such choices were intertwined with increasing concerns over the issue of visual experience, namely, the proper impact of pictures on viewers.

The aesthetic charge (the "stylishness" or "rhetoric of presentation") of scientific images has, recently, been highlighted and reincorporated in the analysis of anatomical illustrations as an integral part of their existence.[82] However, the analytical tools used for this purpose by historians of science remain uninformed by sufficiently historicized approaches to visual culture prevalent in other specialist disciplines such as art history and affiliated fields. The sweeping use of the vague term "beauty," for example, as an all-embracing catchword to describe the competence of wildly differing kinds of scientific images is, from this point of view, characteristic. Equally reductive, yet just as frequent, is the tendency to confine discussion to dry, technical, and un-contextualized evaluations of the "bravura," "virtuosity," or skilful imitation of anatomical pictures. In contrast, I would suggest that Rymsdyk's works contain many subtle references, picked up from the complex art-historical debates of the period concerning the styles most appropriate for the pictorial representation of the human figure and its anatomy. Such debates spilled over into scientific discussions about anatomical illustration. It is thus unsurprising that the defining aesthetic conflict of the period is found raging again in anatomical science, that is, the opposition between official styles of ideal abstraction and the "uncompromising empiricism" cultivated by "the extreme wing of a characteristically British tradition."[83]

Rymsdyk and his chief patron in Britain, Hunter, were at the very forefront of this debate in Britain, and their joint masterpiece, the *Anatomy of the Human Gravid Uterus*, is a polemical monument of emerging styles of extreme naturalism (figure 1.6). The book was published much later, in 1774, but Hunter's collaboration with Rymsdyk predates the painter's employment by Jenty. In his introduction Hunter pitted the unconventional naturalism he adopted against established models of ideal representation, encapsulated by Albinus's "polished," "classicizing and synthetic" approach.[84] He thus contrasted his preferred method of providing a "simple portrait, in which the object is represented exactly as it was seen" against traditional techniques of idealization and formalization prevalent in contemporary scientific depictions. According to Hunter, ideal anatomies are "conceived in the imagination" – recording "such circumstances as were not actually seen," and they bear all "the hardness of a geometrical diagram."[85] True to its name, therefore, the ideal style of official science "gives an idea" of the object, while "close representation of nature," like Hunter's own, "shews the object" and "becomes almost as infallible as the object itself."[86]

Nonetheless, Hunter's reality drive was neither an exclusively scientific product nor solely designed for a scientific audience, as it has been surmised.[87] In fact, it had been first showcased within the highest echelon of contemporary art, the Royal Academy of Arts in London, where Hunter was employed as professor of anatomy. Herein, Hunter aired an unusually extreme version of realism, which alienated the elite directorate of the institution with its neoclassical agendas of ideal beauty and grandeur,[88] as much as it would later divide the polite readership of his atlas.[89] Hunter indeed reiterated in his lectures the provocative assertion that "Representation in the imitative Arts is a Substitute for reality,"

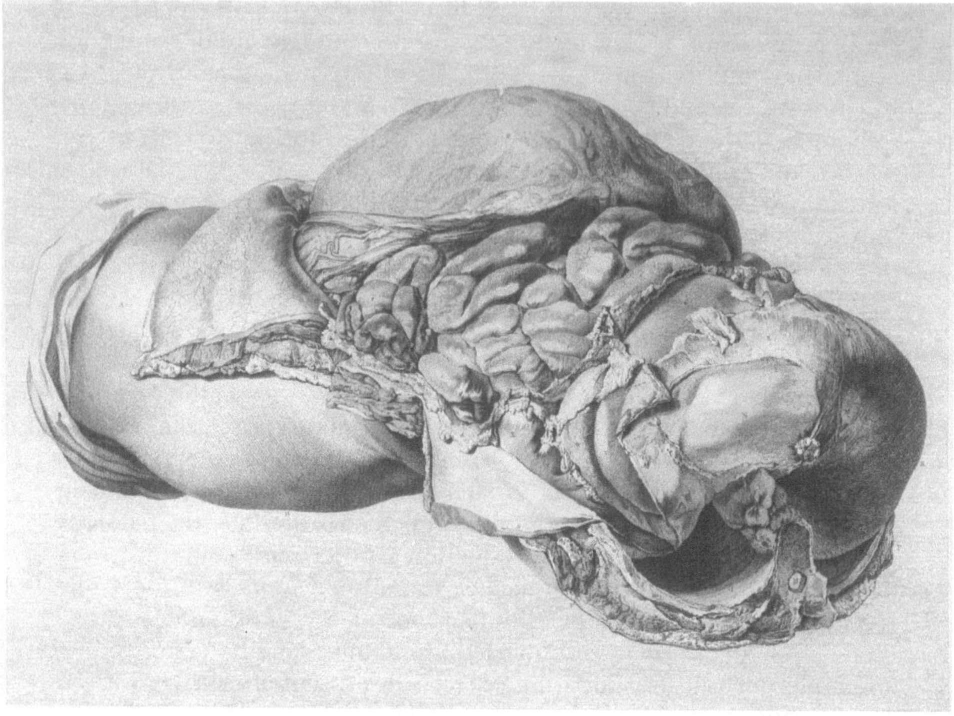

Figure 1.6 Jan Van Rymsdyk, Plate III, from William Hunter, *Anatomy of the Human Gravid Uterus*, line engraving, 1774

affecting viewers by giving them "the impression of the original reality."[90] Thus, it naturally followed that, for Hunter, an artist "cannot copy Nature too exactly, or make the deception too strong."[91] Hunter also spoke at great length about the power and "terror," pain and disorientation caused by accurate imitations. Far from inventing these extraordinary ideas, Hunter had actually imported them from the main source of similar heterodoxies, Burke's *Philosophical Enquiry*. Burke had, indeed, proclaimed that "The nearer [a representation] approaches the reality, and the further it removes us from all idea of fiction, the more perfect is its power,"[92] while repeating at crucial points in the argument his conviction that "frequently the effect of images in painting are exactly similar to those in nature," especially where "real calamities" and "imitated distresses" are involved.[93] Though Burke clearly struggled with these ideas and their implications, falling into a series of contradictions, he still gave sanction to the idea that painted objects – including "a very clear idea of those objects" – could affect us in painting as they "would have affected in the reality."[94]

One of the reasons why Burke was forced to argue in support of amplified imitations in art was his conviction that pleasure of the strongest kind, that is, the sublime, is consequent upon borderline experiences of pain and exposure to spectacles of violence. From the same viewpoint, he grasped correctly that the prevailing perception of art as "no more than fiction" was being put in the service of the very opposite purpose: namely, it provided protective detachment "from the evils which we see represented" and exemplified the spineless attitudes of polite criticism. Consequently, Burke insisted that *both* "in real or fictitious distresses," it is not "our immunity" from pain but rather immediate exposure to "acute suffering" that "produces our delight," and hence the sublime.[95] This approach entailed a new theory of extreme imitations that, contrary to current evaluations of Burke's sublime as an anti-visual and anti-pictorial concept,[96] actually set the ground for a continual amplification of the "realities" of "representations";[97] that is, of the fidelity of artworks as a necessary component for the increase of their effect.

Moreover, if Burke's "realism" harboured an occasional pessimism concerning the limitations of imitative art in matching the intensity of the natural sublime,[98] Hunter was convinced that this gap between art and nature could be closed a little, though never eliminated. The tone and vocabulary he adopted were unmistakeably sublime: "what imitates Nature most is most striking," or, still more emphatically, "in the Fine Arts the more precise the imitation of Nature is, that is, the nearer we come to the point of realising [Nature], the more *striking* I should suppose the effect will be; and therefore the more pleasing."[99] Furthermore, the subjects of pictures should also be carefully selected to accord with the Burkean call for stimulating, even painful experiences: "Whatever raises disgust or horror, gives *unnerving* or pain; likewise, rousing that passion to a certain pitch upon many occasions has a happy effect."[100] Or as Hunter again clarified, "There is certainly much elegance and beauty and grace and dignity in nature," but, far more interestingly, painters ought to realize that "there is [also] animation, spirit, fire, force and violence" in it.[101]

Hunter's statements read like digests, or, often, verbatim transcriptions of Burke's formulations.[102] Yet, the anatomist grasped and expressed something that Burke's sublime was still struggling to articulate: namely, that the vital need to intensify the viewing experience could be combined with a call for the perfection of techniques of simulation in order to achieve *in art* the power of the sublime *in nature*. For Hunter, indeed, the "Life, Soul, and Animation" of pictures lay in processes of visual simulation; otherwise, "the sense will not be properly impressed."[103]

So far it would seem that anatomical realism and the sublime were coextensive phenomena: anatomical realism was sublime because it replicated a whole range of sublime events like, in this case, the experience of dissection. But, I would repeat, this should not be understood to mean that anatomical realism was sublime only because of its subject matter. As Hunter put it, artists may choose "the most stimulating object," but they should also "use every power of rendering the effect striking."[104] In fact, the kind of hard imitation Hunter and Rymsdyk accomplished was the product of laborious exercises in visual rhetoric and technique: anatomical realism constituted a pictorial style. As such, anatomical realism developed a series of distinct, yet heterodox visual qualities by which it is characterized. These included a new emphasis on minute detail and local specificity of time and place, an unflinching focus on ugliness, deformity, or disorder, and, finally, a painstaking sensitivity to experimental contingencies including perceptual errors as well as technical aberrations in the process of anatomical labour.[105]

In this pursuit of powerful reality-effects, details played a key role as visual stimulants, associated again by Burke with the production of the sublime. Burke's section on "Magnificence," in particular, introduced a type of affect which would later claim its proper place in Kant's mathematical sublime, a sublimity of which "number is certainly the cause." Burke explained the special affective powers of sheer number and multiplicity of micro-particularities, tying the "great profusion of things" with "situations of splendid confusion." In one of the most modern twists of his theory of the sublime, Burke praised the astonishing effects of disorder. There are, undeniably, spectacles in nature which "owe their sublimity to a richness and profusion of images, in which the mind is so dazzled as to make it impossible to attend to that exact coherence and agreement of the allusions."[106] The section "Vastness" gave Burke further opportunity to explain the sublimity of scientific details, this time under the name of "littleness" – "the last extreme" of vastness – that "is in some measure sublime likewise."[107] Indeed, taking an example from the science of microscope, whose historical contributions to the progress of anatomy had also been extensively explained by Hunter,[108] Burke described the sublime delights of minuteness: "When we attend to the infinite divisibility of matter, when we pursue animal life into these excessively small, and yet organised beings, that escape the nicest inquisition of the sense ...

[then] we become amazed and confounded at the wonder of minuteness [which] must be infinite."[109] Far from being the exclusive product of privation, Burke's theory of the sublime was thus conceived and executed as a state of sensory plenitude in which visual minuteness had a significant role to play. On the threshold of acute perception and high-power precision, Burke's sublime discovered a treacherous kind of hyper-clarity that dazzles and confounds, while extending the frontiers both of feeling and of science. Scholars have, nevertheless, tended to associate the historical emergence of details as the very "Foundation of the Sublime" with Blake and the Romantic movement, treating everything before this watershed as examples of the "irreconcilability of detail and the sublime."[110] To be sure, Blake's famous motto "to Generalize is to be an Idiot; to Particularize is the Alone Distinction of Merit" encapsulated, early in the nineteenth century, the radical wing of opposition against Reynolds's polite aesthetics of abstraction. However, as demonstrated by Burke's sublime and its powerful influence on eighteenth-century anatomical art, such tensions had already begun to appear much earlier.[111]

Hunter's collaboration with Rymsdyk is an exemplary case of this new economy of details and its aesthetic co-implications. Plate V, in particular, is a powerful spectacle that grips the viewer with its drive towards the faithful replication of microscopic and supernumerary details (figure 1.7). This is a composite representation of three successive layers of the womb revealed, firstly, by a grand cross-section down the middle and, secondly, by delicate acts of drilling and chiselling that peel away slices of the deciduas to show the transparent chorion beneath. The visual result is a rough but highly textured surface loaded with innumerable smears, cuts, cracks, and splinters of encrusted matter.

Part of the image's allure relies, I would propose, on the split viewer responses it accommodates: an appreciation of the profusion and finesse of micro-singularities, as well as a sense of violence amplified by the coarseness of the calcified surface thereby produced. Indeed, most of the fine and minute details recorded in this plate are the products of mini-acts of violence indicating the aggressive intervention of the surgeon. This space of minute visibility was carved with gross gestures, including the breaking, cutting, pulling, and tearing down of membranes and arteries. Most of the arteries recorded on the surface of the womb are wound up and shrivelled as a result of the way in which the anatomist broke apart the vascular networks of the womb. Moreover, the countless surface-effects on the womb's coating also include scattered lumps of coagulated vessels, broken veins, and other sharply marked chunks of flesh, which

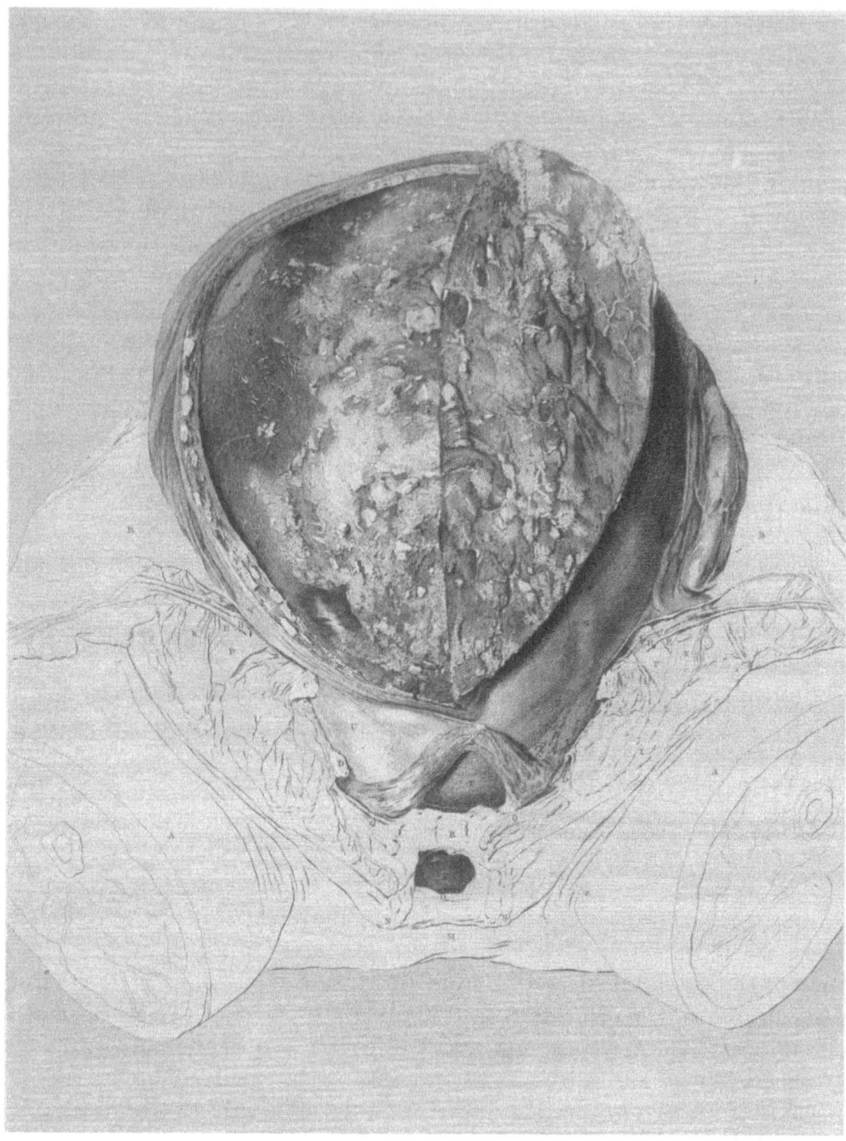

Figure 1.7 Jan Van Rymsdyk, Plate V, from William Hunter, *Anatomy of the Human Gravid Uterus*, line engraving, 1774

are again the products of further technical interventions; namely, injections gone wrong and extravasations of bursting vessels.

Although Hunter used the term "delicacy" to describe the effect, these details actually resulted from clearly indelicate operations. The bond linking crudeness, minuteness and the profusion of "crowded" surfaces is continuous throughout the atlas.[112] And it produced an energizing aesthetic contrast: a finesse of violence and an extreme type of visibility, which bordered on its opposite. As Hunter admitted, the sheer crowdedness and distortion of the result led to "indistinct," confusing, and, ultimately, uncontrollable images. But regardless, Hunter and Rymsdyk proceeded to replicate this disorder with a level of fidelity and resolve that attests to the passion and dazzle of their experience.

Such is the aesthetic frisson of this uncompromising realism that sought no recourse to artifices, refinements, corrections of error, or beautifications of any kind. Martin Kemp and Marina Warner have rightly noted that this "raw directness" was designed to underline "the incisive real-ness of the dissection."[113] In this strict sense, Hunter's style of seeing is an early form of realism: it does not aim to imitate or restore "nature" in its original aspect. Rather, Hunter's intention is to capture visual *reality* – a word which, together with its affiliate term "real," is obsessively repeated throughout the anatomist's lectures at the Royal Academy. What is more, this reality drive was neither an ascetic nor a quietist ideal; on the contrary, it came with its own sensory amplifications, prodigious excitements, and sensual pleasures. The reality that artists began to reverence during this period seems to be situated at that precise point where disorder, profusion, and excess specificity intersected.

Better still, this extreme sensation of reality is further enhanced by the fact that it appeared as the result of the way in which raw bodies, surgical interventions, and equally invasive techniques of artistic reproduction coalesced. The very choice of medium by Hunter, line or copperplate engraving, is a characteristically intrusive technique, matching with its sharp outlines and jagged incisions, the roughness and harshness of the dissection depicted, as well as the demand for precise, distinct, and powerful simulations of it.

Softer Imitations: The Compromises and Failures of Marginal Professionals in Britain

The Jenty/Rymsdyk pictures of the Pennsylvania Hospital form an inseparable part of these developments in anatomical art. And yet, they also vary considerably from them: Jenty's preferred variation constitutes an early and much softer moment in this realist shift. Admittedly, Jenty's preferred style of representation shared Hunter's fascination with optimal imitation, and its power to stimulate.[114] However, the kind of simulation that Jenty sought diverged markedly from Hunter's in a crucial set of visual properties. Jenty, for example, rejected the harshness and sharpness of Hunter's line engravings, choosing instead the medium of mezzotint because of its "softness," which he compared with the softness of painting.[115] In contradistinction to the razor-sharp linearity of Hunter's illustrations, Jenty's mezzotints are notable for their painterly qualities: pliant textures, unity of mass and texture, gentle contrasts, broad and smooth treatment, absence of any sign of cross-hatching and hazy outlines are all visual choices that mark a different path to realism.

The flowing appearance of Rymsdyk's originals in the Pennsylvania Hospital collection was a necessary pre-adaptation to this set of stylistic qualities that prevailed in his final published illustrations. Indeed, Rymsdyk's polychrome pictures display a degree of smoothness, swift brushwork, and broad modelling that invoke a type of painterliness with strong references to "old master" pictorial effects, not least the colourism and facilitá of Baroque painting (figure 1.3). Colour indeed generates here breathtaking effects of sensuality and brilliance, and it leads to visual results very different from the linear sharpness, acute detail, and intensity of Rymsdyk's original drawings for the line engravings in Hunter's atlas. To put it more clearly, such stylistic variations as those respectively adopted by Jenty and Hunter were deliberate and orchestrated phenomena that were intertwined with different choices about techniques of reproduction, as well as variable social aspirations and target audiences.

In associating mezzotint with painting and colour, Jenty attempted to gather and project cultural capital accumulated from one of the politest arts – painting – to one of the most dubious cachet – anatomical illustration. However, what needs to be stressed is that his choice of style and technique seems to have been also determined by his visual notions of what constituted nature, natural vision, and optimal simulation. Jenty emphasized, for example, that mezzotint was selected because it was "capable of exhibiting a nearer imitation of nature than engraving" due to its "well blended and softened" forms.[116] In deploying this language of soft imitation, Jenty made use of a range of contemporary resources drawn directly from the polite discourse of ideal beauty. Crucially, however, Jenty's language of pictorial smoothness did not adopt the classical ideals of abstraction, simplicity, and harmony with which such polite repertoires were also closely associated at the time. Instead of serving neoclassical notions of ideal perfection, Jenty's technique of mezzotint (and his projected use of colour) was intended to *enhance* the very opposite "ideal" of reality-effects. It is in this way, I suggest, that the Jenty/Rymsdyk project maintained its radical and realistic edge: it broke the discourse of beauty down the middle, recombining its polite aesthetic of smoothness with the harsher qualities of sublime imitation. Among such qualities there is perhaps nothing more alien to ideal beauty than the kind of minuteness and superabundance of micro-particularities present in Rymsdyk's paintings for Jenty.

One of the unpublished paintings of "detached parts" from Jenty's human anatomy project emblematizes this tendency (figure 1.4). Jenty praised Rymsdyk's full frontal representation of the lungs and viscera as "more minutely" executed than "could be done even in ... large tables."[117] (Jenty's admiration may perhaps explain why he set this table aside for later publication). The image is an example of exuberant virtuosity in the imitation of exceedingly challenging, tangled, minute, and almost imperceptible particulars. The detailed rendition of the linear webs of fibres, arteries, and veins on the lung surface is astonishing, especially as it is here combined with such holistic pictorial qualities as mass, weight, and volume of the lungs. But where this image excels is in the sensitive representation of the transparency and opacity of membranes, and the light effects produced thereon by significant coagulations and accretions of membranous fluids. The resulting effects are indeed unusual. Detail emerges here at the limits of transparency as the corollary of a subtle variation of light, and it is the product of soft strokes and touches of white paint, rather than linear incisions. A new order of visual detail thus emerges, where singularity maintains its intrusiveness and surfeit, but loses its sharp linearity and harshness.

This is an unusual combination of coarseness and delicacy, smoothness and minuteness, which heralds, yet in a cautious manner, the sharpness of hard imitation that subsequently came to define the aesthetic politics of anatomical realism. In the Pennsylvania pictures, therefore, Rymsdyk performed a balancing act, exploring a mode of pictorial animation that was precariously situated between the past and the future. And he negotiated, without fully accomplishing, a transition from polite idealism to sublime strands of anatomical realism, which he was again destined to emblematize in his later work for Hunter, as well as in his own publications.

This was, I would argue, a plausible compromise. Rymsdyk's anatomical realism for Hunter's atlas was too risky and divisive, and Jenty was sensible enough not to encourage his artist to go down this particular road. His caution had a social logic markedly its own: Jenty's uncertain status as an immigrant professional in London did not allow him such levels of risk taking as Hunter's high-profile position did. The old style of painterliness that Jenty encouraged his painter to adopt, and the smoothness of the published illustrations were both designed to appeal to a civil audience, without, however, compromising Rymsdyk's more dynamic drives for innovation. It is in this sense that this early hybrid of anatomical realism encapsulates well the insecurity and, at the same time, the ingenuity of similar marginal groups within contemporary medical markets.

Such caution was nevertheless not enough. Jenty and his painter, Rymsdyk, were socially disadvantaged in ways which no makeshift compromise at the visual level could successfully redress. Jenty's books proved a market failure, his hopes for upward mobility would soon be frustrated, and his departure for Portugal was thus sped up. On his part, Rymsdyk returned to Hunter's employment in the dissection theatre, and despite his various attempts to climb up the professional ladder by seeking a career in portrait painting,[118] he was forced to come to terms with the unforgiving realities of career organization in the British art world. This was rather expected, as his established reputation in the style of scrupulous fidelity to particular nature ran directly against the "official ideology of British art." Rymsdyk knew that "idealist art theory" had managed "to establish itself as the discourse through which polite discussions of the visual arts were conducted,"[119] and hence his style of minute attention to particulars was bound to shock and alienate polite sensibilities.[120] What is more surprising, however, is that once his hopes for a career in painting were frustrated, Rymsdyk became more, rather than less resolved in deepening, honing, and amplifying his extraordinary abilities for extreme simulations. And further still, he put his ideas in writing, arguing, in an overtly radical language, about the importance of amplified imitation for the much-needed reformation of fine art practices.

Rymsdyk's introduction to the *Museum Britannicum*, published in 1778, is a fiercely polemical manifesto reinforcing the anti-academic, anti-idealist, and anti-establishment nature of eighteenth-century realism in Britain. Rymsdyk turned against influential trends of academic idealism, namely, "abstract," "broad," and other summary styles of representation, "still so much in vogue in Europe,"[121] which he dismissed as bland forms of "nature mending."[122] It is still more fascinating, however, that he managed to entwine his visual realism with a much broader political agenda. Rymsdyk tied up his fierce defence of detailed depictions, first, with a highly politicized attack on the favouritism and elitism of the Royal Academy – which was totally incapable of "mak[ing] a sublime artist";[123] and, second, with a radical call for "merit," "justice," egalitarianism, and social "reform."[124]

It is not surprising, therefore, that, in Britain, the bastions of politeness found it deeply unsettling to engage with anatomical realism in its different variants. Such repertoires proved too much even for the cultural elites of the revolution, which re-enacted the old battle between mind and body, reason and flesh. Roy Porter explains vividly that it was not only anti-Jacobin conservatives, but also the liberal and progressive intelligentsia that gradually saw the kind of "gross corporeality" emblematized by Rymsdyk's realism as the very opposite of their rehabilitated version of the revolution, which promoted the "radical dictatorship of the body by the mind."[125] The emergent secular elites that replaced the clergy "had a stalking-horse and shibboleth of their own: it was mind, and soon the march of mind ... became the secularization of salvation. The doctrine of mind over matter stood for power over the people."[126]

Such a noxious atmosphere of division is not evident in the different context of middle-class supremacy on the other side of the Atlantic: Shippen, himself a supporter and fighter in the American Revolution, did not face serious political problems persuading the local elites and co-professionals about the ideological and epistemic importance of realist anatomy and affiliated forms of illustration.[127] Even American Quakers, so pivotal in the transfer and preservation of these images, seem to have abandoned their notorious visual conservatism, adding another chapter to the dissemination of realism in North America.

The fraught relations of the Quaker community with visual culture have traditionally been seen as expressive of a negative and ascetic or utilitarian approach to vision and art. More recently, however, Marcia Pointon has critiqued such reductive generalizations, providing at the same time a richer and more nuanced insight into Quaker engagements with the materiality of images. Pointon shows how Quakers tended to negotiate "their way between prohibition and acceptance [of visual culture] in some kind of compromise."[128] Enlightened Quakers like Fothergill, for example, avidly collected engravings, shells, views, and botanical drawings without, as it has been routinely assumed, resorting to the usual invocations of education or utility to justify their attraction to images. On the contrary, such Quaker reformers formulated the paradoxical argument that an informed use of visual objects was a far more effective protection against the feared "Lust of the Eye," than a total "abstention" from it, as dictated by traditional Quaker attitudes.[129] This alone explains Quaker acceptance of Rymsdyk's pictures, especially as Fothergill himself, who bought and donated the pictures, was a distinguished member of this reforming Quaker elite for whom the cultivation of the eye was the best resistance to the organ's sensual excesses.

Yet Fothergill's initiative bespeaks a fascination with natural facsimiles that indicates a susceptibility to the pleasures of visual culture still more complex than the compromises described above. To put it differently, the reality-effects of Rymsdyk's simulations of nature seem to be uniquely apt in re-enacting in visual form the same tensions between art and nature – illusion and reality – that, according to Pointon, defined Quakers' fascination with visual culture. Hence, I would argue, the endless oscillations of Quakers "between necessity and superfluity, nature and art, spirit and body, truth and deception"[130] did not just allow some space for the passive acceptance of Rymsdyk's works; rather, this to and fro of contraries found in Rymsdyk's simulations a unique material template where these oscillations are captured, concretized, made explicit, and rehearsed in an art object.

While, in North America, anatomists and the public, including religious communities hostile to vision, endorsed visual innovation, in turn-of-the-century Britain anatomical realism and amplified imitations were still fiercely opposed both by polite men of the establishment and refined revolutionaries alike. In North America, where realism became the dominant style in nineteenth-century art, leaving behind a vibrant pictorial tradition, Rymsdyk's novelties found a friendlier audience and a more appropriate place of public existence. In 1817, the arrival, again from Britain, of Benjamin West's *Christ Healing the Sick in the Temple*, a work openly boastful of its intimate connections with the anatomical realism of the Parthenon Sculptures, opened another chapter in Pennsylvania Hospital's association with novel naturalist trends in high art. On this occasion, the memorable display of West's blockbuster picture at the same place where Rymsdyk's anatomical drawings were also held, foretold, in its own way, the extraordinary reach and complex cultural legacies of anatomy in North America.

NOTES

1 John L. Thornton, *Jan van Rymsdyk: Medical Artist of the Eighteenth Century* (Cambridge and New York, 1982), 93.

2 Michael Sappol, *A Traffic of Dead Bodies: Anatomy and Embodied Social Identity in Nineteenth-Century America* (Princeton, NJ, and Oxford: Princeton University Press, 2002), 48–9.

3 Wendy Moore, *The Knife-Man: The Extraordinary Life and Times of John Hunter, Father of Modern Surgery* (New York, 2005.

4 William Hunter, *Two Introductory Lectures* ... ([London], 1784), 118 and 120.

5 "Preface" in William Hunter, *The Anatomy of the Human Gravid Uterus* (Birmingham, 1774), [not paginated].

6 Ruth Richardson, *Death, Dissection and the Destitute*, 2nd ed. (Chicago, 1992), 52–73.

7 Ibid., 75–99, esp. 99.

8 Susan Lawrence, "Creating Medical Gentlemen in Eighteenth-Century London," in Vivian Nutton and Roy Porter, eds, *The History of Medical Education in Britain* (*Clio Medica*, Amsterdam and Atlanta, GA, 1995), 199–229.

9 Hunter, *Two Introductory Lectures*, 119.

10 Charles Nicholas Jenty, *The Demonstrations of a Pregnant Uterus of a Woman at her Full Time* (London, 1757), 8.

11 Charles Nicholas Jenty, *An Essay on the Demonstration of the Human Structure* (London, 1757), 9.

12 Lorraine Daston and Peter Galison, "The Image of Objectivity," *Representations* 40 (Autumn 1992): 81–128, esp. 85–6.

13 Jenty, *Essay on the Human Structure*, 9.

14 Ibid., 5.

15 Bruno Latour, "Drawing Things Together," in Michael Lynch and Steve Woolgar, eds, *Representation in Scientific Practice* (Cambridge, MA, and London, 1990), 27–44.

16 John Pickstone, *Medicine and Industrial Society: A History of Hospital Development in Manchester and Its Region 1752–1946* (Manchester, 1985) and Susan C. Lawrence, *Charitable Knowledge: Hospital Pupils and Practitioners in Eighteenth-Century London* (Cambridge, 1996).

17 William H. Williams, *America's First Hospital: The Pennsylvania Hospital, 1751–1841* (Wayne, PA, c. 1976), 8ff. See also Kristen A. Graham, *A History of the Pennsylvania Hospital* (Charleston, 2008).
18 Williams, *America's First Hospital*, 31–8, esp. 35 and 38; Elan Daniel Louis, "William Shippen's Unsuccessful Attempt to Establish the First 'School for Physick' in the American Colonies in 1762," *Journal of the History of Medicine and Allied Sciences* 44 (2) (1989): 218–39, esp. 226–7.
19 Williams, *America's First Hospital*, 29–30.
20 For the following references to Fothergill's letter to Pemberton, see the "Abstract" included in the *Pennsylvania Hospital Minutes Book* (8 November 1762). Extensive extracts from the letter can be found in Thomas G. Morton, *The History of the Pennsylvania Hospital* (Philadelphia, 1897 [rev. ed.]), 356–7.
21 Compare this commentary in Fothergill's letter with Hunter's polemical defence of anatomy in his *Introductory Lectures*, 66–9.
22 Louis, "William Shippen's Unsuccessful Attempt."
23 Betsy Copping Corner, *William Shippen, Jr., Pioneer in American Medical Education: A Biographical Essay with Notes, and the Original Text of Shippen's Student Diary, London, 1759–1760* (Philadelphia, 1951), 29.
24 Letter to Edward of Lancaster (Shippen's uncle) dated 10 March 1759, in Corner, *Shippen*, 8–9. See also Shippen's "Diary" in Corner, *Shippen*, 12, 16, 23, 29 and 32.
25 Corner, *Shippen*, 75–7.
26 C. Helen Brock, *The Correspondence of Dr William Hunter, 1740–83*, vol. 1 (London, 2008), 184. Two letters of thanks sent to William Hunter by his anatomy pupils from the period of Shippen's tuition encapsulate the spirit of association, patronage, and ambition cultivated among his students. See ibid., 116–18.
27 Corner, *Shippen*, 92–4.
28 Quoted in full, ibid., 95.
29 *Pennsylvania Hospital Minutes Book*, 9 November 1762; Morton, *History*, 357.
30 Louis, "William Shippen's Unsuccessful Attempt," 235–6.
31 *Pennsylvania Gazette*, 11 November 1762.
32 *Pennsylvania Hospital Minutes Book*, 17 May 1763, 373–4.
33 *Pennsylvania Gazette*, 19 May 1763. The same advertisement appeared again on 23 June 1763.
34 *Pennsylvania Hospital Minutes Book*, February 1763, 339.
35 Letter to Dr Fothergill, ibid., 29 December 1763, 433–4.
36 Williams, *America's First Hospital*, 35–7.
37 Marcia Pointon, "Quakerism and Material Culture," *Art History*, September 1997: 397–431.

38 Letter to Dr Fothergill, *Pennsylvania Hospital Minutes Book,* 29 December 1763, 433.

39 Roy Porter, "William Hunter: A Surgeon and a Gentleman," in Roy Porter and William F. Bynum, eds, *William Hunter and the Eighteenth-Century Medical World* (Cambridge, 1985), 7–34, esp. 12–28.

40 *Pennsylvania Gazette,* 11 November 1762; ibid., 29 September 1763.

41 Ibid., 11 November 1762.

42 Whitfield J. Bell, Jr, "William Shippen, Jr.'s Introductory Lecture, 1762," *Journal of the History of Medicine* 25 (1970): 478–9, esp. 478.

43 *Pennsylvania Gazette,* 17 February 1763.

44 Ibid., 11 November 1762.

45 Ibid., 31 January 1765.

46 Whitfield J. Bell, Jr, "The Court Martial of Dr. William Shippen, Jr., 1780," *Journal of the History of Medicine and Allied Sciences* 19 (3) (July 1964): 218–38. See also Louis, "Shippen's Unsuccessful Attempt," 238.

47 *Pennsylvania Gazette,* 26 September 1765.

48 Ibid., 29 September 1763.

49 Sappol, *Traffic,* 44–7.

50 *Pennsylvania Gazette,* 26 Sept. 1765; and ibid., 11 Jan. 1770.

51 Ibid., 11 January 1770, where the supporting affidavit of his assistant Joseph Harrison also appeared.

52 Ibid., 26 September 1765.

53 Ibid., 29 September 1763; again repeated on 27 September 1764.

54 For Hunter's extensive engagement in art and his precious collections of coins, paintings, drawings, and other cultural objects, see Peter Black, ed., *"My Highest Pleasures": William Hunter's Art Collection* (London, 2007).

55 Shippen was awarded the degree of Master of Arts by the College of New Jersey "in a very crouded, polite and learned assembly" (*Pennsylvania Gazette,* 13 October 1763); got elected fellow of the Royal College of Physicians at Edinburgh (ibid., 12 May 1768), and member of the American Philosophical Society (ibid., 10 January 1771).

56 Morgan's career reveals similar, if not more spectacular, synergies between medical careers and the pursuit of credentials of cultivation; see Louis, "Shippen's Unsuccessful Attempt," 230–1.

57 Lawrence, *Charitable Knowledge,* 200–1. For the various struggles and public rebuffs to which the anatomical and surgical profession was subject due to the unsuccessful management of its fraught associations with dissection, see Simon Chaplin, "The Divine Touch, or Touching Divines: John Hunter, David Hume, and the Bishop of Durham's Rectum," in *Vital Matters:*

Eighteenth-Century Views of Conception, Life, and Death, ed. Helen Deutch and Mary Terrall (Toronto, 2012), 224–8.

58 Ibid., 212–21.

59 Porter, "William Hunter," 29–31, esp. 30.

60 There has now been a great deal of work associating scientific labour in this period and the production of wonder and shock. See, for example, Richard Holmes, *The Age of Wonder* (London, 2008), or Simon Schaffer, "Natural Philosophy and Public Spectacle in the Eighteenth Century," *History of Science* 21 (1983): 1–43.

61 Philadelphia was, unsurprisingly, the place where James Graham, the legendary medical entertainer and quintessential impresario of spectacular science in the eighteenth century, picked up many of his notorious techniques. Lydia Syson, *Doctor of Love: George Graham and His Celestial Bed* (London, 2009).

62 Ibid., 51; see also 55.

63 William Shippen, *A Course of Anatomical Lectures Delivered by W. Shippen Professor of Anatomy and Surgery in the College of Pennsylvania*, 1766 (bound copy of autograph student notes kept in the National Library of Medicine, Bethesda, MD).

64 Shippen's approach to anatomy was clearly influenced by Galen-based natural theology and related notions that "the examination into nature was a species of theology." But, his fascination with anatomy is rife with the kind of tensions that marked Hunter's own sublime approach to the topic. See Bell, "Shippen's Introductory Lecture," 478–79, esp. 479.

65 Hunter, *Introductory Lectures*, 64, 81, and 83.

66 For the dark connotations of grave robbing in lay cultures and the riots they frequently caused, see Richardson, *Death*, 3–29 and 75–99.

67 Extract from the advertisement of Chovet's private lectures on anatomy and physiology in 1774–5, quoted in Morton, *History*, 360.

68 Sappol, *Traffic*, 33–4.

69 Ibid., 74–97, esp. 80–8.

70 Ibid., 77–8.

71 I have elsewhere explained the emergence of contemporary definitions of the sublime as an aggravated state of extreme contradictions, in which the extreme polarities of anatomical practice seem a nice fit. See Aris Sarafianos, "The Contractility of Burke's Sublime and Heterodoxies in Medicine and Art," *Journal of the History of Ideas* 69 (1) (January 2008): 23–48.

72 David Bromwich, "The Sublime before Aesthetics and Politics," *Raritan*, Spring 1997: 30, 33–4. See also David Bromwich, *The Intellectual Life of Edmund Burke* (Cambridge, MA, 2014), 65–96, esp. 68–9 and 89–91.

73 Edmund Burke, *A Philosophical Enquiry into the Origins of Our Ideas of the Sublime and Beautiful* (London, 1759), 77 and 79.

74 Ibid., 72–5.

75 Ibid., 24.

76 Richard Payne Knight, *An Analytical Inquiry into the Principles of Taste* (London, 1805), 89.

77 Burke, *Philosophical Inquiry*, 156–7.

78 Ibid., 52–3.

79 Denis Diderot, *Diderot on Art*, vol. I, trans. John Goodman (New Haven and London, 1995), 213–14. I analyse in detail such disturbing amalgamations of extreme affects and sensations in a forthcoming piece, "The Scaffold, the Stage and the Gallery: The Politics of Suffering and the Contested Power of 'Real and Imitated Distress' (1757–1816)" in *Performing and Beholding Pain, 1600–1800*, ed. Cornelius van der Haven, Tomas Macsotay, Karel Vanhaesebrouck (Manchester, 2016).

80 Hunter, *Introductory Lectures*, 62, 64, 81, and 83.

81 Burke, *Philosophical Inquiry*, 24.

82 Daston and Galison, "Image of Objectivity," 84–7, and Martin Kemp and Marina Warner, *Spectacular Bodies* (London, 2000), 68.

83 Martin Kemp, "True to Their Natures: Sir Joshua Reynolds and Dr William Hunter at the Royal Academy of Arts," *Notes and Records of the Royal Society of London*, January 1992: 77-88, esp. 79.

84 Kemp and Warner, *Spectacular Bodies*, 44–6.

85 "Preface" in William Hunter, *The Anatomy of the Human Gravid Uterus* (Birmingham, 1774 [not paginated]).

86 Ibid.

87 See, for example, Kemp, "True to Their Natures," 79–81.

88 Ibid., 80–6.

89 Hunter's preface reveals an acute awareness of existing divisions and tensions: "With regard to this work, which is a faithful representation of what was actually seen, the judgment of the public will probably be divided." See "Preface," in Hunter, *Anatomy* (not paginated).

90 "The Text of William Hunter's Lectures to the Royal Academy of Arts, 1769-1772," in Martin Kemp, *William Hunter at the Royal Academy of Arts* (Glasgow, 1975), 40.

91 Ibid., 39, 41, and 40.

92 Burke, *Philosophical Inquiry*, 75–6.

93 Ibid., 107 and 75.

94 Ibid., 101–2.

95 Ibid., 78.

96 W.J.T. Mitchell, "Eye and Ear: Edmund Burke and the Politics of Sensibility," in *Iconology: Image, Text, Ideology* (Chicago, 1986), 116–49, esp. 140.

97 Burke, *Philosophical Inquiry*, 76.

98 Ibid., 75–7.

99 "Text of Hunter's Lectures," in Kemp, *William Hunter*, 38.

100 Ibid., 39–40.

101 Ibid., 43–4.

102 Compare with Burke's sections on tragedy, sympathy, and imitation; Burke, *Philosophical Inquiry*, part 1, sections 12, 15, 16.

103 "Text of Hunter's Lectures" in Kemp, *William Hunter*, 40.

104 Ibid., 39.

105 Michael Sappol, *Dream Anatomy* (Bethesda, MD, 2006), 33–4.

106 Burke, *Philosophical Inquiry*, 141.

107 Ibid., 128.

108 Hunter, *Introductory Lectures*, 56.

109 Burke, *Philosophical Inquiry*, 128–9.

110 Naomi Schor, *Reading in Detail: Aesthetics and the Feminine* (1987) (London, 2007), 18 and 15. For another example of the same exclusive association of "detailism" with Romanticism, see Alan Liu, "Local Transcendence: Cultural Criticism, Postmodernism, and the Romanticism of Detail," *Representations* 32 (Autumn, 1990): 75–113.

111 For a brief account of similar tensions in British art, see Harry Mount, "Van Rymsdyk and the Nature-Menders: An Early Victim of the Two Cultures Divide," *British Journal for Eighteenth-Century Studies* 29 (2006): 79–96, esp. 84–6.

112 Similar cases of intimate collusion among fine detail, high numbers of marks, and violent acts of tearing through tissues are sensationally described in Hunter, *Anatomy*, plates XXVIII (fig. II, key O) and XXIX (fig. I, key BBB).

113 Kemp and Warner, *Spectacular Bodies*, 50.

114 Jenty, *Essay on the Human Structure*, 6–7.

115 Ibid., 7.

116 Jenty, *Pregnant Uterus*, 9.

117 Ibid., 50.

118 See Betsy Copping Corner, "Dr. Ibis and the Artists: A Sidelight upon Hunter's Atlas," *Journal of the History of Medicine* 6 (Winter 1951): 1–21, esp. 18ff.

119 Mount, "Van Rymsdyk," 85–6.

120 See Corner, "Dr. Ibis and the Artists."

121 John (Jan) and Andrew van Rymsdyk, *Museum Britannicum* (London, 1778), iv.
122 Ibid.
123 Ibid., vi.
124 Ibid., vi–vii.
125 Roy Porter, *Flesh in the Age of Reason* (London, 2004), 472–3.
126 Ibid., 474.
127 For the diverging histories of anatomy's role in the modernization of medicine in Britain and antebellum America, and, more particularly, the various institutional barriers to anatomical medicine in Britain's medical establishment, as opposed to the "anatomical enthusiasm" of antebellum America, contrast Russell Maulitz, *Morbid Appearances: The Anatomy of Pathology in the Early Nineteenth Century* (Cambridge, 1987), 110, 136–7, 175–6, 229, and Sappol, *Traffic*, esp. 53–73.
128 Pointon, "Quakerism ," 422.
129 Ibid., 426.
130 Ibid., 404.

chapter two

Disavowed and Reprobated: Anti-Quakerism in an Age of Revolution

SARAH CRABTREE

In 1764, an anonymous author from Philadelphia – later revealed to be Hugh Williamson – unleashed a torrent of anti-Quaker sentiments in his popular pamphlet *The Plain Dealer.* He remained embittered at Friends' opposition to the recent war and, as a result, spearheaded a movement to expel them from elected office. He claimed that these legislators had "cheerfully and liberally espoused the cause of our Indian enemies, inflamed their anger against the province, and thereby occasioned the massacre of many a hundred innocent people."[1] He also charged that "many of us are by them reduced to extreme poverty and famine and continue in hourly terror of loosing [*sic*] the miserable remains of life."[2] Here, Williamson propagated two common suspicions: first, that the Friends were Indian sympathizers and, as such, dangerous to their fellow colonists and disloyal to the British crown. Second, affluent Quakers continued to hoard the colony's wealth to the detriment of all others. Building on these misgivings, he reminded his audience that "we have abundant reason to conclude that they are not consulting our happiness, nor the growth of this province, but are prosecuting some scheme to continue their own power and our misery."[3] The Friends – deceitful, conspiratorial, and disloyal – were unfit to lead or to serve the colony of Pennsylvania.

Only twelve years later, another anonymous pamphleteer from Philadelphia similarly lambasted the Quakers for their failure to support a second war. Characterizing them as disingenuous and disloyal in his *Common Sense,* Thomas Paine appended an appeal entitled "To the Representatives of the Religious Society of the People called Quakers" to its second edition.[4] Indeed, despite the fact that the Friends had withdrawn from participation in formal politics, Paine remained irked that they "dabbled in matters, which the professed Quietude of your Principles instruct you not to meddle with." Paine was particularly angered at the Philadelphia Yearly Meeting's recently published appeal for restraint, moderation, and peace. Accusing them of "departing from the right way," he reproached the Society for ignoring the best interests of the people and instead "putting in for a share of the business." He further alleged that they exhibited "a tendency to undo that continental harmony and friendship" that Paine valued and that the rebel cause needed, and concluded by cautioning the Friends that they risked being "disavowed and reprobated by every inhabitant of America." The Quakers – corrupted, hypocritical, and seditious – undermined the revolutionary cause and were thus dangerous to the America nation and the American people.

Both of these propagandists identified the Friends as members of a dangerous political minority. Each labelled the Quakers as duplicitous and warned others of their avarice. Neither believed that the Friends had the best interests of their compatriots at heart. And yet, at the same time, there were striking differences between these two portrayals. For Williamson, Quaker legislators were unqualified to lead the colony and poor subjects of the British crown. For Paine, the Quakers themselves were unsuitable citizens of the American nation and aliens in this new country. These areas of divergence reveal an important tension between religion and nation in the late eighteenth century – a conflict between religious and political identity that many scholars have overlooked because they have accepted these depictions of the Quakers at face value. If we compare the Williamson and Paine pamphlets, however, the contrasts between them introduce a series of important questions: How can we reconcile these strikingly similar characterizations of Friends with these seemingly conflicting portrayals of their political positions? Why did these two authors expend such a disproportionate amount of time and energy criticizing a small, marginalized religious sect? How should we understand the political divide between Friends and their critics? And what were the consequences of this sustained and very public persecution of the Society of Friends?

The key to answering these questions is understanding how and why the Quakers' critics depicted the Society of Friends before and after the watershed of the American Revolution. Taken at face value, it seems difficult to reconcile Williamson's charge that Quakers were insufficiently loyal to the Crown with Paine's accusation only a decade later that they were too devoted in their attachment to Britain. If we turn these critics' claims inside out, however, the conflict between the Friends and their detractors becomes clearer. In other words, the Quakers' political stance had not changed in over a century, but the world the Friends and their opponents inhabited had changed a great deal in the last decade. Friends had espoused pacifism from the inception of their religious sect during the English Civil War and had no more supported the Seven Years' War than the War for Independence. Nor had they switched allegiances during the interwar period. They had remained unwavering in their commitment first and foremost to fellow members of the Society wherever they lived and they had continued to pledge their fealty only to divine authority and law. The Friends' religious and political positions had remained consistent.

But political tides had changed, and the realignment of the 1770s had larger consequences than the independence of the thirteen colonies. The very notions of belonging and loyalty, authority and obedience, involvement and identity had changed dramatically. The Revolution transformed those people who lived within the borders of the United States from British *subjects* to American *citizens* and this evolution had dire consequences for the Friends. As subjects of an empire, Friends could distance themselves from the actions of the state by choosing to "render unto Caesar." Society members invoked this scriptural reference to justify their compliance with worldly authority, particularly when paying their taxes, their only real direct contact with the Crown. This apportionment (rendering unto Caesar what is Caesar's and unto God what is God's) also allowed them to disconnect from the identity of state. The Crown was a remote actor, uninvolved in their daily life. This perception allowed them to build stronger relationships with their coreligionists, the people with whom they identified most intimately. As a result, their relationship to the state was more secondary and mediated than their closer and more direct relationship with their fellow Society members.

This distance was near impossible to maintain during the War for Independence as revolutionaries struggled to unite the population behind an American *nation*. Leaders decried the Quakers' difference and their diffidence, as they were impediments to the cultural and political homogeneity required to generate an independence movement, to forge a nation, and to solidify control over a citizenry. The peculiarities of the Friends, of course, were not new to their critics. Politically, the Friends had angered many people with their staunch commitment to pacifism, their refusal to swear oaths, and their frequent objections to tithes. Their opponents also had long lampooned the Quakers for their distinctive culture, including their unique dress and speech patterns as well as their idiosyncratic dating system. And yet while these practices provoked some of their neighbours and frequently aggravated those in power, they alone did not seal the Friends' fate. Amidst the nationalist movements of the late eighteenth century, it was their notorious tribalism that marked them as seditious.

This core commitment to one another could exist in the British Empire but not in the American nation for two reasons. First, an overwhelming majority of Friends were British subjects in the era before the War for Independence. Whether in the Caribbean, Ireland, Scotland, or the American colonies, the Quakers' devotion to their transatlantic coreligionists did not challenge the unity or the authority of the British Empire. The fragmentation of the Empire, however, forced Quakers to favour either their religious or their political allegiances. Their choice to align themselves principally with other Society members now meant that they actively supported foreigners. Perhaps even more importantly, the Revolution turned this trans*atlantic* community into a trans*national* community. In the years during and after the war, the Friends worked tirelessly to preserve unity within the Society. This bond was intolerable to American nationalists, as the active effort by Friends to choose their coreligionists over their compatriots hindered the movement for independence. It undermined nationalist ideologies as well by questioning the calls for citizens within set geopolitical boundaries to see themselves as part of the same nation. In this context, to identify first and foremost with "foreign" Quakers was to *dis*-identify with the nation in which they lived. Put another way, the Friends' investment in their religious community required a divestment from their geopolitical community – an identity for which there was room in an empire, but not a nation.

The tenets of empire that had allowed the relationships among distant Friends to flourish thus ended with the American Revolution. Friends' loyalty to the Society rather than to the nation in which they lived was a brazen statement amidst the wars and revolutions of the nineteenth century. This allegiance undermined claims to both political and cultural nations and highlighted the artificial and arbitrary nature of nation states. It was perhaps unsurprising, then, that as the nationalist fervour initiated by the American Revolution spread across the Atlantic World during the late eighteenth century, clashes multiplied between the Society of Friends and the governments under which they lived. French, British, and Irish Quakers soon experienced the same troubles at the turn of the nineteenth century as the Society members in the American colonies had endured a decade beforehand. Of course, Quakers neither had the large population nor wielded the same political power in these areas as they had in Pennsylvania, but the reactions by their opponents unfolded in comparable ways. The condemnations of Friends, confined to their public personas and political power during the Seven Years' War, had become an attack against Quakerism itself during the American Revolution and into the nineteenth century.

The outbreak of the Seven Years' War forced the Friends' hand. For years, Friends on both sides of the Atlantic dutifully had paid taxes to the British crown, arguing that this action did not violate their pacifist principles. They maintained that even if the government used these monies to conduct warfare, the Friends merely "rendered unto Caesar" and were not directly responsible for the Crown's actions. Quakers were loyal subjects of the Empire and made every effort to fulfil those responsibilities that did not conflict with their religious principles. Society members even assumed leadership roles, serving as legislators and governors in Pennsylvania and other colonies. This delicate balancing act ended, however, when the king directed the Quaker leaders in Philadelphia to fund the war on the frontier directly. What's more, the colonial legislature voted over Quaker objections to place a reward on Indian scalps brought back from the frontier. The hair-splitting position of the Quaker legislators thus became untenable, as the escalation of the conflict, the reformation afoot within the Society, and the changing composition of the colonial government forced the issue. Friends recused themselves from public office by the end of the war and the Quaker Party, led by Benjamin Franklin, became Quaker in name only.[5]

Friends' peace testimony reminded those inside and outside of the Society of their inability to serve worldly governments. For their part, ministers on both sides of the Atlantic initiated a "Reformation" that sought to return wayward members to the core tenets of the Society.[6] They demanded that all Friends condemn the violence emanating out from the American frontier and reverberating throughout the Atlantic World. Noted British Public Friends such as Catherine Payton, Mary Piesley, and Samuel Fothergill joined American ministers like John Woolman, Israel Pemberton, and Anthony Benezet in pressuring Quaker legislators to resign from the legislature and Friends in general to withdraw from worldly society altogether. As Anthony Benezet observed, there was "an impossibility for us, as a People … in times of War … to maintain the Government & be Honest & true to that noble, evangelike Testimony which God has given us to bear as a People."[7] Here, the Quaker reformation encouraged Friends to leave their roles in government and their close association with political society in order to re-establish the distance from the state afforded them by the structure of empire. They had to leave the seat of government in order to remain true to their religious principles, but they did not have to renounce the British Empire.

Their critics supported this mass exodus wholeheartedly. Incensed by the Quaker legislators' opposition to the war, Friends' detractors launched a print crusade against them. Significantly, these authors directed their outrage towards the Quaker Party and its leaders, rather than the Society of Friends itself. Indeed, as Peter Silver remarked, the pamphlet war was noteworthy for its "tolerant intolerance," and the attempt by at least Rev. William Smith, the leading anti-Quaker author, "to somehow keep up his attacks on Quakers as a political class, and on the German role in supporting them, without seeming to vilify these groups as groups."[8] This parsing was evident in nearly all the prominent anti-Quaker authors. In his *The Quaker Unmask'd*, David James Dove wanted to avoid all efforts to "condemn the Lump of Quakers,"[9] while Smith was quick to distinguish in a later pamphlet between the majority of Friends and the "pacifistic Quaker legislator" who was "a Betrayer of his Country."[10] Hugh Williamson, the most well-known of these authors, similarly lambasted the Quaker Party while avoiding impugning the Society itself. He entreated his readers to vote them out of office, querying, "Are we always to be slaves, must we groan forever beneath the yoke of three Quaker counties?"[11] Here, Williamson chafed against the disproportionate political power brandished by the Friends, but largely refrained from denouncing the Society itself.

Illustrators also skirted this fine line, as anti-Quaker images tended to focus on two notorious individuals: Israel Pemberton, an important Public Friend who incessantly lobbied the legislature against the war, and Abel James, another Public Friend and clerk of the Friendly Association. Cartoonists blamed these men for the obstructionism of the Quaker Party and, while certainly deploying stereotypes about the Friends to satirize these prominent members, confined their criticisms to their political actions (or, perhaps more accurately, to their political *in*actions). A famous drawing entitled "An Indian Squau King Wampus Spies" accused a lustful Israel Pemberton of being "in bed with the enemy." The caption accused the Friends of ignoring the dangers faced by those in the backcountry while disingenuously lecturing their fellow citizens about the duties of conscience. As such, they continued to permit the Indians to murder white residents, to plot the overthrow of the government, and to impoverish the colony. Another widely distributed image from the period depicted Abel James handing out tomahawks to American Indians to use on non-Quakers. The implication was clear in this illustration as well: Friends actively supported the colony's enemies while ignoring the desperation of their (white) neighbours.

The anti-Quaker campaign during the Seven Years' War was thus directed primarily at the Quaker Party. As pacifists, the Friends were unreliable and dangerous legislators. Their refusal to wage war made them unfit for governance and the main focus of the print war was removing the Friends from public office. Their peace testimony meant that they could not serve as agents of the Empire or as direct representatives of the state. As subjects, however, Friends were acceptable members of society. Quakers were troublesome during times of war, to be sure, but they certainly posed no threat to the British Empire. In fact, even when these pamphlets deployed more sweeping criticisms of the Society as a whole, detractors indicted them for aiding the enemy, but not of *being* an enemy. In other words, their critics lambasted the Friends for their supposed support of American Indians, and thus for being flawed and irresponsible subjects, but they still recognized them as Pennsylvanian and as British. They were part of the Empire – an infuriating and regrettable part, perhaps – but undoubtedly members of the imperial community.

This attitude began to change in the American colonies during the aftermath of the Seven Years' War. The fury against the Quaker Party sparked by the war seemed to arouse deeper suspicions about the Society itself and to unearth long-simmering resentments against the Friends as a whole. Burgeoning nationalist sentiment contributed to this antipathy, as Americans began to see themselves not only as separate and distinct from Britain but also as a unified people with a shared history and culture. These anti-Quaker authors maintained that the Friends' cultural and political divergence from their compatriots signified their fundamental "apartness" from the rest of society and that these very visible and vocal differences threatened the harmony of the new nation. Some of their critics went even farther, suggesting that the Friends' very existence challenged the stability of their government. These opponents held that the Quakers' belief in their status as a chosen people was merely a pretext for their notorious tribalism and that this insularity had the potential to shake the very foundation of civil government. In fact, one anonymous author concluded his first anti-Quaker tract by quoting the political philosopher David Hume:

> Factions subvert Government, render Laws impotent, and beget the fiercest Animosities among Men of the same Nation, who ought to give mutual

assistance and protection to each other ... They naturally propagate themselves for many Centuries and seldom end but by the total Dissolution of that Government, in which they are planted. They are besides, weeds which grow more plentifully in rich Soils and tho' despotic Government are not quite free from them, it must be confessed, that they rise more easily, and propagate themselves faster in free Governments.[12]

Here, the author built on the resentment against the Quaker Party that was expressed by Williamson in order to express a growing apprehension about the problem posed by the Society of Friends itself. This passage cautioned that the diversity of peoples was fundamentally de-stabilizing for a government and criticized his compatriots for being too tolerant of the religious, ethnic, and national difference within its borders.

This development – a movement from an antipathy towards the Quaker Party to a hostility towards the Society as a whole – signified an important political transition within the American colonies. During the Seven Years' War, critics alleged that the Quakers were incapable of leading the colony. This conflict arose more acutely during outbreaks of war when the state required of its leaders a commitment to military campaigns, the assessment of wartime levies, and the swearing of loyalty oaths. The discord between the Quaker Party and the British crown during the Seven Years' War, therefore, was one between nonconformist legislators and the state and did not extend to the Society as a whole. Neither Quakers nor Quakerism threatened the tenets of empire because imperialism accommodated difference. By their very nature, empires contained "nations within nations," while its strong, centralized state held together a diverse array of people.[13] The imperial state did not require a homogeneous citizenry, only an obedient one. It did not rely on its subjects subsuming alternative identities, and it did not demand that they take up arms for its military campaigns. It required only that its officials carry out its orders and that its subjects obey these commands. In return, the British "empire-state" would provide them with protection from its enemies.[14] In this context, the Quaker Party was the problem, not Quakerism itself.

And yet as "Philadelphienses" forewarned, "factions" such as the Society of Friends threatened to "subvert Government." The rhetorical shift portended the rise of an American *nation*, manifested in its earliest stages as a nascent patriotism or nationalism. This worry that the Quakers' marked difference from their compatriots disrupted the affective bonds between "Men of the same Nation" connoted a need for homogeneity among a budding American nation that did not exist within the

British Empire for several reasons. First, a nation relied on its citizens to identify with one another and to invest themselves in the "imagined community" of the nation.[15] Shared theological world views reinforced feelings of kinship among a population and gave credence to assertions of a unified homogeneous citizenry. Religious difference highlighted the dissimilarities between nationalities and fuelled antagonism between rival nations. If these divisions existed within a state or an empire, they could disrupt the perception of homogeneity that several scholars have argued must be attained in order for a population to come together as a nation.[16] Indeed, as some historians have maintained, those in authority recognized that such internal discord could portend rebellion, secession, or civil war.[17] Second, the Quakers were connected only to each other. They felt an affinity not with their nearest neighbours but with their fellow Society members – even those who resided in foreign countries. Finally, Friends rejected the affective appeal of the nation, divesting from the geopolitical community in order to devote themselves to their religion. As the American nation attempted to separate itself from the British state, this kinship and this *dis*-identification undermined the process by which it cohered and established legitimacy. As a result, the harassment and persecution of the Friends that began during the Seven Years' War and escalated exponentially during the War for Independence.

The anti-Quaker campaign during the Revolution also assumed a different tenor. The stakes were now higher, as the Friends were not unreliable leaders or untrustworthy subjects but dangerous imposters. The harassment therefore intensified, moving from attacks in the press and vigilante harassment to higher-profile and even officially endorsed targeting of the Friends. Most of the anti-Quaker sentiment once again centred in Philadelphia, because the highest proportion of Friends resided in and around the area, because the city was the political centre of the Revolution, and because American and British forces clashed repeatedly in the area. The tensions mounted throughout the war as the series of anti-Quaker broadsides and individual acts of persecution gave way to government-sanctioned prosecution of Society members.

Towards the beginning of the conflict, Friends' enemies took to the press again. Thomas Paine led the way with his address to the members of the Society of Friends in the second edition of *Common Sense*. He was responding to the *Caution* published by a select committee of Friends only months beforehand. In it, they urged their compatriots to move forward slowly and to be prudent and circumspect in their actions. Many scholars have used this document as evidence of Friends' loyalty to the

British crown, but the Friends merely wanted to preserve the protection afforded them under the 1689 Act of Toleration – a recognition of religious liberty, it should be noted, that was granted to nonconformists within the British Empire and not for some time within the American nation. Paine resented the Friends' defence of Britain and their admonition of their compatriots. He bitterly told Society members to "preach repentance to *your* king," perhaps deliberately taking advantage of the linguistic slippage between the titles used for both King George and the Christian divine. This anti-Quaker trope became commonplace, as another author similarly employed this sardonic play on words when complaining that "too great a number of the members of this State are the avowed votaries of *submission to higher powers.*"[18] Clearly, these authors used these accusations of disloyalty in order to mark the Friends as interlopers and to suggest that their allegiance rested elsewhere. They existed outside the boundaries of the American nation – an accusation, it bears repeating, that critics did not lob against the Society during the Seven Years' War. Detractors warned of the peril in which Quaker *leadership* placed the colony, but they did not deem the mere existence of the Friends a threat to its survival. The nationalist fervour sparked by the American Revolution changed this outlook, however. As Paine's diatribe made clear, the Friends exhibited "a tendency to undo that continental harmony and friendship" that Paine valued and that the rebel cause needed.

Following these salvos against the Friends, the infamous "Spanktown controversy" then filled the newspapers from New England to the Carolinas for over a year.[19] In 1777, a packet of papers was delivered anonymously to Congress. The contents purportedly originated with the "Spanktown" meeting of the Society of Friends and contained secret intelligence intended for the British regarding the movements of the American forces. Friends proved beyond a doubt that there was no such meeting and that the papers were counterfeit, but the firestorm of anti-Quaker sentiment that ensued in the wake of the Spanktown scandal illustrated the continued distrust of the Friends by their compatriots. Quakers were once again suspected as traitors to the cause and accused of committing acts of sedition against the governments under which they lived. The authors of the forgery seized on the common assumptions that the Quakers were traitors, that they actively plotted against the government under which they lived, that they cared not a whit for the safety or security of their compatriots, and that they used the cloak of religion to conceal their true motivations and actions. Their opponents now considered all Quakers to be dangerous to the war effort and Society meetings themselves to be fertile ground for sedition – a marked departure from the careful ways that their critics minced their words during the Seven Years' War.

The allegations contained in these pamphlets inflamed the anti-Quaker sentiment already extant in the colonies. Towards the beginning of the war, the anti-Quaker sentiment remained confined to mostly non-official channels. Anonymous broadsides censured the entire Society and impugned the reputations of its members. Mobs gathered outside of Quaker homes and businesses, breaking the windows of their residences and storefronts, and crowds confronted members of the Society when they attempted to attend weekly meetings for worship.[20] As the war wore on, the campaign against the Friends spread further across the population and began to rise through the ranks of government and the anti-Quaker campaign began to operate via pseudo-official conduits. For example, Pennsylvanian ministers Robert Walker and his wife were shot at by a group of American militiamen who then proceeded to ransack their home and steal their food, furniture, and specie.[21] New York minister Daniel Sands and his wife were also victims of these semi-official attacks. According to his account, 500 soldiers surrounded their home. He overheard several of them discussing whether or not to kill him and his wife, and one of the guards stationed outside their house did shoot at them through their window. The militia then plundered their home, stealing most of its contents.[22]

In both cases, the soldiers later claimed that these acts were retribution for the Friends' repudiation of the Revolutionary cause: if the Quakers refused to support the American war effort, in other words, the militiamen would ensure that they contributed one way or another. Neither Walker nor Sands ever uncovered any proof that officers had directed these soldiers to target Society members, but both men certainly believed that the militiamen felt justified in attacking a prominent Friend because of his religious principles and that they suffered fewer consequences because of the anti-Quaker sentiment of the military, the government, and the population at large. In this way, these acts of violence against Quakers, just for being Quakers, could be categorized somewhere between vigilantism and the sanctioned targeting of Friends by an arm of the government – a clear escalation from the anti-Quaker sentiment during the Seven Years' War, when government or military officials never became involved in the persecution of Friends.

As the war progressed, those in power took a more active role in both forcing the Friends to contribute to the war effort and in punishing them for their observance of the peace testimony. All over the colonies, nearly every Friend suffered from the distraint of property imposed by the government in lieu of war taxes, as Elizabeth Drinker famously and meticulously detailed in her diary.[23] The Friends also lost much of their collective property, as their meeting houses were used as headquarters and makeshift hospitals by both sides during the conflict, and were damaged or destroyed as a result.[24] In Massachusetts, a wealthy Nantucket whaler, William Rotch, was charged with treason for abetting the British and the Pennsylvania authorities hanged two Friends for treason for providing directions on a river crossing to a British officer.

The starkest examples of government prosecution occurred during the difficult years of 1777 and 1778, when the American cause was perhaps at its nadir. The Pennsylvanian government exiled – without trial – fourteen prominent Philadelphian Quakers and one British Public Friend to Virginia under suspicion of treason.[25] Under a Congressional Resolution passed in late August of 1777 (conspicuously in the immediate wake of the Spanktown controversy), government officials were "requested to call all persons, within the respective states, notoriously disaffected, forthwith to be disarmed and secured, until such time as they may be released without injury to the common cause." The act was particularly aimed at containing the threat posed by those "who have not manifested their attachment to the American cause" and demanded that the proper authorities conduct "a diligent search" for "firearms, swords, and bayonets" of all such persons. The government also seized all their "political papers," which, revealingly in the case of the Friends, included all their correspondence with British Quakers.[26] The experiences of the so-called Virginia Exiles were much publicized and served as a warning to Friends everywhere that the government itself would remand its own citizens without formal charges, thereby denying them the very liberty the war purportedly was fought to secure. Indeed, even upon their release, these men were treated as "prisoners of the State of Pennsylvania" – in other words, as enemies of the state.

These anti-Quaker feelings were thus shared by many people, including high-ranking officials, during the Revolution. The Friends were enemies and traitors who hid behind religious rhetoric in order to disguise their attempts to undermine the war effort and to undercut the government. These misgivings – already present before the armed conflict began – were shared even more widely during and after the war. Their opponents interpreted the Friends' opposition to the Revolution as an impediment not only to the war effort but also to the process of nation building. Post-war editorials spell out this conflict even more plainly. Following Paine's lead, one author labelled the Friends "British subjects, aliens, and cowards who had no share in the declaration of independence, in the formation of our Constitution, or in establishing them by ARMS."[27] This author's branding of the Friends as "aliens," or people living outside the purview of the governments under which they lived, was striking indeed. The Quakers, for their part, recognized this attempt to mark them as outsiders, remarking after the war's conclusion that they were "*treated as aliens and enemies to their country.*"[28] The transition here from their poor showing as imperial subjects to their fundamental incompatibility as citizens of a nation is clear. During the Seven Years' War, the attempt was to remove them from power. During and after the American Revolution it was to demarcate them as outside of the polity.

The Society insisted that its membership had "*remained committed to itself, and not to a foreign land.*"[29] Noteworthy, of course, was the striking absence of any attempt to affirm its loyalty to the American cause. Friends sought repeatedly to reassure their critics that they did not ally themselves with the enemy but could not bring themselves to pledge their own allegiance to the governments under which they lived. Thus, British minister Thomas Colley promised the king on his embarkation to America, "We have no plot to facilitate, no friends to serve, no interest at state, but that of all mankind,"[30] while Pennsylvanian John Pemberton pledged on taking his leave for Great Britain: "I have no sinister view, or worldly concern to promote, but singly, the honest and upright Discharge of a duty."[31] The Society was willing to disavow its allegiance to the opposing side but unwilling to identify itself with the nation or empire in which Friends lived. It "remained committed to itself" rather than align itself with any worldly nation.[32]

This positionality, however, posed a threat to the very foundation of the nation state. Fledgling governments could not abide a people living within the borders of "their" country but refusing to identify with it or, more importantly, to recognize its authority. The author continued:

> These men certainly are not in earnest, when they talk and write of *liberty* and of the *sacred rights of conscience.* Their conduct contradicts all their speeches and publications; and if they were truly sensible of their folly and wickedness in opposing the new government, instead of trying to excite a civil war (in which they will bear no more part than they did in the late war with Great Britain) they ought rather to acknowledge, with gratitude, the lenity of their fellow citizens, in permitting them to live among us with impunity, after thus

transgressing and violating the great principles of liberty, government, and conscience.[33]

Echoing Paine's claims, this author contended that the Friends "transgressed and violated" the very underpinnings of the new American government – a sense of belonging and of fraternity as well as a belief in a shared commitment to and willingness to sacrifice for the nation.

The Friends, however, rejected this national fraternity, choosing instead to reaffirm their commitment to one another during these times of political realignment. Pennsylvanian minister John Woolman, for example, wrote to Irish Friend Susannah Lightfoot that Quakers remained "members of one body," who shared a "fellowship of true and unfeigned love," and thus "if one member suffers the other suffers with it and if one rejoices and abounds the rest are rejoiced in a degree of the same abounding love."[34] New York minister David Sands reflected the biblically infused language of the London Yearly Meeting when he pledged to William Jackson that "we being many are one Bread being Baptized by the one Spirit in the one Body."[35] And Massachusetts minister Mehitabale Jenkins wrote that the bond among Friends was one "which time nor distance I believe will wear out."[36] She further believed that the "yunaty of brethren and sisters is pracsus thing to me" and reflected on the love "that causes us to remember and pray for won another if we are unduly separated in bodey. I can not expras the lov to the full that I feal to som of you in tham parts. Oh may it continue."[37] In each of these cases, American Friends reassured themselves that American independence did not sever the ties between their British coreligionists and themselves. Their travels and epistles during the immediate post-war period illustrated their attempts to comfort their membership that the fragmentation of the Empire would not cause a fragmentation among the Society.

At every level of the Society, Friends endeavoured to heal the fissures caused by the late war. In this regard, the London Yearly Meeting led the way. Its annual epistles reflected an overt attempt to maintain the connection among the British and American Yearly Meetings in spite of the political partition. Thus, in the closing years of the war, the London Yearly Meeting reassured its American correspondents that "though outwardly separated from you, beloved friends, yet as brethren of one family, and united in the same glorious cause, we partake of your burthens and exercises."[38] After the war concluded, the proclamations became even more forthright, as when the London Yearly Meeting comforted its membership, promising that "United in the same religious fellowship, and baptized by one spirit, into one body, we salute you in the sympathy of the gospel of Christ and remain your FRIENDS and BRETHREN."[39]

Perhaps even more importantly, Friends discounted the importance of the nation during this crucial period. New York minister Henry Hull, for example, told his British audience that "before him all the nations of the Earth are but as the small dust of the balance."[40] And Rhode Island minister Job Scott, in a famous prophesy made from his deathbed, warned Friends not to be distracted by the "great commotions and overturnings in the nations," as they were insignificant in comparison to "the [divine] foundation that cannot be moved."[41] During this period of intense political instability, the Friends actually increased their transatlantic travel, despite the fact that many ministers believed it was "harder to travel now in this day and time than ever was in any age of the world since we were a people."[42] The volume of correspondence also rose markedly, as attested by the epistles and letters that flew back and forth between American and British meetings and members during this period. This period was also one of marked expansion for the Society, as the warfare that engulfed Europe in the late eighteenth century actually increased their membership. Soldiers who encountered the Friends' wartime protests carried information about the Society back to their homes countries, as was the case for several Norwegian soldiers who deserted their posts in France after stumbling across Quaker anti-war pamphlets.

Those in power were disquieted by the rapid spread of Friends' principles, and this relationship between the Quakers and the European governments under which they lived during the French Revolution and the wars that followed illustrate the continued clash between Quakerism and nationalism during the late eighteenth and early nineteenth centuries. Non-Friends harboured the same suspicions and animosity towards Society members on the other side of the Atlantic, accusing them of undermining the war effort, plotting against those in power, and corrupting the nation with their rabble-rousing. Once again, the backlash against Friends was the most serious in countries with revolutionary movements – namely, France and Ireland. Even in Great Britain, however, the government moved against the Friends during the Napoleonic conflicts – a period that several scholars have identified as one of burgeoning nationalist sentiment.[43] The Quakers, no matter how much time elapsed or how far they travelled, could not elude the antagonism that others harboured towards them.

There was perhaps no better example of Quakerism's inescapable stigma than William Rotch, a wealthy whaler and Public Friend from Nantucket. Born to a prominent family, he counted among his acquaintances some of the foremost families in Massachusetts. He had amassed significant political and economic capital by the eve of the American Revolution, and until that point, had experienced little conflict between his business empire and his Quaker convictions. The war, however, destroyed this harmony. Caught quite literally in the crossfire between the British and the Americans, Nantucket was devastated. Despite repeated pleas by the islanders, neither the British army nor the Massachusetts government provided adequate supplies to the island. William Rotch attempted to seek help from both sides, alternately leading a group of men aboard a British vessel to request provisions and then writing to the American army imploring them to send any rations they could spare. He was, for the most part, unsuccessful. Even if either camp could have spared any materials for Nantucket residents, neither was much inclined to help Rotch of all people. He had gained notoriety after sinking an entire ship filled with bayonets rather than allow them to be used for "blood-letting" by the resource-starved Americans. He was put on trial for treason during the early years of the Revolution, and, though he was acquitted, his reputation mirrored the island's economy: neither ever recovered. In the last years of his life, Rotch was still defending his action in his autobiography, *Memorandum: Written by William Rotch in the eightieth year of his age* and in a series of terse letters with former United States president John Adams.[44]

Until this point, Rotch's experiences were in keeping with the difficulties encountered by several other Friends during the American Revolution. His situation turned exceptional, however, when he made the decision to relocate his entire whaling operations to France only a few years before the outbreak of the French Revolution.[45] Louis XVI had recruited the Rotch family to build a whaling industry in Dunkirk and Rotch had negotiated with the king to secure the right to practice his religion freely. Unfortunately, these promises vanished with the monarchy, and in perhaps one of history's greatest ironies, he and his son were summoned in 1791 by the Revolutionary government to answer for their refusal to support the cause of liberty. Upon hearing the news, Rotch wrote to his wife: "I little expected ever to be in the midst of another Revolution after that of America was completed but here we are."[46] He and his son Benjamin delivered a speech to the members of the assembly entitled "The Respectful Petition of the Christian Society of Friends called Quakers delivered before the National Assembly." The content of the appeal bore what for both Rotch men must have been a disquieting resemblance to their protests against the American *and* the

British authorities during the War for Independence. While choosing not to indict him, the revolutionaries nevertheless ignored his pleas for religious tolerance, and thus, only a short time later, Rotch was forced to petition again both the National Assembly of France and the local officials in order to request permission not to illuminate his house in observance of French victories.[47] In another ominous parallel, riotous mobs had descended on the Rotch home when they heard of his plans to keep his windows dark. They threatened to burn the house to the ground with its inhabitants trapped inside. Frustrated and fatigued, William and Benjamin Rotch finally fled France for Great Britain under the cover of night shortly afterwards.

These fifty or so Nantucketers were not the only Friends to run into problems with the French government, as the regime reacted even more harshly to native-born French Quakers. Revolutionaries, who had previously admired the tenets of the Society, now found them ill-suited for the French nation. They began to investigate the tiny meetings in Congenies and imprisoned the well-known Public Friend Jean de Marsillac. Marsillac had become convinced of Quaker principles years beforehand, but had kept silent about his conversion for fear of retribution. He gained the courage to organize a meeting for worship in Paris only as a result of his friendship with William Rotch, who warned him that he needed to prepare himself for "the mocking and scoffing that are so commonly the attendants" of Quakerism.[48] He came to the notice of the authorities in 1793 when he attempted to establish a school and college for 150 children orphaned by the ongoing wars in Europe. That same year, he also petitioned the National Assembly to request that all Friends be exempted from military duty and wartime taxes. He offered to pay an annual fee to the local government on the condition that it not be used to finance the war effort or the Catholic church.

Although he argued that the establishment of regular Society meetings and a Quaker school would "advance the sentiment of fraternity" and that it was in the "national interest to encourage [the efforts of] such disinterested and generous men," the French government remained suspicious of his motives.[49] Marsillac persisted, promising the authorities that the meeting for worship and its school would attract Friends from England, Ireland, Holland, Germany, and even the United States and that their visits would encourage the "free exchange of ideas" by men who were "well adapted to a republican style."[50] Still, the revolutionaries remained unmoved. They distrusted the influence of foreigners and remained wary of Friends' principles. They lauded Quaker tenets in *theory*, but could not abide them in practice – let alone within their borders or in the midst of such turmoil.

Unfortunately for Marsillac, he could convince neither politicians nor local non-Quaker citizens of his honest intentions. He received a letter from the authorities declaring that the people within the district of Vendome were "taking alarm at the dangerous doctrine of Friends"[51] and their increasing celebrity.[52] They also claimed that the principles of Friends were "out of harmony" with the French nation and that their dangerous lifestyles "would be difficult to hold in check."[53] The government was convinced that Quakers would indoctrinate their membership as well as the children attending their school to manifest a lack of loyalty to the state.[54] Marsillac's efforts to appease the French authorities failed, and he eventually abandoned the project. The meeting for worship likewise withered and the Society of Friends in France disappeared for almost a generation.

The extraordinary experiences of William Rotch and Jean de Marsillac during this tumultuous period in France demonstrate the ways in which revolutionary leaders and nationalist governments in Europe continued to perceive Quakerism as a threat to their movements. The reactions by the authorities were similar to those in America, as each branded the Friends as "aliens" who were "out of harmony" with the nation. Their compatriots distrusted Society members' commitment to their coreligionists and maintained that their faith practice prevented them from fulfilling the most basic duties of citizenship.

Across the Channel, British Friends began to encounter the same hostilities as their American and French counterparts. Though they were exempt for much of the eighteenth century from the most strident accusations and the harshest persecutions, this tolerance evaporated when the British people felt directly threatened by a French invasion. After fleeing the oppression in France, William and Benjamin Rotch were appalled to discover that the British authorities were inspecting their private correspondence for evidence of sedition.[55] Benjamin was further shocked when his neighbours accused him of being a spy for Napoleon. Apparently, they thought that his Quaker garb was evidence of his 'foreign-ness' and thus his disloyalty to the Crown.[56] British Friends responded to these kinds of allegations differently. Some insisted that their relationship to the Crown had not changed and that they could continue to "render unto Caesar." Others drifted away from the Society, or left it altogether, frustrated by its intransigence regarding pacifist doctrine. But in yet another striking parallel to the years in between the Seven Years' War and the War for Independence, British Friends re-initiated a reformation. They turned out those members who profited from the war in any way and launched a new wave of protests against the wartime levies imposed by the Crown. Scores of Friends were imprisoned all over Britain; a particularly intransigent group became infamous for their extended incarceration at York Castle and their very public protests against these taxes.

Friends also came under fire from the British government for their vocal support of Ireland in the years before and after the 1798 rebellion. Here again, the Irish nationalist movement stemmed from a struggle for independence – a parallel noted by Irish and American Friends.[57] British officials accused the Friends of inciting an uprising and of aiding the rebels during the conflict. This action prompted several American Quakers, including New York minister Hannah Barnard, and numerous British Friends, such as Benjamin Rotch, to act decisively in defence of their Irish coreligionists. They insisted that while their sympathies remained with all "distressed creatures," they remained detached from worldly tumult. Once more, government officials distrusted these assertions of impartiality and repeatedly burned Quaker homes, ransacked their businesses, and seized their meeting houses. One author attempted to explain this treatment in an account published after the rebellion:

> When a kingdom is divided in itself, it is difficult for any to remain neutral ... The members of a Society which neither united with the political nor the religious views of these factious bands, might naturally be looked upon with suspicion by both; at least they were not likely to be considered as friends; as a part of the community, which did not exert itself actively in aiding the [unintelligible] it was bound, in all cases of purely civil obligation, to obey, in order to suppress a rebellion, the motives are objects of which it could not possible approve, the Society, in its relation to the government, seemed to manifest but a spurious loyalty.[58]

Here again, those in power had accused Friends of disloyalty, insisting that their lack of investment in or dedication to the government under which they lived signalled their status as outsiders, as those "not likely to be considered ... as a part of the community."

During these heady years at the turn of the nineteenth century, the fledgling communities of Quakers in Pyrmont and Minden endured similar struggles to those in France, Britain, and Ireland. Prussian authorities arrested not only the leaders of these meetings but also those American and British Public Friends who visited these tiny outposts during the 1790s. This small community – never more than fifty members strong – continued to struggle with the government. They refused to swear oaths of allegiance, to celebrate national holidays, or to serve in the military. These far-flung Friends wrote to the London Yearly Meeting that they endeavoured to secure "toleration" from the government under which they lived, but that the prospects were not favourable. The Prince of Prussia himself claimed that "the Quakers, whose confession of faith excludes its followers from the most important civil duties in an independent state ... Even to tolerate them is a favour, which must not be extended too far, lest the state should suffer by it."[59] After this declaration, the prince forbade any new members from joining the Society and denied the existing members the right to purchase any property for their use. The community – cut off from any foreign or domestic support – withered.

By the turn of the nineteenth century, the Atlantic world had been witness to almost fifty years of continual warfare. The violence of imperial expansion and the upheaval of nationalist movements had impacted countless people, changing the ways that they related to their governments, to each other, and to themselves. And yet while the Age of Revolution had inspired new feelings of belonging for some, it had defined others as outsiders. Quakers were one example of this exclusion. The reaction of their critics to the transnational orientation of the Society illustrates what was lost as nation states emerged as the primary means of political organization in the modern world.

Members of the Society of Friends became caught up in these political and religious realignments as both actors and symbols. Their distinctive dress and speech interrupted the cultural homogeneity that nationalists employed as evidence of a cultural nation. As a result, the Friends' visible and audible difference disrupted the underpinnings of a nation in ways that it did not for an empire. The Quakers' peace testimony also dismayed the governments under which they lived, as it challenged the obligations of citizens more than it ever did the responsibilities of subjects. The most significant challenge of Quakerism, however, was their reticence. Friends were notorious for their tribalism – an insularity that could exist quite easily within the British Empire, but ran afoul of the new political boundaries between Great Britain and the

United States. When Friends lost the unifying identity provided by the British Empire, they focused all their efforts on preserving their religious bonds. In order to do so, Quakers declined to invest in the new "American" nation and proceeded to divest from the British Empire. Their ties with their coreligionists were upheld only after severing those of their compatriots.

This orientation complicates our ideas about the consolidation of political power in the eighteenth century and challenges us to recognize the alternative forms of community and nationalism that existed (and clashed) during this important era. Indeed, after considering this conflict between religion and nation, one Friend was led to reflect: "When patriotism is made to supersede this vital spring of all virtue [the Gospel], then the glory of this world is made to eclipse the brighter glory of that which is to come … for the patriotism of a Christian is continually aiming at the highest interests of man; and … needs not the aid of the sword."[60] At last, the Friends and their critics had found something on which to agree: Quakerism and nationalism were incompatible. Understanding the reasons behind and the consequences of this conflict will allow us to unpack the fraught relationships between religion and nation, patriotism and dissent, and revolution and reform that continue to impact similar discussions today.

NOTES

1 Hugh Williamson, *The Plain Dealer, or Remarks on Quaker Politics in Pennsylvania* (Philadelphia, 1764), 23.

2 Ibid., 22.

3 Ibid., *The Plain Dealer*, 24.

4 Thomas Paine, *Common Sense: Addressed to the Inhabitants of America … A New Edition, with Several Additions in the Body of the Work. To Which is added an Appendix; together with an Address to the People called Quakers* (Philadelphia, 1791).

5 See Jack Marrietta's important work *The Reformation of American Quakerism, 1748–1783* (Philadelphia, 1984), 150.

6 Ibid., esp. chapters 7 and 8.

7 Ibid., 158.

8 Peter Silver, *Our Savage Neighbors: How Indian War Transformed Early America* (New York, 2008), 197.

9 David James Dove, quoted in Peter Silver, *Our Savage Neighbors*, 206.

10 Rev. William Smith in Peter Silver, *Our Savage Neighbors*, 199.

11 Williamson, *The Plain Dealer*, 22.

12 "Philadelphienses," in *Remarks on the Quaker Unmask'd or Plain Truth found to be Plain Falsehood Humbly address'd to the Candid* (Philadelphia, 1764), 8.

13 The British, for example, comprised English, Irish, Welsh, and Scottish "nations," to say nothing of the Catholic "nation" or the Jewish "nation" as well as an endless list of dissenting Protestant sects.

14 Here, I have borrowed and appropriated Elizabeth Mancke's term "empire-state." For her discussion of this phrase, see Elizabeth Mancke, "Empire and State," in David Armitage and Michael J. Bradick, eds, *The British Atlantic World, 1500–1800* (New York, 2002), 175–95. Mancke coined this term as a means of describing the British government as it colonized distant lands throughout the eighteenth and nineteenth centuries; however, I have made use of it here in order to describe the ways in which many nation states – from their inception – had imperial designs.

15 Benedict Anderson, *Imagined Communities: Reflections on the Origin and Spread of Nationalism* (New York, 1983).

16 I am thinking here in particular of Ernest Gellner and Linda Colley. See Ernest Gellner, *Nations and Nationalism* (Ithaca, 1983) and Linda Colley, *Britons: Forging the Nation, 1707–1837* (New Haven, 1994).

17 Two of Eric Hobsbawm's works in particular have influenced my thinking in this regard. See E.J. Hobsbawm, *Nations and Nationalism since 1780: Programme, Myth, Reality* (Cambridge, 1992) and *The Age of Revolution, 1789–1848* (London, 1962). The work of Anthony Marx is also helpful in this context. While he is concerned with competing nationalisms, I have used his conclusions to understand the challenges posed by Friends' religious (trans)nationalism. As he has argued, "When nationalism does not coincide with a state, it de-legitimates it, potentially threatening that state's coercive power." Anthony Marx, *Faith in Nation: Exclusionary Origins of Nationalism* (New York, 2003), 7. The Friends' community, as well as their transnational orientation, support this assertion. Marx also maintains that "the masses then perceived themselves to be members of varying 'imagined communities,' but these did not neatly overlap with political boundaries. These divergent communities reflected culture, language, and then most prominently faith, as well as class interests and estates. But amid conflict within and between such communities, imagination by itself did not effectively bind the masses and it certainly did not bound them within units coinciding with state boundaries. Such coincidence

would only emerge through explicitly political processes … with faith and secular identities reinforcing each other within particularist communities of nationalism." Marx, *Faith in Nation*, 19. Again, the eighteenth- and nineteenth-century Society of Friends provided an example when faith and secular identities did not reinforce one another but rather opposed each other.

18 *Pennsylvania Gazette*, 9 October 1776. Emphasis in original.

19 A full description of the "Spanktown" controversy, complete with copies of the forged documents and the Friends' response, may be found in Thomas Gilpen's *Exiles in Virginia* (Philadelphia, 1848). It should also be noted that the "Spanktown" hullaballoo re-emerged during the War of 1812 as newspapers republished articles regarding the controversy.

20 Henry Drinker's store, for example, had its windows smashed when Drinker refused to close his store during national days of prayer or to illuminate his windows in celebration of American victories.

21 A full account of Robert Walker's experiences may be found at the Library of the Religious Society of Friends in London, England, collection TEMP 869.

22 Sands's experiences were described in a manuscript entitled "Some Remarkable circumstances attending the pillaging of David Sands house in North America." This item may be found in the Portfolio collection 14.113 at the Library of the Religious Society of Friends.

23 For a fascinating glimpse into the experience of one woman – wife to one of the Virginia exiles – during the American Revolution, see Elizabeth Sandwith Drinker, *Extracts from the Diary of Elizabeth Drinker* (Philadelphia, 1889). For a more modern interpretation, see Elaine Forman Crane and Sarah Blank Dine, eds, *The Diary of Elizabeth Drinker: The Life Cycle of an Eighteenth-Century Woman* (Boston, 1994).

24 Though officials on both sides occasionally offered monetary compensation for the use of their meeting houses and for the damaged property, Friends could not accept what they deemed to be tainted money.

25 The arrest and subsequent exile of John Pemberton – one of the fourteen so-called Virginia Exiles – is quite a remarkable story. When the authorities came to take Pemberton away, he claimed he was not "easy" to allow it, and remained seated at his desk. Despite the authorities' best attempts to dislodge him, they were forced to dodge his wife, who tried to chase the men out of her house, carrying him out still sitting in his chair, over an hour later. When he and the thirteen other exiles were later led out of town, the free black community – in a moving and courageous gesture – lined the streets

as a demonstration of their loyalty and support. The wives of the exiles led a campaign to secure the release of their husbands, petitioning both governmental and military officials until they realized their objective.

26 Gilpen, *Exiles in Virginia*, 35.

27 *Pennsylvania Gazette*, 23 January 23, 1788. Emphasis in original of both quotations.

28 Gilpen, *Exiles in Virginia*, 34. Emphasis in original.

29 Ibid., 53. Emphasis in original.

30 "Old Patriotic Quaker" (thought to be British Friend Thomas Colley), *Letters to the King from an Old Patriotic Quaker, Lately Deceased* (London, 1778), 14–15.

31 John Pemberton's address to the Pennsylvania legislature during the American Revolution may be found in the Pemberton Papers collection, vol. 36, no. 130 at the Historical Society of Pennsylvania, Philadelphia.

32 This opinion clearly continued for a long while, as when Rev. Hubbard charged that "the Quakers have assumed the *name* friends, to distinguish them from other denominations, whereas they are not *friends* to any, except their own order." Rev. Billy Hibbard, *Errors of the Quakers Laid open with plainness, by a Plain Man and a lover of honesty* (Printed for the reader, December 1808).

33 *Pennsylvania Gazette*, 23 January 1788. Emphasis in original of both quotations.

34 Letter from John Woolman to Susannah Lightfoot found at the Library of the Religious Society of Friends in London, England, collection Port 31.88.

35 Letter from David Sands to William Jackson dated 28 February 1782. Item found at Swarthmore College, Friends' Historical Library, Swarthmore, PA, collection RG5/217.

36 Letter from Mehitable Jenkins to Mary England dated 31 May 1784. Item found at Haverford College Library, Haverford, PA, Quaker Special Collections, collection 1006, box "Evans family – Z," folder "Jenkins, Mehitable."

37 Letter from Mehitable Jenkins to David Bacton Barwich dated 18 November 1790. Item found at Haverford College Library, Haverford, PA, Quaker Special Collections, collection 1006, box "Evans family – Z," folder "Jenkins, Mehitable."

38 London Yearly Meeting, *Epistle*, 1781. Item located in London Yearly Meeting Epistle collection, box 3 in Quaker Special Collections at Haverford College, Haverford, PA.

39 London Yearly Meeting, *Epistle*, 1784. Item located in London Yearly Meeting Epistle collection, box 3 in Quaker Special Collections at Haverford College, Haverford, PA.

40 Henry Hull letter undated, but probably 1785. Located in collection JT 280 at the Library of the Religious Society of Friends in London, England.

41 This transcript of Job Scott's 1793 prophesy of "trouble looming for Great Britain" may be found at the Library of the Religious Society of Friends in London, England, collection Port 5.8.

42 Letter from Jane Watson to Richard Chester dated 7 May 178? (Watson travelled in 1787, so it is likely from that year). This item may be found in the Portfolio Collection 34.54 at the Library of the Religious Society of Friends.

43 In addition to Linda Colley's superb *Britons*, I was also influenced by Krishan Kumar, *The Making of English National Identity* (Cambridge, 2003), chapter 6 in particular.

44 William Rotch, *Memorandum: Written by William Rotch in the eightieth year of his age* (Boston, 1916). Rotch also sent a series of exasperated and pointed letters to John Adams, beginning in April 1823, explaining once again the motives for his actions during the American Revolution. In particular, Rotch was incensed that Adams had instructed the Massachusetts Old Colony Memorial to insert "word for word" a description of Rotch as a traitor to the United States. Rotch insisted that he had only followed his conscience and refused to apologize for his actions. See in particular the letter from William Rotch to John Adams dated 10 April 1823 in the Rotch Family Papers, Ms N-474, box 2, folder "1823" at the Massachusetts Historical Society.

45 After the American Revolution, Rotch struggled to obtain the support of the US government to rebuild Nantucket's whaling industry. When it failed to materialize, he and his eldest son sought opportunity elsewhere. In a move he would later defend in a series of terse letters exchanged with John Adams, Rotch invited the British government to invest in his whaling venture. He promised to move the people and infrastructure necessary to launch a base on the coast of England and in return asked for an exemption from several levies and duties as well as the freedom to observe Quaker principles in peace. He was disappointed, however, as despite the support of the prime minister, the king showed little interest and offered only mediocre terms. In the meantime, his son had approached French officials and they had proposed a better arrangement. The agreement included considerable financial resources in addition to a pledge from Louis XVI to allow the Quaker community to practise their religion freely. The king also promised to exempt them from military duty

and ecclesiastical levies. These unparalleled conditions made the decision easy for Rotch, and so he, his family, and his whaling operation moved to Dunkirk in northern France.

46 This letter, dated London 18 February 1792, may be found in the Rotch papers at the New Bedford Whaling Museum, Collection S-G 1, series A, folder 4.

47 Letter from William Rotch to Samuel Rodman dated Dunkirk 12 November 1792. Item located at the Massachusetts Historical Society, Rotch Family Papers, folder "Transcripts #1." As a fascinating aside, when Rotch told the local officials why he could not illuminate in celebration of French victories, one of the men recognized Rotch from the petition he delivered to the French National Assembly. He explained further that he believed that the new French government was modelled after William Penn's Pennsylvania and so excused his actions.

48 This letter, dated London 18 June 1791, may be found in the Rotch papers at the New Bedford Whaling Museum, Collection S-G 1, series A, folder 4.

49 For an account of Marsillac's efforts, as well as copies of his communications with British Friends and the French government, see MSS collection Q3/5, 2 at the Library of the Religious Society of Friends in London, England.

50 Ibid., Q3/5, 12.

51 Ibid., 20.

52 Ibid., 27.

53 Ibid., 17.

54 Ibid., 5.

55 Rotch was so incensed (and perhaps paranoid) that he numbered all of his letters and insisted that his correspondents do the same in order to determine whether or not British officials had seized or delayed his letters. For at least two examples of this, see Rotch papers at the New Bedford Whaling Museum, Collection S-G 1, series A, folder 2.

56 This quote was taken from the diary kept by Benjamin Rotch's daughter. See Rotch papers at the New Bedford Whaling Museum, Box 11, sub-series 12, series B, volume 1.

57 Thomas Hancock, *The Principles of Peace Exemplified in the Conduct of the Society of Friends in Ireland during the Rebellion of the Year 1798 with some Preliminary and Concluding Observations* (Boston, 1825), 96–7. The document quoted here reads: "We retain in affectionate remembrance the sympathy of Friends in your nation and the generous relief you afforded to our brethren who were much stripped of their property by the war in this country some years since; and we are thankful in feeling a degree of the same brotherly

love, by which we are made one in the Lord, wherever dispersed or situated." The American Friends thus collected 2852 pounds, 15 shillings, and 10.5d to distribute to Irish Quakers affected by the rebellion.

58 Ibid., 29.

59 Frederick Schmidt, *An Account of the Origin and Progress of the Christian Society of Friends at Minden.* This quote was taken from p. 47. The manuscript item may be found in collection 975a in the Quaker Special Collections at Haverford College, Haverford, PA.

60 Hancock, *The Principles of Peace,* 105.

chapter three

British Atlantic Catholicism in the Age of Revolution and Reaction

CATHERINE O'DONNELL

If, as Tip O'Neill proclaimed, all politics is local, no one knows that better than men trying to build nations and empires. And if we can add the corollary that all religion is local, no one knows that better than men trying to build a universal Catholic church. Sustaining such enterprises requires strategies that acknowledge the power of the local, in order to transcend it. In the late eighteenth century, as Great Britain faced the collapse of the first phase of its imperial reach, its metropolitan government sought to create dominions whose residents would not follow the path of the American rebels, but rather would continue in harmonious, profitable subordination. Parliament began to sanction local identities and allegiances, including Catholicism, long deemed incompatible with Britishness. Across the Atlantic, founders of the new American nation created a composite republic, seeking to build national institutions and loyalty out of thriving and sometimes hostile regional, ethnic, and religious allegiances.[1] In Rome, the cardinals of the Propaganda Fide, tasked with overseeing the worldwide Church, manoeuvred to maintain authority without provoking schism. The Church could live with diversity, if diversity could live in orderly fashion inside the Church.

In 1789, British empire, American nation, and Roman Catholic Church confronted the sudden emergence of a new power, Revolutionary France. Great Britain and Rome's immediate opposition to the Revolution's ideology and ambitions threw into bold relief lurking commonalities between them: a mistrust of radical innovation, a respect for hierarchy, and, above all, horror at the possibility of a powerful, hostile, and expansionist Continental polity. In the United States, the French Revolution had its admirers, but members of the Federalist party joined in ideological and strategic opposition to it.

Through the cycles of revolution and counter-revolution Catholic clergy in England and the United States watched, calculated, and strategized. How might they and the members of their flocks demonstrate their loyalty to their countries and to their church? What should such loyalties consist of? What did it mean simultaneously to offer allegiance to polities that insisted on their distinctiveness, and to a church that insisted on its universality? How might the threat of the French Revolution be countered – and used? In this essay, I will explore English and American Catholic leaders' efforts to create sustainable churches in an era of state building, Revolution, and reaction.

In the United States, the crucial strategist was John Carroll (1735–1815), who would in 1790 become the first bishop of the new nation and in 1808 its first archbishop. In England, clergymen such as Charles Plowden (1743–1821), who like Carroll trained as a Jesuit, and Joseph Berington (1746–1827), a secular priest, set the terms of debate as they battled over how to negotiate the claims of the local and the universal. Leading Catholic gentry, members of the Catholic hierarchy, and members of Parliament, most notably Edmund Burke, joined the fray as well. In the shifting positions of these figures can be seen the evolution of the ideas and strategies that shaped British North Atlantic Catholicism, and those that failed to. At stake in both England and America was the institutional structure of the Catholic Church, its formal status within the polity, and its members' integration into the culture. At stake as well was whether once incompatible religious and political allegiances could coexist, in polities and in minds.

At the onset of the Age of Revolutions, British Atlantic Catholicism was a small world defined by its connections to larger ones, the Roman Catholic Church and the Protestant polity. In both England and America, elite Catholics created networks through which money, status, and brides circulated. In England, families such as the Howards, the Arundels, the Welds, and the Throckmortons constituted a sometimes beleaguered but hardly powerless Catholic gentry. This gentry, which had members both great and small, paid for priests and maintained private chapels, effectively directing English Catholicism during centuries when there could be no official hierarchy, schools, or seminaries, nor even publicly recognized clergy. English Catholics faced a wide range of prohibitions: they were allowed only greatly truncated participation in politics, law, the military, and medicine, and they faced fines and extra taxation.[2] The extent of their persecution ebbed and flowed over the centuries, rising, predictably, during the reigns of Charles II and James II, at the time of the Glorious Revolution, and during threats of Jacobite uprising. Perhaps surprisingly, Catholic gentry continued to enjoy wealth and position despite the challenges. Lord Petre, a leader of the community, was rumoured to have the immense income of £30,000 per year in the early 1790s; many members of the gentry employed "legal legerdemain," often with the support of Protestant neighbours and kin, in order to preserve estates and status. [3] The small Catholic community, constituting perhaps 1 per cent of the English population, did face constant attrition due to members' conversion to Protestantism. Yet even such attrition may have had its uses, making it possible for Catholic clans to benefit from relationships with Protestant branches. Across the centuries, English Catholic families also maintained ties to the Jesuit order, which provided more priests to the country than any other order. Some English Catholic families, such as the Plowdens, saw men from several generations and sub-branches educated in Jesuit schools abroad (Liège and Douai) and inducted into the Society of Jesus.[4]

In colonial British America, the only substantial Catholic population lived in Maryland, which had been founded as a refuge for Catholics. As in England, intermarried clans – which in Maryland included influential families such as the Carrolls and the Fenwicks – knew both wealth and restriction. Catholics early on lost control of colonial government, and faced extra taxation, bans on public worship, and the threat, albeit always forestalled, of confiscation of their estates. The intensity of persecution rose and fell in response both to events in England and to politics within the colonies. Maryland families such as the Carrolls also had strong ties to Ireland, and knew of the confiscatory policies applied to Catholics there. And like its English counterpart, Catholicism in the thirteen colonies was entwined with the Jesuit order. Jesuits constituted the greatest number of priests in the colonies, and prominent Catholic families sent sons to Liège and Douai for education. Some, such as John Carroll, entered the order.[5]

English and American Catholic clans faced distinctive circumstances: English families knew greater wealth and status than their American counterparts, and more intense persecution. But the communities were linked by their shared possession of two allegiances – to a vaguely defined Anglo-American republicanism, and to an imperfectly defined but often intense Catholicism. Furthermore, Catholics both in England and in the colonies knew that many of their fellow subjects considered popery to be a relentless enemy. The opposition had, for centuries, been literal: Catholic Spain and France made war on England, the pope deemed Elizabeth I worthy of deposition, and partisans of the deposed Stuarts were often Catholics who made matters worse by seeking support from Catholic nations. In the colonies, the Catholic French and their Indian allies attacked towns and lurked as an ever-threatening presence; Puritan families who lost members to Indian captivity lamented the risk of conversion to Catholicism as bitterly as the risk of death, and Catholic Spain nibbled at the southern and western edges of colonial land claims.[6] The enmity between popery and Englishness was not limited to such straightforward conflicts, however, but constituted as well a kind of existential opposition, rooted in history and sprouting tendrils in rhetoric, law, and culture. That Catholicism was considered an internal threat as well as an external one only made the opposition more intense. Burning bright was the figure of James II, whose Catholicism was, in the minds of many Englishmen, inseparable from his aspirations of absolute rule. Thus, the Glorious Revolution's ban on Catholic succession and political participation seemed inextricable from its defence of Parliament and constitution. In succeeding generations, republicanism's animating enemy was popery: papists' slavish obedience to a foreign power was the defining opposite of British republicans' independent-minded patriotism. After 1707, the construction of a British identity out of ill-aligned English and Scottish parts also drew on the mortar of antipopery.[7]

Nonetheless, by the early 1770s, many Catholic clergy and laity were convinced that their faith was compatible with their political loyalty and that Protestant Britons could learn to see it as such. Natural law provided a foundation for arguments for toleration. But that was not all. Antipopery had created a rhetoric of tolerance – more precisely, a rhetoric of indignant contempt for Catholic intolerance, as exemplified in the Inquisition – that could be turned, ironically enough, against antipopery itself. An extensive empire reliant on trade, moreover, potentially would be more cosmopolitan than a "little England." Also promising were theories of civil society. It was no coincidence that such theories developed in tandem with an empire built on managed inequalities. They described and sought to create relationships that bound people in sympathy and mutual improvement, even within the structure of brittle and oppressive political and economic relationships. Disenfranchised British elites were among civil society's great promoters: "They had to find a way," James Livesy suggests, "of explaining how one might enjoy all one's rights without sharing in sovereignty, a way of describing a community in which identity was not political."[8]

The era thus held out many possible ways of arguing for civil and political liberties. But well-connected Catholic clergy and laypeople knew that rupture was as likely as quiet progress. And rupture came. The first great blow to the British Atlantic Catholic world was the 1773 suppression of its most important order, the Society of Jesus. The Jesuits' strength had always been their ability to move between an insistence on the Church's universal truth and authority and a recognition of the claims of idiosyncratic local cultures and sovereigns. That empowering flexibility attracted enemies. Other Catholic clerics, some influential within the Holy See, mistrusted the order for its willingness to adapt to local mores and form allegiances with non-Catholic powers. Catholic and non-Catholic sovereigns alike, for their part, mistrusted the Jesuits for their insistence on the authority of the pope. Jesuits' ability to weave argument out of subtle distinctions meant that the word "Jesuitical" was an insult in almost every European language. And the education, multilingualism, and organization that made Jesuits seem preternaturally powerful also made them seem targets for containment. Across the eighteenth century, the order found itself banished by more and more sovereigns seeking to assert their authority. In 1773, the order was suppressed by a pope seeking to appease the Bourbon monarchs and avoid further nationalist assaults on the Church as a whole.

The second great rupture of British Atlantic Catholicism came in the form of the thirteen colonies' rebellion. In 1774, after years of increasing tension and defiance, Parliament enacted the Coercive Acts and the Quebec Act. Lumped together by furious colonists as the Intolerable Acts, the Coercive Acts and the Quebec Act were in reality quite distinct. The first, in retaliation for the Boston Tea Party, sought to preserve empire through punishment and division, by closing the port of Boston and suspending the Massachusetts government. The Quebec Act was a different kind of effort to strengthen the empire. As one of its central provisions, Parliament mandated that Catholicism could remain the established religion of Quebec. Harmony and potential profitability were more important than antipopery. Parliament would extend civil liberties while restricting political liberties, and in that way maintain control over Canada. It seemed worth a try: the thirteen American colonies had, despite their liberties and their overwhelming Protestantism, proved themselves unruly and unprofitable. Colonists, however, reacted with outrage, not only to the obviously punitive Coercive Acts, but also, and with equal intensity, to the Quebec Act's protection of Canadian Catholicism.[9] Parliament may have begun to move away from the equation of Britishness and liberty with antipopery. American colonists had not.

As war drew near, John Carroll – by then a broken-hearted former Jesuit – returned to the colonies as a secular priest. He was immediately sent on a mission to try to gain Canadian support for the American Revolution: the Continental Congress, it seemed, now joined Parliament in seeing the value of a strategy that accepted Catholics in the service of state building. The mission failed – the colonists' red-faced opposition to the Quebec Act had not gone unnoticed in Quebec. But Carroll remained hopeful that independence would be achieved. He hoped for a new nation in which Catholicism could flourish free from the oppressions of government and from the corruptions of superstition and a Roman power-mongering of which he had bitter experience.

Carroll's optimism sprang not only from a conviction that recent ideas would lead to ever greater toleration, but also from a hard-headed consciousness that both the English and American governments needed the loyalty of Catholic citizens in a time of war. In the colonies, the religious patchwork created by England's mixture of Crown and private colonization ensured that there could be no unitary national religion. During the conflict, moreover, several colonies reduced restrictions on religious liberty in an effort to attract loyalty and soldiers. After the war there was no serious move to reinstate disabilities, and Carroll believed (correctly, in hindsight), that the nation was on a path towards the total abandonment of established religions. Despite the antipopery demonstrated in reaction to the Quebec Act, and without any concerted action on the part of lay Catholics or clergy, Carroll looked forward to a post-Revolutionary increase in liberty.[10]

In England, matters were more complicated. In some ways, the era appeared auspicious for Catholic relief: in addition to the state's need for loyal subjects and the growing power of the ideal of toleration, Catholics could point to their rejection of rebellion in 1745, and to the absence of any recent plots, as they asked for greater liberties. But the elaborate English and British framework of establishment and restriction would not dismantle itself. Thus, English Catholic gentry and clergy began a process of organizing, arguing, and petitioning that would change both the community's relationship to the state and its internal organization.

The British surrender at Saratoga offered the crucial opportunity. Concerned about a Franco-American alliance and an ever-widening war, Lord North decided to survey leading British Catholic opinion in an effort to secure support. Sir John Dalrymple was sent to Scotland to learn what might be necessary to secure Scottish Catholic enlistments in the army. There, Bishop Hay suggested the possibility that Catholics be permitted to hear Mass and to have greater protections for their property; Hay also suggested that Dalrymple appeal to English Catholics. Dalrymple's queries prompted leading English Catholics to meet to discuss the situation. From those April 1778 meetings emerged a group of influential Catholics who styled themselves "the Catholic Committee." The committee soon distanced itself from Dalrymple's tactics (Dalrymple suggested, at one point, that the Catholic gentry offer to pay the government for their liberties). And they decided to seek English Catholic liberation independently from either Scottish or Irish Catholic liberation.[11]

The committee had clergy members, such as the secular priests Charles Berington and John Douglass. Berington's brother, the priest and author Joseph Berington, would become closely associated with it and its successor, the Cisalpine club; he had first caused a stir with a seminary dissertation in which he rejected Descartes's theory of innate ideas, and was, at the time of the committee's formation, already publicly attempting to reconcile Catholicism with the moderate Enlightenment and with English politics and culture. But the committee was initially directed not by these clergymen but by members of the gentry families – Petre, Throckmorton, Sheldon – who had led English Catholicism since the Reformation. (The committee's most aristocratic member was aristocratic indeed: the Duke of Norfolk was both a Catholic and "the first commoner of the realm," ranking just below the royal family.) The committee was modelled on the kind of civil society association that during the era fostered sociability among its members and good works in the outer world – libraries, hospitals, historical societies. "Associations," James Livesy explains, "performed many of the functions that had been filled by privileged corporations before the eighteenth century ... A new kind of urban elite was created that exerted itself in an alliance with Parliament, an alliance cemented by the membership of MP's in the plethora of new associations."[12] Associational life was particularly important to imperial subjects who had wealth, but, because of their provincial status and lack of political standing, and for the English Catholic gentry who led the Catholic Committee, associational life held out a similar promise. It would serve the public good from outside the political realm, it would be governed by the rules of sociability and accord, and it would demonstrate the merit of its participants. As an organization of like-minded, patriotic Englishmen, the Catholic Committee, and perhaps by extension, the Catholic community, would be one among many respected, benevolent English associations – and therefore not an alien, Rome-based cabal.

In early 1778, the Catholic Committee met in London to discuss how a petition for relief might be crafted and brought to the king. Their campaign demonstrated three central elements of the English Catholic community: its privilege, its disabilities, and its lurking internal divisions. The Catholic Committee knew they enjoyed the support of a number of well-placed non-Catholic Whigs. Catholic families had abandoned Jacobitism and, by the last quarter of the eighteenth century, had in the main embraced Whiggery's promise of greater liberty and inclusiveness. The committee's most important supporter was none other than the conservative Whig Edmund Burke. Burke was a latitudinarian with a Catholic mother and a Catholic wife, and he had since at least the late 1750s argued that both justice and good sense demanded the extension of civil liberties to Catholics in Ireland and England.[13] "I have been a steady friend, since I came to the use of reason," Burke would write in 1780,

> to the cause of religious toleration; not only as a Christian and protestant, but as one concerned for the civil welfare of the country in which I live … I never thought it right … to force men into enmity to the state by ill treatment, upon any pretense either of civil or religious party; and I never thought it wise in any circumstances, still less do I think it wise, when we have lost one half of our empire by one idle quarrel, to distract … the other half, by another quarrel not less injudicious and absurd.[14]

Burke's primary concern was in fact Ireland, but he was hopeful that mitigation of the English penal laws would demonstrate the safety and desirability of improving the lot of that country's Catholics. Burke backed the Catholic Committee's efforts.[15] Thus, the committee was confident both in its friends and in the propitiousness of the moment.

The committee faced challenges as impressive as its allies. Catholics did not have the right to appear in the king's presence: the fascination that underlay British loathing of popery was clear in this prohibition, which stemmed from the apparent fear that a Protestant monarch might be turned towards popery by a cunning papist granted even a few moments' audience. Catholics also could not serve in Parliament, so even the duke of Norfolk could not take his seat in the House of Lords. Unable to present directly their petition to the king nor their bill to Parliament, the Catholic Committee would need to rely on others' aid.

As they contemplated strategy, Catholic Committee members asked Richard Challoner, an elderly and beloved vicar apostolic, what relief he would wish for the community. Challoner first proposed a repeal of all the penal laws. Cautioned that this would be seen as overreaching, Challoner suggested they ask only for protection of the priesthood. Having asked Challoner's advice, the committee did instead as its members saw fit. Such were the habits of the leading families of English Catholicism.[16]

Members of the Catholic Committee decided to craft a petition of loyalty to king and country. In stirring language that owed much to Burke, the petition declared that English Catholics owed only spiritual loyalty to the pope, and maintained an undivided political loyalty to their native land. After the petition was presented to the king, and warmly approved and praised, the committee had an ally bring forth a bill removing two of the most onerous penal laws: that prohibiting public worship and that making inheritance favour Protestants. This second prohibition had been, for the gentry families of the committee, nearly as galling as the first: in a nation building an elite on stable property holding, Catholic families could not control the inheritance of their estates. A family member who converted to Protestantism could claim everything, even if he was not otherwise the heir; the current Catholic Duke of Norfolk had claimed his title and lands, after eighty years in which both were in Protestant hands, only because there was no Protestant claimant to be found. These two provisions recommended themselves for attack not only because of their impact on the gentry, but also because they seemed likely to be approved. Public worship was a civil liberty, not a political one; the English Catholics were asking for the kind of privilege granted to colonial subjects in the emerging plan of empire, the kind of privilege that was intended to promote order and loyalty. Rendering Catholic inheritance of estates straightforward and predictable, moreover, accorded with the developing sense that property rights and the stability of property ownership were essential to the polity. The protection of Catholics, not their persecution, could be presented as serving the interest of the modern British state. At the Catholic Committee's behest, Sir George Savile thus presented a bill that offered those liberties in exchange for an oath English Catholics could quite readily accept: it required only that they reject the Pretender and all claims to temporal authority by the pope, including the right to depose. The bill was readily passed. Five days later, to Edmund Burke's delight, the Irish Parliament repealed the Act of Queen Anne, thus creating the possibility of greater Catholic civil liberties in Ireland as well.[17]

Along with the Quebec Act, the 1778 Relief Act demonstrated the possibility that the British state might no longer have antipopery at its heart. To some British subjects, that seemed not progress, but treason. Chief among the angry: British evangelicals. Though growing religious toleration helped evangelicals as well as Catholics, evangelicals continued to see Catholicism as the antithesis of Britishness and Christianity. Leaving the Established Church did not mean embracing its established foe. The Relief Act in fact prompted George Wesley to cease meandering between benign and malign views of Catholicism and settle firmly on the latter. In *Popery Calmly Considered*, Wesley argued that "the Romanists ... worship saints," and that the Church dealt in "anathemas" tending "utterly [to] destroy the love of our neighbor."[18] In January, 1780, Wesley further opined that "no government, not Roman Catholic, ought to tolerate the Roman Catholic persuasion."[19]

Startlingly, evangelical members of Parliament tended to vote in support of Catholic relief, despite the objections of their brethren outside the circle of political power.[20] Since antipopery continued to matter deeply to those not tasked with piecing together Great Britain and its empire, the apparent capitulation of Parliament only made the sense of threat more acute. In the immediate wake of the Relief Act of 1778, a loose coalition called the Protestant Association struck up a festively glowering opposition. "Tracts and broadsides were spread about," writes one historian. "Songs were sung, poems written. It was rumored that some twenty thousand Jesuits hid on the Surrey side of the Thames, plotting to blow up the Embankment and drown London, that there was to be a mass assassination of the King and his ministers."[21] Even across the Atlantic, John Carroll noticed the surge in anti-Catholic English print culture.[22] The old equation of Englishness with antipopery was far from dead. On the contrary, it now lent its emotional and rhetorical power to a new mistrust: that of the modernizing elites who seemed to give their allegiance to ideals and institutions that had little to do with the English past.

Resentments of class, ideology, and religion soon leapt off the page and onto the streets. After riots in Edinburgh and Glasgow in 1779, a mass meeting in London on 2 June 1780 produced a march on Parliament and six days of street violence. Rioters targeted properties associated with Catholics. Grandees such as Lord Petre feared for their magnificent residences, but it seems likely that it was mainly poor Irish Catholics who actually lost their scant possessions.[23] Perhaps as a result, the well-heeled Catholic cleric and committee supporter Charles Butler described the riots with considerable sangfroid. He wryly sketched the torching of a brewery – "I don't think an Eruption of Mount Vesuvius could be more terrible" – and described the Protestant Association as "composed chiefly of Methodists, and the most insignificant Bodies of Sectarians. There was hardly to be found among them a Man of learning, of ffamily, or of ffortune." Butler concluded his account by noting approvingly that Savile Row had survived (despite Lord Savile's association with the bill), and he added sanguinely that in the colonies, Sir Henry Clinton had captured "Charlestown."[24]

Butler's double-ff'ed backhanding of the rioters might seem nothing more than unilluminating class prejudice, and his reference to the siege of Charleston to reflect nothing more than a quaint running together of dramatically different events. But to many observers in England, the American Revolution and the Gordon emerged from a similar source. Charles Plowden suggested as much to John Carroll; Carroll was indignant, but Plowden voiced an opinion widely held among the political class.[25] The duke of Richmond went so far as to suggest that the Gordon Riots were, like the colonial rebellion, a response to the Quebec Act. George III himself, thanking Parliament for its support in the conflict with both the colonies and the rioters, warned, "Rebellious insurrection either to resist or reform the laws, must end either in the destruction of the persons who make the attempt, or in the subversion of our free and happy constitution."[26] To attack popery was to attack the British constitution! This was something new under the pale English sun. Thus, on the one side stood those who saw the American rebellion and the Gordon Riots as ill-bred, irrational spasms of protest against necessary political reform and imperial expansion. And on the other were those who mourned and feared this apparently sudden decision to change the rules of the old, loved game.

Within three years of the Gordon Riots and the siege of Charleston, of course, the Americans had succeeded in driving Great Britain to sue for peace. The Americans would have their nation, and the British would turn their attention to a new kind of empire. Catholic clergy in England and America set out immediately and self-consciously to face the new challenges and take advantage of the new possibilities. They did so with the bonds of their own communities – and of their shared transatlantic community – stretched by disagreements over strategy, over the proper relation of religion and politics, and over the proper relation of Anglo-American Catholics to Rome.

In the United States, John Carroll quickly decided that he wished to manoeuvre Rome into establishing a hierarchy of bishops and eventually archbishops, rather than relying on the system of vicars apostolic that had long characterized England. Carroll believed that only a true hierarchy would allow the creation of a church that would be free of corruption and allowed to exist within the Protestant United States. Carroll's friend and fellow former Jesuit, Charles Plowden, heartily agreed and worked closely with Carroll to convince Rome to appoint Carroll a bishop. The two used their network of former Jesuits to gather and relay information, and they did not hesitate to exaggerate the threat of antipopery in the United States in order to convince Rome that appointing a fully empowered bishop, rather than the vicars apostolic of the English mission, would allow Catholicism to thrive. While they manoeuvred, Carroll and Plowden worried that Roman cardinals mistrusted all former Jesuits and thus might hesitate in empowering Carroll. They were right to worry. Members of the Propaganda Fide were suspicious of any resurgence of the Jesuit order, for fear the order would be a competing power base within the Church (and one that offered a different understanding of the proper relationship between the local and the universal). Nor were those cardinals wrong to imagine that former Jesuits wished to see the recreation of their order: they did. Former Jesuits, including Carroll and Plowden, shared news of the order's continued existence in Russia, and rumours of possible restoration by Rome. Their mistrust of Rome was as profound as Rome's mistrust of them. Nonetheless, Carroll and Plowden, with the help of other former Jesuits, continued working to convince the cardinals of the Propaganda Fide that Carroll and only Carroll could suture the American church to Rome while not attracting opposition from the Protestant nation surrounding him. The fact that both Rome and the former Jesuits wanted to create a locally sustainable Catholicism that was also loyal to Rome, led to mutually earnest, if mutually mistrustful, persistence in the efforts.[27]

Even as Carroll worked with Plowden to gain the trust of Rome and the bishop's mitre, he contemplated changing certain practices in the American church. Here, he found a comrade not in Charles Plowden, who mistrusted innovation and, given historical precedent, reformation. Plowden was a kindred strategist, but for a kindred thinker, Carroll turned instead to Joseph Berington. Berington had pressed beyond the Catholic Committee's petitioning for civil liberties, arguing for a more aggressive integration of Catholicism into British society. Carroll and Berington agreed that popes should not possess temporal power, and that even their authority over priests was (in an undefined way) limited. Both men opposed all religious establishment as corrupting of church and state. Both argued that justice and national fellow feeling required that Catholics be granted full civil and political liberty in England and

America. Finally, both were willing, even eager, to reform some of the practices of Catholicism, in order to purify it of the superstition that alienated Protestants and corrupted what they viewed as the purity of the early Church. Carroll wrote to Berington expressing his admiration: "That your writings have been censured by a few, even the Friends of Virtue and Religion, I have no Doubt," Carroll wrote in 1784,

> since you have dared to express yourself with Freedom on some Subjects, which the timid wished never to be touched upon; and to declare openly your Opposition to many opinions, particularly on the Subject of Toleration, which the authority of some of our great schoolmen had rendered too prevalent. But I am well persuaded from the Firmness of your mind visible in every feature of your Compositions, that you will not suffer yourself to be discouraged from rendering to Religion the Services, you are capable of affording her.[28]

Carroll and Berington took to print in order to persuade the Catholic community and Protestant onlookers that Catholicism was compatible with reason and republicanism. Carroll wrote and published a long response to the accusations levied by Charles Wharton (not only a former Jesuit, but a friend of Carroll's and a fellow Marylander) that Catholicism prevented its followers from reading the Bible and from exercising their own reason, and that Catholic doctrine held all non-Catholics were destined for Hell. Carroll repudiated Wharton's charges, insisted that the Church did not claim to sit in judgment of others' salvation, and insisted even that he lamented public religious disputation itself.[29] In his own pamphlet, Berington joined the fray, praising Carroll as "[a] learned, a judicious, a respectable, and a candid Churchman," and asserting their shared interest in removing the "abuses" and "extraneous matter" that had crept into Catholicism over the centuries.[30] Both Carroll and Berington were intent on making a public case for an enlightened Catholicism that could thrive in and contribute to England and America.

Carroll and Berington's shared interest in creating a purified Catholicism was rooted in English and American culture, but not exclusively. Both men were aware of broader initiatives in European Catholicism that sought to return the Church it to its ostensibly pure, ancient roots.[31] English and American Catholicism seemed as if they might be exemplars of a streamlined, enlightened Catholicism suited to modernity and less vulnerable to the mockery and mistrust of Bible-reading, plain church-attending Protestants. Bereft of the accumulated, highly localized ritual and material culture of European Catholicism, British and American Catholicism might, ironically enough, also be particularly suited to their locales.

To say that not all Catholics shared Berington and Carroll's strategies and hopes, is to put it mildly. Leading the opposition to these reforms was Carroll's friend and ally, Plowden. Plowden deeply mistrusted Berington and disagreed more cordially with some of Carroll's proposals, including the translation of the Mass into English. Where Berington and Carroll saw Latin as archaic and separatist, Plowden saw Latin as the symbol of the Church's claim to universality. Thus, a reform that to Berington and Carroll promised to expand the meaningfulness and the appeal of Catholicism, to Plowden threatened only the Church's contraction and diminishment. It was an argument over the point at which adaptation to local circumstances undermined the Church rather than extending its reach, an argument strangely akin to that occurring, in print and in the streets, over whether the British Empire's accommodation of Catholics would lead to greatness or to destruction.

Carroll's concern was with creating a viable US Catholicism, and he kept his eyes on the prize. He calmly allied with Berington in matters regarding reform of the Church's practices and limitation of its claims to temporal authority, while relying on Plowden's counsel as he sought to achieve the authority necessary to institute such changes. Navigating between his two incompatible counsellors, he created an American Catholicism with strong internal hierarchy, confidence in its compatibility with Rome and the United States, and a spiritual affiliation to Rome as steadfast as it was vague.

In England, there was no dominant intellect and voice such as John Carroll's. Vicars apostolic, former Jesuits, and leading Catholic gentry presented a range of views about what English Catholicism should look like. Throughout the 1780s, the divisions that had faintly appeared in the run-up to the Relief Act of 1778, and that had become manifest in the disagreements between Plowden and Berington, brightened and hardened. The heart of the disagreements lay in disputes over the nature of religious life, its relation to civil society, and its relation to politics.

Berington and Sir John Throckmorton – who employed Berington as chaplain at his estate, Buckland – led the effort to create a Church fully compatible with British sensibilities. Doing so meant, ironically enough, turning to France as a model, since the French state had successfully gained control over clerical appointments and limited papal influence. In 1790 Sir John published two letters advocating that England adopt a

Catholicism that sharply limited papal control and accepted the national government's influence over appointments. The Quebec Act and the 1778 Relief Act, Sir John argued in his second letter, demonstrated that it was indeed possible to craft a Catholicism that would allow its members to stake their claim to British liberties. Berington republished, with only slight revisions, an English tract from the previous century, asserting the possibility of loyalty to Church and to nation if all inappropriate claims of Rome were rejected.[32] Those who supported such a model simultaneously undertook to craft a new oath proving Catholic loyalty. This was a perilous undertaking. Since the Reformation, Catholics had been required to sign oaths of loyalty, and refusals to sign oaths were a staple of English Catholic martyrology.[33] A simple forswearal of papal political authority and acceptance of the House of Hanover would likely have found favour with most Catholics, perhaps even with Plowden and his ilk. But in 1789, the supporters of the Cisalpine Club proposed an oath that denied "any spiritual authority, power, or jurisdiction whatsoever" that might compete with British sovereignty. That seemed a bridge too far. The oath also seemed at odds with the civil-society ethos of the people who had created it: it was a vow to think certain things, never others, and it was a submission of the mind, albeit a voluntary one, to the direct authority of the state. It was a strange child to its fathers.[34]

The committee's efforts to codify and define Catholicism and loyalty thus led to a torrent of pamphlets and responses, claims and counterclaims – to a proliferation of disagreement, not to unity. Even Joseph Berington in the end turned away from the oath his own publication had inspired. No one should have been surprised. Institutions of civil society have at their heart two incompatible dreams: self-expression for all their members and collective harmony. Civil society does not cope well with the inevitable clash of interests that puts its two dreams in conflict.[35] The Catholic Committee, and the wider community of English Catholics drawn into conversation and print communication during the 1780s, inevitably found itself confronting the fact that disagreements would proliferate unless a single view were imposed through vote or decree. Civil society had proved an impossible vehicle through which to create a unified voice of the Catholic community. Charles Plowden, of course, did not need to turn to the theory of civil society to explain the problem. The Reformation had demonstrated that when large numbers of people pay close attention to texts and claim the ability to interpret them, schism results, and chaos follows.

Watching from the United States, Carroll repeatedly demurred offering a strong opinion about the oath. It was not his country, he noted, and he had also begun to withdraw from disputation in print and even in private correspondence, strategically preferring a misty consensus to a parsed conflict.[36] But in a letter to Plowden in early 1790, Carroll revealed his thoughts on the proposed oath. "I am clearly of [the] opinion," he wrote, "that Catholics ought to speak a manly language &, after giving such proof of their attachment to their country, as any government ought in reason to be satisfied with, to demand equal protection *as a right*, & not suppliantly sue for it, as *a favour*."[37] Carroll's distaste for the oath resulted from his belief that the state did not have the power to "tolerate" religion, since religious liberty existed before the state. Charles Plowden also rejected the oath, but did so because he thought it undermined Catholic doctrine and dignity. Plowden accepted that the state created religious liberty. The Quebec Act and the Relief Act, in contrast to the riots that greeted them, seemed to demonstrate that without a powerful state, Catholics in the British Atlantic could not hope for safety, let alone freedom of worship. On this crucial point, Carroll and Plowden would agree to disagree.

The question of whether the state generated religious liberty, even if it had no right to, could remain theoretical. The question of how the English Church should govern itself was immediate and emotionally charged. The gentry's clubbishness provoked the long placid vicars apostolic to assert their authority. A club run by the rules of sociability did not appeal – in either sense of the word – to a religion of bishops, or even of vicars apostolic. ("I must know first by what I authority I am called upon" to explain his views, the vicar apostolic Thomas Talbot wrote angrily to Sir John Throckmorton, adding "B[ishop]s in the Catholic Church have hitherto been allowed to be teachers and Judges of Doctrine, and not subject to be catechized by every individual." "I hope it is not Catechizing you or Mr. Gibson too much," Throckmorton crisply wrote back, "to desire to know the result of your deliberations.")[38] An ethos of conversation and consensus was incompatible not only with hierarchy and the creation of a single public voice, but with Catholic claims to a coherent tradition. For all Carroll's belief in learning and the exercise of reason, he, like Plowden, insisted that only Catholic conveyance of knowledge through the priesthood offered an escape from chaos and ignorance. Catholicism was the path back to Christ. Off the path, one was divorced from communion and so from knowledge of God. Off the path one was not in the cosy confines of a club, but in the howling wilderness. Far from simply clinging to status, Carroll and Plowden were defending what they believed was access to the Word.

While England bickered, the Church in the United States was entering on just the path Carroll and Plowden had hoped the nation would follow. Rome became convinced that Carroll was the man to further the Church's interest in America, and appointed him a bishop in ordinary in 1790. Carroll chose to sail to England to be consecrated among his beloved former Jesuits, at Ludlow Castle. During his trip, in Carroll fashion, he paid his respects both to his friend and ally Plowden, and to Lord Petre, a member of the gentry associated with the most radical wing of the Catholic Committee. Two months later, Plowden published *A Short Account of the Establishment of the new See of Baltimore in Maryland,* in which he attempted to use Carroll's consecration and the new nation's acceptance of a Catholic hierarchy as a way to shame England's government into extending more liberty to Catholics. But Plowden also hoped, it seems, to use Carroll's professed loyalty to Rome (whatever his private mistrust of individual cardinals and even popes) as a way to shame the Catholic Committee into backing away from their Gallicanism and, more specifically, their crafting of objectionable oaths.[39]

Even as Carroll serenely assumed his see, disagreements between English clergy became more bitter, and the variety of disagreements more broad. Berington became – as Plowden had predicted – more radicalized. He amplified his argument that the pope had only limited authority, outstripping Carroll in his emphasis and, perhaps even more importantly, in his explicitness.[40] Berington also began more directly to question the necessity of monastic celibacy.[41] Vicars apostolic split among themselves over the proper severity and directness of a response, and over the proper relationship to Rome. The death of a vicar apostolic in 1790 led to dramatic concerns about which priest, bearing which ideals and allegiances, would be appointed to fill the vacancy. Gentry such as Lords Throckmorton and Petre made clear that priests who did not support their vision of a British church, should not expect their continued financial support.[42] Charles Plowden grimly predicted schism.[43]

What would have come of this profusion of positions, had the Estates General in France not been summoned, the Bastille stormed, and the king and queen, along with thousands of other Frenchmen, sent to their deaths, is unknowable. The British and American Catholic worlds contained a multitude of nuanced, unexpected points of concord and disagreement. But then the engine of the French Revolution moved through, first lumping and then splitting. It left in its wake an equation in British minds of tradition with religion, patriotism, and order, and of radical change with statism, anticlericalism, and chaos. Thus, arguments against

British Catholic Church reform that might have seemed wild slippery-slope fantasies in 1787, seemed to many by 1791 like bland descriptions of fact. In 1790, church property was seized in France and a constitutional clergy created, which had to swear allegiance to the new French state. Many French clergy refused to become "constitutional" clergy and also refused to recognize any rites performed by those priests who did take on that mantle. The pope declared the Revolution an enemy of the Church. "Dechristianization" had begun, and with it flowered the equally totalizing opposition of the Counter-Enlightenment, which saw in the French Revolution the enemy to God, hierarchy, beauty, and even love.[44]

Authors such as the French Jesuit Augustin Barruel opposed the Revolution by arguing for an alliance of throne and crown more absolute than had existed under Louis XVI. Catholic thinkers in England and America shared the conviction that traditional hierarchies of society and religion must be defended. Events in France made reform seem like revolution, and the Revolution seemed to possess the unravelling power of the Reformation. But English and American Catholics such as Carroll and Plowden did not think the answer to the crisis lay in a tighter union of church and state. On the contrary, in the French state's confiscation of church property and its assault on Christian practice and display, they saw support for their view that religion must occupy its own ground, literally and figuratively. Those who had objected to the Catholic Committee's willingness to swear oaths of allegiance saw in France's constitutional clergy confirmation of the dangers of a religion abasing itself before the state.

The French Revolution also seemed to demonstrate that the British state should not hitch its wagon to antipopery. Parliament had already begun to decouple antipopery from British self-definition and policy. The Revolution now presented a far more immediate and powerful enemy than popery. Its ideology assaulted British conceptions of patriotism, order, and the good society, and its geographical ambition – as grand as that of Louis XIV – threatened Britain's empire. And the Revolution itself was anti-Catholic. (In contrast to the powerful Revolution, the pope, Burke wrote in 1792, was only "a commodious bugbear (who is of infinitely more use to those who pretend to fear him than to those who love him)."[45] England began offering refuge to clergy, nuns, and Catholic aristocrats who fled French dechristianization. In June 1791, Parliament passed a second Relief Act, which included in its provisions permission for Catholics who agreed to swear allegiance to the Protestant succession, to have houses of worship (albeit without bells and steeples), to maintain schools, and to practise law. In 1793, the Irish Parliament followed suit. Watching from the United States, Carroll rejoiced when leaders of the Catholic college at Liège removed to England. The path of exile had been reversed. French priests also fled across the Pyrenees, and then into the United States, bringing with them their revulsion at the Revolution and an interest in shaping the American Catholic Church. Carroll even hoped that "the late convulsions in Europe, when traced to their real sources," would persuade "the governing powers" to seek the restoration of the Jesuits.[46]

Rhetoric pivoted on the axis of the new allegiances. Edmund Burke again led the way. Just as he had earlier crafted arguments for Catholic relief, so did he now present a vision of the changed relationship between Catholicism and Great Britain. Burke's *Reflections* was the most famous conservative response to the Revolution, selling thousands of copies and inspiring accolades and attacks. Its central argument, that individuals must honour tradition and respect the organic beauty and coherence of a society built on hierarchies, was deeply compatible with a Catholic ethos. Burke also specifically pointed to France's assault on Church property as a central instance of the Revolution's depraved overreaching. Any "superstition" that may have characterized French monasteries, Burke wrote, was far less pernicious than the "superstition of the pretended philosophers of the hour."[47] What had lurked in George III's remarks to Parliament after the Gordon Riots, roared to life in Burke's prose: an assault on Catholicism could be – extraordinarily – the essence of anti-Britishness.

In the *Reflections*, Burke did more than argue that the Revolution's assault on Catholicism was essential to its nature. The French state, he declared, confiscated Church property not only because it loathed Christianity, but because it accepted no limit in its pursuit of money. In several passages, Burke implied that it was Jews who facilitated and benefited from that pursuit. "Are the church lands to be sold to Jews and jobbers?" he demanded. Because of the levelling French Revolution and its embrace of unfettered economic gain, Burke snarled, "the next generation of the nobility will resemble the artificers and clowns, and money-jobbers, usurers, and Jews, who will be always their fellows, sometimes their masters."[48] That Lord Gordon, the eccentric British peer associated with the anti-Catholic riots of 1780, had since converted to Judaism, only made Burke's prose flow more smoothly.

Burke had no history of intolerance of this kind; on the contrary, in 1781, he had described Jews before the House of Commons as the group "whom of all others it ought to be the care and the wish of human nations to protect."[49] But "Jews" appear in this essay not as members of a persecuted faith, but as symbols of what Burke deemed the Revolution's unholy alliance: that between deracinated and selfish individuals and an unfettered state. In Burke's telling, such an alliance both emerged from and nurtured the Revolution's ongoing assault on traditional relationships and hierarchies. Not Jesuits but Jews were the powerful, alien cadre who infiltrated communities, acting in their own interests and in the interest of a dangerous master. Burke's ability to reorient British rhetoric should not be overstated: antipopery remained a force in English (and American) culture, one that would resurge more than once in the nineteenth century. But the galvanizing power of patriotic anxiety and animosity could also, Burke demonstrated, be generated from a different source.

The rejection of the French Revolution, whether in the *Reflections* or in the horrified responses of Carroll, Plowden, and other observers, was in no small measure a defence of the local: particular ties, idiosyncratic traditions, moss-covered walls of monasteries, all must be defended against the Revolution's intention to remake man and society for all times and all places. Catholic Church, British empire, and American nation also, like the Revolution against which they set their faces, claimed to defend universally desirable principles. But their leaders, and inhabitants such as John Carroll and Charles Plowden, claimed also that these expansionist institutions derived their legitimacy from their respect for the particularities of place and the uneven contours of human nature. Cast irony to the winds; patriotism and Catholic faith would coexist and together battle a new enemy.

For Catholic leaders, local circumstances mattered strategically and not simply ideologically. English and American Catholicism necessarily continued on separate paths throughout the decades of the Revolution and Napoleonic rule. In America, Carroll and the prelates who joined him created a hierarchy of bishops and archbishops. Catholics faced fewer and fewer political or civil disabilities as the United States' rejection of established churches took hold. Carroll's insistence that the authority he and others possessed as priests and bishops extended only to those who chose to enter the Catholic communion, succeeded in creating a Catholicism of strong internal hierarchies with a tolerant public face. Ethnic rivalries flared occasionally, as did rhetorical uses of antipopery, but a real challenge for Catholics would not arise until the surge of Irish and German immigration in the 1840s.

In England, the campaign for full Catholic liberation ground temporarily to a halt, largely due to the personal conviction of George III that allowing Catholic liberty would violate his coronation oath. Inside the English Catholic community, the influence of men such as Joseph Berington and Sir John Throckmorton withered. They found their form of religion – reformist, eager for a full partnership with the state, grounded in the ethos of civil society – increasingly discredited by association with the radical absolutism of France. By 1796, when Berington proposed that British bishops be elected by fellow clergy, with the British government more important to the process than Rome, the moment had long since passed. Even Berington didn't see fit to publish his plan.[50] He would continue to question Catholic practice and tradition, but a Gallican British church was not to be, nor would a church governed by gentry power cloaked in the ideals of civil society flourish.

Instead, in England as in America, the rise of powerful nation states would be accompanied by the rise of a Church stripped of political authority but (or rather, therefore) unabashedly ultramontane.[51] Its leaders, in both England and America, distanced themselves from the mistrust of Rome that had animated English and American clergy, and from the interest in reform that had once been shared by Carroll and Berington. The Church's flock and eventually its leaders, in both England and America, came to be dominated not by genteel Anglo-American clans, but rather by recent immigrants, predominantly Irish. Discredited by Revolution, a reformist, nationalist vision of Catholicism would be made irrelevant by demography. The arrival of waves of intensely, and Carroll might have thought, primitively Catholic immigrants would revive the kind of antipopery that had fuelled the Gordon Riots and that flowed through evangelicalism in both the British Isles and the United States.

But cultural rejection would not be accompanied by significant state-sponsored restrictions on liberty. The logic of the composite republic and the expanding empire demanded otherwise. In 1829 – after the death of George III – English Catholics were granted the remaining civil and political liberties that their faith had denied them; in 1850 English Catholics were permitted a structure of bishops and archbishops. Irish Catholics, too, gained political liberty, not least because the calculus of managing difference suggested to Parliament that enfranchising propertied Catholics would counter the nationalist ambitions of Anglo-Irish Protestants.[52] In America, the Know-Nothings flared across the public stage seeking to impose political disabilities on Catholics and utterly failing to do so. Politicians in both Great Britain and America in fact courted

Irish Catholic support. Powerful nation states had created the conditions in which a Catholic Church directed from Rome, but adapted to the nationalist loyalties of its members, flourished. A new configuration of the local and the supra-local, had been born.

NOTES

1 John L. Brooke, "Cultures of Nationalism, Movements of Reform, and the Composite-Federal Polity: From Revolutionary Settlement to Antebellum Crisis," *Journal of the Early Republic* 29 (2009): 1–33.

2 R.W. Linker, "English Catholics in the Eighteenth Century: An Interpretation," *Church History* 35 (3) (1966): 294–5; John Bossy, *The English Catholic Community, 1570–1850* (New York, 1976).

3 Linker, "English Catholics," 288–92, 295–6.

4 Eamon Duffy, "Ecclesiastical Democracy Detected," parts 1–3, *Recusant History*, 1969–70; Peter Marshall and Geoffrey Scott, eds, *Catholic Gentry in English Society: The Throckmortons of Coughton from Reformation to Emancipation* (London, 2009); Jane Silloway Smith, "English Catholics and the Forging of the British Nation, 1778–1829," PhD diss. (Northwestern University, 2009).

5 Ronald Hoffman and Sally Mason, *Princes of Ireland, Planters of Maryland: A Carroll Saga, 1500–1782* (Chapel Hill, NC, 2000); Maura Jane Farrelly, "Papist Patriots: Catholic Identity and Revolutionary Ideology in Maryland," PhD diss. (Emory University, 2002); Tricia T. Pyne, "Ritual and Practice in the Maryland Catholic Community, 1634–1776," *American Catholic Historian* 26 (2008): 17–46; Peter Guilday, *The Life and Times of John Carroll, Archbishop of Baltimore* (Westminster, MD, 1954).

6 Peter Silver, *Our Savage Neighbors: How Indian War Transformed Early America* (New York, 2008); John Demos, *The Unredeemed Captive: A Family Story from Early America* (New York, 1974).

7 Colin Haydon, *Anti-Catholicism in Eighteenth Century England, c. 1714–1780: A Political and Social Study* (Manchester, UK, 1993).

8 James Livesy, *Civil Society and Empire: Ireland and Scotland in the Eighteenth-Century Atlantic World* (New Haven, 2009), 77.

9 Elizabeth Fenton, "Birth of a Protestant Nation," *Early American Literature* 41 (1) (2006): 29–30 and 37–40.

10 Catherine O'Donnell, "John Carroll," *William and Mary Quarterly* 68 (1) (2011); Chris Beneke, "The 'Catholic Spirit Prevailing in Our Country': America's Moderate Religious Revolution," in Chris Beneke and Christopher

S. Grenda, eds, *The First Prejudice: Religious Tolerance and Intolerance in Early America* (Philadelphia, 2011), 265–85.

11 Smith, "English Catholics," 83–100; A. Paul Levack, "Edmund Burke, His Friends, and the Dawn of Irish Catholic Emancipation," *Catholic Historical Review* 37 (1952): 396–400. The presence of the large Catholic community in Ireland was also always a factor both in Parliament's efforts to create stability and in the calculations of the English and Scottish communities over how best to pursue their own emancipation. At this point in the Revolution, Irish Catholics had gained some favour by being far less pro-American than were Irish Presbyterians, Irish landlords were interested in ensuring the loyalty of their tenants, and the North ministry was considering measures for Irish Catholic relief.

12 Livesy, *Civil Society and Empire*, 17.

13 Nigel Aston, "Burke, Christianity, and the British State," in N. Aston, ed., *Religious Change in Europe 1650–1914* (New York, 1997) 185–211; Derek Beales, "Edmund Burke and the Monasteries of France," *The Historical Journal* 48 (2005): 415–36; Thomas H.D. Mahoney, "Edmund Burke and Rome," *Catholic Historical Review* 43 (4) (1958): 401–4. Conor Cruise O'Brien's argument in *Edmund Burke* (London, 1997) that Burke may have at least considered conversion to Catholicism has been generally rejected; scholars agree he was sympathetic to Catholicism while being a committed Protestant.

14 Burke to Mr Watts, Bristol, 10 August 1780, quoted in Levack, "Edmund Burke, His Friends," 385.

15 On Burke's well-known concern for Ireland, see, for example, Beales, "Monasteries," 422–5, and Mahoney, "Burke and Rome," 407–8.

16 Smith, "English Catholics,"103–7.

17 Ibid., 103–17; Mahoney, "Burke and Rome," 401–4.

18 John Wesley, *Popery Calmly Considered*, in *Works of the Rev. John Wesley*, vol. 15 (London, 1812), 184, 195.

19 John Wesley, "To the Printer of the Public Advertiser," 12 January 1780, http://wesley.nnu.edu/john-wesley/the-letters-of-john-wesley/wesleys-letters-1780a/; also discussed and quoted in Hexter, "The Protestant Revival and the Catholic Question in England, 1775–1829," *Journal of Modern History* 8 (3) (1936): 299–307.

20 Hexter, "The Protestant Revival and the Catholic Question," 306–8.

21 Ibid., 291.

22 John Carroll to Charles Plowden, 27 February 1785, in *John Carroll Papers*, vol. 1, ed. Thomas O'Brien Hanley (Notre Dame, 1976), 168 [hereafter *JCP* 1].

23 Colin Haydon, *Anti-Catholicism in Eighteenth-Century England, c. 1714–1780: A Political and Social Study* (Mancheter, UK, 1993) rejects the "class bias" argument of George Rude, "The Gordon Riots: A Study of the Rioters and Their Victims," *Transactions of the Royal Historical Society*, 5th ser., 6 (1956), as does Linker, "English Catholics," 308.

24 Quoted in Linker, "English Catholics," 307–8.

25 "I am glad that you have not to fear a renewal of Ld G. Gordon's mobs," Carroll wrote, "but cannot agree with you they were fomented or in any way encouraged by the leaders of the opposition of that time; or, as you call them foment[ers] of the *Rebellion*"; John Carroll to Charles Plowden, 26 September 1783, in *JCP* 1, 79.

26 David Milobar, "Conservative Ideology, Metropolitan Government, and the Reform of Quebec, 1782–1791," *International History Review* 12 (1) (1990): 48.

27 O'Donnell, "John Carroll," *WMQ*; Ronald A. Binzley, "Ganganelli's Disaffected Children: The Ex-Jesuits and the Shaping of Early American Catholicism, 1773–1790," *U.S. Catholic Historian* 26 (2) (Spring 2008): 47–77.

28 John Carroll to Joseph Berington, 10 July 1784, *JCP* 1, 147.

29 Carroll, *An Address to the Roman Catholics of the United States of America by a Catholic Clergyman* (Baltimore, 1784). A rough sequence of the pamphlets relevant to this discussion includes Berington, "State and Behaviour of English Catholics," 1780–1 (1st and 2nd editions); Wharton, "Letter to the Roman Catholics of Worcester," 1784; Carroll, "An Address to Roman Catholics on Wharton," Fall 1784 ; William Pilling, "Caveat to the Catholics of Worcester against the insinuating Letter of Dr. Wharton," 1785; John Hawkins, "An appeal to scripture, reason, & tradition, In Support of the Doctrines contained in a letter to the Roman Catholics of the city of Worcester," 1785; Wharton, "A Reply to an Address to the Roman Catholics of the United States of America," 1785; and Arthur O'Leary's 1786 review of Wharton, Carroll, and Hawkins. Joseph Chinnici's work is essential to contemplation of all these figures and their intellectual and spiritual milieu; I have drawn particularly on *The English Catholic Enlightenment: John Lingard and the Cisalpine Movement* (1980) and *Living Stones: The History and Structure of Catholic Spiritual Life in the United States* (2nd ed., 1996).

30 Berington, *Reflections Addressed to Hawkins*, 17, 2, 22.

31 Dale Van Kley, "Religion and the Age of 'Patriot' Reform," *Journal of Modern History* 80 (June 2008): 278–80.

32 Marshall and Scott, "Introduction," *English Catholic Gentry*, 25–6; Smith, "English Catholics"; Berington may not have known that the text he republished had originally been written in response to the persecutions following the fictitious Oakes plot.

33 Thomas M. McCoog, SJ, "Construing Martyrdom in the English Catholic Community, 1582–1602," in Ethan Shagan, ed., *Catholics and the 'Protestant Nation': Religious Politics and Identity in Early Modern England* (Manchester, UK, 2005), 95–127; Johann P. Sommerville, "Papalist Political Thought and the Controversy over the Jacobean Oath of Allegiance," in Shagan, ed., *Catholics and the 'Protestant Nation,'* 162–84; Linker, "English Catholics," 302.

34 Duffy, *Ecclesiastical Democracy* 2, 31–14, and Thomas W. Jodziewicz, "*A Short Account ... of the Consecrating of the Right Rev. Dr. John Carroll* (1790); Two Intersecting Roman Catholic Stories," *Catholic Social Science Review* 12 (2007): 261.

35 Charles Taylor, "Invoking Civil Society," in *Philosophical Arguments* (Cambridge, MA, 1995), 200; Livesy, *Civil Society and Empire*, 6–7.

36 "It is probable that I shall hear much on the subject of the oath when I am in England," Carroll wrote to fellow clergyman John Troy. "Hitherto I have never seen it, though I have heard of the disagreement amongst the VV.AA. [Vicars Apostolic] I shall be very cautious in forming, and more so in uttering, any opinions whilst I am there." London, 23 July 1790, in *JCP* 1, 452.

37 John Carroll to Charles Plowden, 24 February 1790, in *JCP* 1, 432.

38 Quoted in Duffy, *Ecclesiastical Democracy*, 2: 311.

39 Jodziewicz, "*Short Account*," 257–60.

40 Berington, *Reflections Addressed to Hawkins*, 69. John Carroll to Joseph Berington, 29 September 1786, in *JCP* 1, 218.

41 Joseph Berington, *The Lives of Abeillard and Heloisa, comprising a period of eighty-four years, from 1079 to 1163* (London, 1793).

42 Smith, "English Catholics," 172–95; Duffy, *Ecclesiastical Democracy*, 2: 319–21.

43 Duffy, *Ecclesiastical Democracy*, 2: 318.

44 Darron McMahon, *Enemies of the Enlightenment: The French Counter-Enlightenment and the Making of Modernity* (New York, 2001).

45 Quoted in Mahoney, "Burke and Rome," 418.

46 John Carroll to Charles Plowden, 16 March 1790, in *JCP* 1, 434.

47 Quoted in Beales, "Monasteries," 430; Beales's fascinating discussion of Burke's comments is more nuanced than I can discuss here.

48 *Reflections*, 8.105 and 8.1000, quoted in Frans De Bruyn, "Anti-Semitism, Millenarianism, and Radical Dissent in Edmund Burke's *Reflections on the Revolution in France*," *Eighteenth Century Studies* 34 (2001), 582. DeBruyn notes that this strain of *Reflections* has received fairly scant attention, and brilliantly sets forth the "intermixing of religious and economic stereotypes in [Burke's] anti-Jewish characterizations."

49 Speech on 14th May 1781, quoted in De Bruyn, "Anti-Semitism" 579.

50 Duffy, *Ecclesiastical Democracy*, 2: 327.

51 Although it is outside the scope of this essay, Spain participated in this general trend as well. Van Kley describes the "affective, clerical, and peasant-based nature of Spain's post-Napoleonic "national and ultramontanist Catholic patriotism," in "Religion and the Age of 'Patriot Reform," *Journal of Modern History* 80 (June 2008): 279.

52 The strategic possibilities of this alliance had been evident since the mid-eighteenth century, but could not be acted on until this later date. See Levack, "Edmund Burke," 387.

chapter four

Mary Wollstonecraft's Two Lovers: Convergence and Divergence in Trans-Atlantic Literary Radicalism

ANDREW CAYTON

In the last five years of her life, Mary Wollstonecraft fell in love with two men with whom she thought it possible to practise the principles she had outlined in *A Vindication of the Rights of Woman.* Wollstonecraft imagined that the American Gilbert Imlay and then the Englishman William Godwin would find her as necessary to their happiness as she found them to hers. Together they would demonstrate that the surest path to revising the immoral, unjust, artificial, and patriarchal world in which they lived lay in social rather than political reform. Two lovers or a community of friends would reveal the power of the paradox at the core of their shared vision: achieving individual independence required embracing social dependence. No human being was capable of managing his or her body alone; no one could make sense of the torrent of sensations that washed over individuals without an empathetic and honest companion (or companions). Centuries of European history had proved that coercion and superstition were counterproductive; they intensified rather than restrained the instincts of human beings to seek security from fear and want impulsively and violently. Only through natural commerce – a practice shaped by education, devoted to mutuality, and embodied in manly exchanges of information, perspectives, and sentiments – could individuals achieve some degree of autonomy. The most powerful expression of this commerce was romantic love, defined neither as a transcendent state of being nor as an anti-social passion, but as the ordinary experience of people who understood that the origin of human progress lay in acknowledging their own frailty.[1]

Although many people around the North Atlantic embraced a version of this vision in the early 1790s, most dismissed it by the end of the decade as an exercise in hubris, a celebration of perfectionism and anarchy. Nothing contributed more to their judgment than public revelations about Wollstonecraft's relationships with Imlay and Godwin. Reaction was less monolithic, indeed, subtler and more conflicted, than we think because different people understood the behaviour – and the writing that explained it – in different ways. The one thing that virtually all commentators had in common was a flawed understanding of Wollstonecraft and her lovers. But that outcome should not surprise us. For Wollstonecraft, Godwin, and Imlay also misunderstood each other, interpreting each other's words and actions differently. Scholars investigating their conflicts tend to locate their problems in personal divergences inflected by essentialist notions of gender. If Godwin and Wollstonecraft worked together better than Imlay and Wollstonecraft, the reason is the choice of a sadder and wiser woman, scarred by the predictable behaviour of a bad boy following his penis, to ally herself with a shy, bookish virgin who wanted to comment rather than participate in a world dominated by soldiers, sailors, bankers, entrepreneurs, and politicians.

In this chapter, I consider the differences between Godwin and Imlay as embodiments of a divergence between Great Britain and the United States that we sometimes overlook in our eagerness to emphasize commonalities around the North Atlantic, one that was built into the conversation long before the so-called conservative reaction against the excesses of the French Revolution, one that perpetuated the nasty civil war within the British Empire that was the American War for Independence.[2] Character, or what we would call personality, was, as writers since at least the middle of the seventeenth century had been arguing, a dynamic mixture of influences. Because Imlay and Godwin were products of different environments, issues of nation and class intersected with gender to nurture divergent interpretations of love and sexuality.

Superficially, Imlay and Godwin lived parallel lives. Imlay was born in a village in New Jersey around 1754; Godwin was born in a village in Cambridgeshire in 1756. After military service in the War for American Independence, Imlay engaged in land speculation and the slave trade before he travelled to London in the late 1780s.[3] Godwin, unhappy at the prospect of a life like his father's, abandoned a career as a Dissenting minister and moved to London in the 1780s to prosper as a writer.[4] In their late thirties, both men achieved considerable literary success. Imlay's *A Topographical Description of North America* and his novel *The Emigrants* established him as an expert on trans-Appalachian North America. Godwin's essay *An Enquiry concerning Political Justice* and his novel *Things as They Are, or, The Adventures of Caleb Williams* were among the most influential texts to appear in English in the 1790s. Yet as quickly as each man emerged into prominence he faded into obscurity. Imlay disappeared, lost to the historical record until his death in 1828. Godwin continued to write, but became so invisible that Percy Bysshe Shelley introduced himself to Godwin in 1811 by expressing surprise that he was still alive.

Both Imlay and Godwin betrayed Wollstonecraft. Her first lover and the father of her daughter Fanny, Imlay left mother and child for another woman less than two years after he and Wollstonecraft met in Paris in April 1793. Her second lover, only legal husband, and the father of her daughter Mary, Godwin compromised his wife's reputation as well as those of Imlay and himself in *Memoirs of the Life of the Author of A Vindication of the Rights of Woman.* Written immediately after Wollstonecraft's death in September 1797, the book prompted one of the first transatlantic celebrity scandals. Taking readers into his wife's "closet" and blurring any distinction between public and private, Godwin laid the foundation of Wollstonecraft's reputation as a writer whose inability to control her own body undermined her literary efforts to vindicate the rights of woman. Their relationships with Wollstonecraft were also turning points in Imlay and Godwin's careers. A widespread perception of their treatment of Wollstonecraft as ungenerous undermined their reputations. Literary radicals, pushing affectionate paternalism that had become the mark of a civilized man towards a more egalitarian practice of mutuality, found much to criticize in both men.[5] Godwin has subsequently fared better than Imlay, largely because his influential oeuvre makes him a substantial figure. We would care about Godwin had he had never met Wollstonecraft, although she had a decisive impact on his writing. No one would make the same claim about Imlay.

Despite their similarities, Wollstonecraft's lovers were variations on a theme that suggest a late eighteenth century Atlantic-wide "cosmopolitan" cultural discourse that was as fractured in its origins as it was in its disintegration. A Romantic national identity became more prevalent in the United States in the early nineteenth century, but a sense of American distinctiveness mattered even in the 1780s and early 1790s. If British and American men and women writers frequently deployed the same words, they often understood them differently because of divergent experiences shaped by a combination of politics and gender.[6] Imlay and Godwin read the same books, loved the same woman, and revered the possibilities of mixed-gender social commerce. But the ambitious American was an angry post-colonial national, a rebel against the British Empire who would settle for nothing less than absolute independence.

Godwin the ambitious Englishman, like Wollstonecraft, defined himself largely within the British Empire as a Dissenter, not a rebel; he interpreted the potential of social commerce through the lens of class, an identity that transcended borders and emphasized interdependence and community more than independence and individuals.

1

With a population approaching one million people in 1800, London was the most important city in the world. Its few square miles contained the institutions of a constitutional monarchy, the bureaucracy of a nation state, a global capitalist economy, the Church of England, and the civil society that the British developed more fully than any other people. London was not all glitter, of course. "In this great city, that proudly rears its head, and boasts of its population and commerce," Wollstonecraft asked pointedly in 1790, "how much misery lurks in pestilential corners, whilst idle mendicants assail, on every side, the man who hates to encourage impostors, or repress, with angry frown, the plaints of the poor?"[7] But the city of poverty and filth, of local gossip and personal rivalries, of fascination with its own problems and possibilities, was also the global nexus of political, economic, social, and cultural capital. The signs, symbols, and instruments of empire were ubiquitous. The residents of London witnessed more than they suffered from the great waves of warfare and revolution that gripped much of the world from the 1750s through the 1820s. If the city had its share of violence, it alone among the great European capitals escaped the devastation of war. British males died all over the world, but the British population endured nothing like what Mexicans endured in the 1810s. The British experienced war in the decades after the Seven Years' War as Americans experienced the Second World War, as the world's most powerful and privileged citizens observing from a distance and ironically benefiting from the ways in which war intensified their city's status as the epicentre of financial and social networks, the ultimate arbiter of taste and expertise.

Like all centres of power, London attracted a large number of ambitious provincials who equated empire with opportunity. Many sought advancement within the imperial institutions of Parliament, government offices, the army, the navy, the Church of England, banks and other financial organizations. Others, such as Godwin and Wollstonecraft, established themselves as critics of those institutions. Precisely because of the concentration of political, financial, and cultural capital, London was a hothouse of social experimentation and cultural creativity, the nexus of overlapping and sometimes competing networks of artists, intellectuals, and activists. Among the chief characteristics of these radicals was their remarkable diversity. Beyond a shared indictment of European society lay profound disagreements about how to eliminate corruption and correct injustice. The widespread enthusiasm in the English-speaking world for the French Revolution quickly disintegrated into vitriolic arguments even among its most fervent advocates, let alone its critics. Both process and outcomes were controversial.[8] Godwin, Wollstonecraft, and Imlay represented a strand of radicalism that tended to focus on revolution achieved through conversion and conversation rather than legislation or coercion.

The Godwin circle was a free-floating class of educated individuals, many of them women, for whom imaginative writing itself constituted a revolutionary act. Often marginalized as narcissistic dilettantes because of their preference for natural commerce, Godwin, Wollstonecraft, and others shaped cultural discourse around the English Atlantic in the 1790s. Radical writers did not merely call for revolution; they attempted to advance in their professional and personal lives. They had grown up in a world in which the individual acquisition of imperial power depended primarily on a reputation as a well-informed person intimately connected with other well-informed and well-positioned people. The major institution was the extended family, or the household, a network of relationships created by birth, marriage, and service, coerced or consensual, mirrored in the structure of merchant houses, political factions, churches, and voluntary societies. Literary radicals put a premium on information and connections. But influenced in many cases by their experience as religious Dissenters who grew up outside the Church of England, they rejected a model of household networks created through birth in favour of a model of networks created by choice. Their ideal was a community of friends who formed relationships and exchanged information freely in an egalitarian world of print. Repudiating the artificial inequities of monarchy, slavery, and patriarchy, radical writers defined themselves against the behaviour of people, rich and poor, who neither read nor wrote regularly. They assumed the value of a life that merged intellectual and social worlds, forgetting that the well-examined life was a luxury few people could indulge, let alone afford. Exploiting their power to manipulate words, they ignored the power inherent in their appropriation of meaning. They valorized their concerns as universal ones, especially their commitment to negotiating relationships as the central activity of human beings.[9]

No one was more significant in radical literary London than the printer and bookseller Joseph Johnson, who convened meetings over meals that resembled the social gatherings of neighbours in small towns. Like many of his peers, Johnson was a Dissenter from the Church of England. The son of Baptists from a village near Liverpool, Johnson had been apprenticed as a youth to a bookseller in London. In the early 1760s, when he was in his mid-twenties, he opened his own shop and published books on medicine and Dissent, later moving into works sympathetic to the American Revolution and against the slave trade. By the 1780s, his shop was one of the most successful in the densely concentrated community of booksellers along Paternoster Row. He occupied what was probably the largest building in St Paul's Churchyard and stocked a variety of books, not all of them his own publications. His medical and religious texts underwrote less profitable works on Unitarianism and political reform. Like his peers, Johnson kept his shop open twelve hours a day, seven days a week, inviting customers to drop in, browse, and chat. He devoted himself to nurturing relationships with authors.[10] Writers were his friends and his house a kind of salon managed by a man rather than a woman. When Johnson died in 1809, Godwin eulogized him as "a man of generous, candid, and liberal mind" who "delighted in doing good," and who presided over a shop that was "the perpetual resort of all his connections in seasons of difficulty and embarrassment."[11]

Johnson cultivated Wollstonecraft from the moment she arrived in London. In the late 1780s, he published her first (and most popular in her lifetime) book, *Thoughts on the Education of Daughters*, and her first novel, *Mary*. When she, like most of her friends, was outraged by Edmund Burke's *Reflections on the Revolution in France*, he encouraged her to compose a reply that ultimately constituted two books, *A Vindication of the Rights of Men* and *A Vindication of the Rights of Woman*. Neither Johnson nor Wollstonecraft saw their relationship in the eighteenth-century manner of patron and client or in the nineteenth-century sense of employer and employee. They were, or so they imagined, friends who found satisfaction in each other's company. He claimed later that "she spent many of her afternoons & most of her evenings with" him.[12] At his house she "met the kind of company" she found "most pleasure in."[13] Wollstonecraft called Johnson her "only friend – the only person [she was] intimate with."[14] Friends such as Johnson were welcome alternatives to relatives. "Involuntarily lament[ing] that I have not a father or brother," Wollstonecraft (ignoring her father and brothers) informed Johnson, she found solace in his kindness and that of "a few others."[15] When "harassed, which was very often the case, she was relieved by unbosoming herself & generally returned home calm, frequently in spirits."[16]

Wollstonecraft was not the only woman in London's literary circles. Taking advantage of the "flood of writing by women," male publishers printed thousands of books between 1780 and 1830 by and for women, thereby nurturing "a climate of encouragement of, even fascination with, women's writing." Middling women saw writing as a more palatable occupation than being a governess or owning a shop. Repulsed by the prospect of degrading domestic labour, they required income sufficient to hire at least one servant to look after them while they devoted themselves to reading, writing, attending the theatre, and talking with people whose aspirations were similar to theirs. Acutely conscious of their dependence on publishers and booksellers, they asserted themselves as women to such an extent that the "1790s in Britain form[ed] the arena for the first concerted expression of feminist thought in modern European culture." Lacking "real authority," they nonetheless "kept writing, continuing a professional career by which many secured their independence." Wollstonecraft was very proud of making £200 in 1788. She was a published author who was able to follow "the peculiar bent of [her] nature."[17] In addition to writing books, she contributed reviews to the *Analytical Review*, a journal Johnson and Thomas Christie founded in London in May 1788.[18]

Women such as Wollstonecraft were hardly naive about the patriarchal culture in which they lived. Committed to promoting equality and mutuality through education, they believed that one caricature of women they could change almost immediately was that of a delicate creature permanently incapable of reasoning as well as a man. In the culture of print, authority – the right to speak and to command respect – amounted to a demonstration of a mastery of the craft of writing. To engage other authors and to create arguments was to demonstrate publicly education and intelligence. Books themselves were physical refutations of demeaning dismissals of women as flighty prisoners of weak bodies and fickle sensibilities. They constituted a literary means to a political end. For it seemed that the most likely way to get men to reform, even to overthrow, patriarchal structures was persuasion. If men understood how they would benefit from female equality and mixed-gender mutuality, they would consent to change a system that they mistakenly thought served their interests. As Mary Hays explained in her *An Appeal to the Men of Great Britain in Behalf of Women*, she was "a petitioner," "a friend and companion" eager to reason. The education of women would be good for everyone.

Liberty-loving British men ought to "wish to counteract the benevolent designs of Providence in their favour." To improve "the understandings, the talents, and the hearts" of women, "to restore female character to its dignity and independence," was to improve men as well as society as a whole.[19]

Wollstonecraft went even further in *A Vindication of the Rights of Woman*: revolution required mixed-gender social commerce. True independence could be achieved only through manly (meaning open and direct) connections with other people. "The world cannot be seen by an unmoved spectator, we must mix in the throng, and feel as men feel before we can judge of their feelings. If we mean, in short, to live in the world to grow wiser and better, and not merely to enjoy the good things of life, we must attain a knowledge of others at the same time that we become acquainted with ourselves." If the sexes were integrated rather than segregated, women would learn to be rational and strong rather than "cunning, envious dependents" and men, those "voluptuous tyrants," would control their desire to dominate others. Equality and mutuality would become the prerequisites of all successful relationships – and improve the condition of all human beings. "[R]ational fellowship" rather than "slavish obedience" would nurture better daughters, sisters, wives, and mothers – "in a word, better citizens." Women would "love with true affection" because they would "respect" themselves." They would become their husbands' "companions rather than their mistresses." Men would understand love as "esteem" and "affection" rather than "selfish gratification."[20]

Wollstonecraft and Hays embodied revolution personally as well as professionally. That was something they could do because they knew a significant number of men in London and Paris who were apparently available for persuasion. Complications ensued when friends became lovers, or when one friend wanted to become or to stop being lovers, and when abstract discussions of love, in which questions of power were largely ignored, gave way to talk of sexuality, money, households, and children, all of which were all about power. Suddenly, it became obvious that men and women did not understand mixed-gender mutuality in quite the same ways. Even male writers who were exceptional imagined mutuality as benevolent paternalism, something that did not require serious sacrifice. To the contrary, attacks on marriage and celebrations of love were welcomed by many males eager to celebrate sexuality as a right, a natural pursuit of pleasure to which all human beings were entitled.[21]

The Atlantic world in the 1790s had more than its share of men who moved from partner to partner at will and demanded, coerced, or purchased the use of women's bodies. Some scorned mutuality altogether, constructing women as passive facilitators of male pleasure whose social importance was entirely post-coital, an attitude reinforced by new ideas about reproduction that denied female agency in the process of conception. No less important, the seduction of multiple (especially virtuous) lovers could secure their reputation as men of formidable talents. But promiscuous behaviour was also dangerous, partly for health reasons, and partly because it could as easily ruin as make a man's reputation. Few characters were more prominent in contemporary novels than the rake, a man who destroyed himself along with virtuous women because he enslaved himself to desire. A rake, especially one of middling rank, who raped or abandoned a respectable woman might escape the law, but he would likely face ostracism or scorn in polite company. Indeed, libertinism was one of the first charges male rivals hurled at each other. In his 1790 novel, *Les Bohémiens*, Anne Gédéon Lafitte, marquis de Pelleport, caricatured his former friend Jacques-Pierre Brissot for believing that the "pursuit of pleasure, unimpeded by social constraints" is "the only value worth pursuing."[22]

Still, more than a few male friends of Wollstonecraft persisted in seeing attacks on patriarchy, particularly male domination of the institution of marriage, as a licence to indulge the rights of man broadly understood. Just as they were free to migrate geographically and politically, so too could they migrate sexually. Consent given to a relationship could be rescinded when in the eyes of at least one partner the relationship no longer served its original purpose, as the American rebels had done with the British Empire in 1776. After he moved to Paris in 1789, Thomas Christie, co-founder of the *Analytical Review*, formed a liaison with a married Frenchwoman, who gave birth to their child. Back in London while the couple awaited her divorce, Christie fell in love with Rebecca Thomson, the granddaughter of a wealthy carpet magnate, and married her, abandoning his previous lover and their child. The Christies immediately set off for an extended honeymoon in Paris. It was in their house that Wollstonecraft and Imlay met. Thomas Paine, an ardent advocate of divorce who had abandoned two wives before he reached Philadelphia in the 1770s, detested marriages contracted out of the rashness of "ill-grounded passion" or a utility in which men sought "a wife as they go to *Smithfield* for a horse." But he also believed that virtually all unions, no matter how mutual and ecstatic their origins, tended to "indifference" and "neglect" that promoted "separate pleasures" and "utter aversion" and eventually led to "mutual infidelity" and "mutual complaisance."[23]

Men, even empathetic men, simply did not fully understand women. Joseph Johnson, a confirmed bachelor with no apparent interest in sex who was as likely as any man to be a true friend to a woman, could not grasp why Wollstonecraft resented her "irksome" "state of dependence" on him. "Your sex generally laugh at female determinations," she told him in 1787, "but let me tell you, I never resolved to do, any thing of consequence, that I did not adhere resolutely to it, till I had accomplished my purpose, improbable as it might have appeared to a more timid mind."[24] When Johnson proposed marriage in 1790 through an intermediary in order to support her financially, she rejected his clumsy advance because she did not love him. The problem was more than sexual. Her ideal lover was not a well-intentioned paternalist but a companion who would find her as necessary to him as she did him. Johnson qualified as an ally, as a friend, but never as a lover.

2

Mary Wollstonecraft found that man when she met Gilbert Imlay in Paris in the spring of 1793. By summer, they were lovers. In August, Wollstonecraft was certain that they had made a long-term commitment. Imlay could "scarcely imagine with what pleasure I anticipate the day, when we are to begin almost to live together." He would "smile to hear how many plans of employment I have in my head, now that I am confident my heart has found peace in your bosom." Wishing him good night, she wanted to kiss him, "glowing with gratitude to Heaven, and affection to you." She liked "the word affection, because it signifies something habitual; and we are soon to meet, to try whether we have mind enough to keep our hearts warm."[25] Thirty-four-year-old Wollstonecraft had found the fulfilment of a rational desire in the arms of a natural man who imagined the future in terms she recognized. By fall, she was pregnant. And by the time she gave birth to their daughter Fanny, in the early summer of 1794, Imlay was drifting away. As he found a new lover, the relationship continued erratically until reaching a final conclusion in the spring of 1796. In retrospect, we wonder why a woman as smart and assertive as Wollstonecraft allowed herself to be deceived by Imlay. But we should not deduce motive from outcome. Imlay's interpretations of words diverged from those of Wollstonecraft because he was an American male. His nationality underlay his appeal to Wollstonecraft. But what she thought he was and what he thought he was were not necessarily the same.

Wollstonecraft shared an image popular among late eighteenth-century European radicals of Americans as natural people who already lived in a world organized around commerce. Americans were, she wrote, more likely to maintain "moderation and reciprocity" than Europeans. They "appeared to be another race of beings, men formed to enjoy the advantages of society, and not merely to benefit those who governed."[26] Her opinion was hardly unique. Americans supposedly held a critical advantage because they overthrew their ancien régime when they seceded from the corrupt British Empire. So romanticized were Americans that radical writers greeted men such as Imlay and his friend Connecticut-born Joel Barlow with unabashed enthusiasm. Many seriously considered migrating to the United States. When the ambitious middling Englishman Frank Henley, the hero of Thomas Holcroft's popular 1792 novel *Anna St. Ives*, contemplates where a man like him should live, he thinks of "sailing to America." There he "may aid the struggles of liberty, may freely publish all which the efforts of reason can teach me, and … form a society of savages, who seem in consequence of their very ignorance to have a less quantity of error, and therefore to be less liable to repel truth than those whose information is more multifarious."[27] Most famously, in 1794, Samuel Taylor Coleridge and Robert Southey planned a pantisocracy ("government by all") in the Susquehanna Valley of Pennsylvania. Neither Coleridge nor Southey migrated to America, but others like them did, including the friends Thomas Cooper and Joseph Priestley.[28] Wollstonecraft herself told her sister that she and Imlay intended to settle in America.

The idealization of the new republic was not completely fanciful. There was in fact a greater degree of political liberty for white males in the United States, although that had less to do with nature than with the relative availability of land, the strength of local communities in a widely dispersed nation, and the absence of entrenched trans-local institutions or communities, including literary circles. Moreover, Americans were susceptible to persuasion by Europeans because they had no serious literary culture of their own. Even talented writers mimicked the styles, genres, and questions of British writers until the second quarter of the nineteenth century.[29] But what no one saw fully at the time was the impact on the United States of its size, its demographic composition, and its history. In the 1790s, religious, ethnic, and class differences were compromised, if not completely obscured, by the increasing tendency of European Americans to construct themselves as the independent and refined antitheses of enslaved Africans and savage Indians. Nearly a half-century of warfare against Indians and the British was producing a national discourse that exalted the civilized actions of free white men and denounced the barbarous behaviour of deceitful Indians and their British allies.[30]

Literary radicals such as Wollstonecraft did not see this United States because they lacked adequate information about the new republic. As important was their ardent self-identification as critics of the structures of power in Great Britain. Champions of values that served their interests, which embodied their expectations of a more moral world, they were blind to their role as imperial agents, as advocates of imperial notions of intimacy "educating the proper distribution of sentiments and desires."[31] What they considered a natural form of social intercourse was a celebration of mutuality developed in the specific context of eighteenth-century Britain, including a long tradition of religious dissent, the expansion of print, the emergence of women as consumers and writers, and humanitarian reform (such as the assault on the slave trade) encouraged by the American and French Revolutions. Assuming that mixed-gender social commerce would thrive in a rural setting distant from the artificial sources of cultural and financial capital, Wollstonecraft imagined America as an idealized extension of London literary circles. Her local world of friends and neighbours was hardly a provincial one.

American men such as Imlay struggled to fit into that world because they were organized differently, to use a favourite phrase of Wollstonecraft's, not just from women but from men such as Godwin. Although North American men grew up with multiple models of masculinity, they tended to define themselves in opposition to other kinds of men, not just Indians and Africans, but "hen-pecked" married men and wild youths who refused to accept the responsibilities of domesticity.[32] As Imlay's career would show, to be an American male was to honour independence, defiance, secession, and a sexual prowess admired by even the most refined and educated women. Indeed, Imlay, like many of his middling American peers, lacked a clear sense of what constituted success beyond a vague sense of independence as freedom from constraint, and resistance to personal as well as political oppression. Reluctant to emulate – indeed, eager to defy – parents, neighbours, and any and all imperial masters, Imlay and others were happy to join in the great eighteenth-century enterprise of transforming multitudes of strangers into circles of friends. But it was never clear that American men understood the operations of those circles in the same ways as their British counterparts.

Born to a solid family in New Jersey, Gilbert Imlay came of age during the American Revolution. A veteran of the nasty civil war that scorched New Jersey in 1776–7, he never married or settled down like his father and grandfather. Instead, he went to Kentucky as an agent for land speculators, got in over his head in the midst of a severe post-war economic contraction, and fled his creditors. Along the Atlantic coast in the mid-1780s, he attempted to salvage his reputation by investing in a slave ship and recruiting investors in land in the Ohio Valley. He failed. Imlay left the United States for Europe, probably in 1786. We know almost nothing about him for the next six years until he pops up as a marginal member of London's literary community. *A Topographical Description of North America* was published on 21 May 1792 by the well-respected John Debrett and went through several editions. Less than a year later, on 12 March 1793, just before Imlay and Wollstonecraft met in Paris, Alexander Hamilton published Imlay's novel *The Emigrants.* (An earlier edition may have appeared in late 1792.)[33] Imlay's modest success as a writer suggests he had had a decent education in literary genres and commonplace intellectual attitudes. But a literary career involved more than literary knowledge.

Making a book was a speculative enterprise on its own terms, as Wollstonecraft knew, yet another way to secure an income, meet people, and influence public opinion. It was also a way through a classic colonial double bind: striving to carve out an independent existence and perform the conflicting roles of vulgar opportunist or natural gentleman assigned to Americans by educated Europeans. Americans were eager to claim the title of citizen of the world, which some contemporaries equated with vagrant, because it blurred occupational and national distinctions and allowed them to pursue multiple opportunities. Our assumption that writers scorned politics and business is a legacy of the early nineteenth century, when a new generation of male poets defined themselves publicly against vulgar capitalism. Imlay's generation, by contrast, moved easily among publishers, merchants, and politicians and indeed saw their work in all three areas as interrelated.[34]

Like New York City in the middle of the twentieth century, London and Paris attracted multitudes eager to acquire reputation and fortune, to experiment with what seemed to be almost complete freedom. A visitor from Philadelphia observed in 1791 that Paris abounded "in spongers – fellows who are well dressed, but live by their wits." They included several Americans "anxiously watching the times in order to cut in and carry off a slice, either by preying upon or administering to the wants of the disordered state." Like Imlay, they had rejected a local world where a man became somebody by serving the interests of his household, his village, his church, and occasionally his king; they did not know a nineteenth-century national world where a man would become somebody by learning to temper ambition through extended education, professional occupation, and devotion to domesticity and public service. They seem inconsistent because they were inconsistent. In their eagerness to get ahead, they betrayed friends, embroidered accomplishments, ignored setbacks, and broke promises; they were forever eager to legitimize their behaviour as respectable and demonize that of their enemies (or competitors) as barbaric.[35]

Americans in Europe could never forget that they were Americans, because nobody, whether friend or critic, would let them forget it. Like many of his peers, Imlay specialized in the discourse of the post-colonial nationalist; an exile from America and an outsider in London, he was always more interested in freedom as escape, freedom as liberation, freedom as an attack on power. In Europe, Imlay traded on being an American because it gave him the cachet of an expert. To some extent, he gave people what he thought they wanted, especially when he could do so by celebrating the superiority of Americans. *A Topographical Description* contrasted "the simple manners and rational life of the Americans" in the Ohio Valley "with the distorted and unnatural habits of the Europeans." "We have more of simplicity, and you more of art. We have more of nature, and you more of the world ... You have more hypocrisy – we are sincere."[36] Imlay was as much at the mercy of his imagination as Wollstonecraft. But if their imaginations converged in envisioning a natural society of sociable men and women, they diverged in the details of that brave new world. Where Wollstonecraft focused on women and education, Imlay came to Paris to harness the resources of the French republic to develop North America in ways that would benefit men like him. He sought state power to encourage rebellion in the Americas.

Neither Wollstonecraft nor Imlay allowed their affair to isolate them from their friends. They spent some of the early summer of 1793 with a floating collection of friends later termed the British Club, many of whom gathered at Thomas Paine's house in the Rue de Faubourg in St Denis, a village about seven miles north of central Paris. A wall surrounded the house and its yard full of ducks, turkeys, geese, rabbits, and two pigs. An adjacent garden of roughly one acre produced delicious oranges, apricots, and plums that were "the best [Paine] ever tasted."[37] The friends spent much of their time in the garden reading newspapers, writing letters, and playing marbles, chess, whist, and cribbage. With the rise of the Jacobins, recalled one member of the circle, they "used to pass [their] Evenings together very frequently either in conversation or any amusement [which] might tend to dissipate those gloomy impressions."[38] Jean-Jacques Rousseau had celebrated mixed company in a setting not unlike the house in St Denis. Their meals would be "neither orderly nor elegant." Independent people would enjoy each other's company because they chose to do so, because it pleased them. "From this cordial and moderate familiarity there would arise ... a playful conflict a hundred times more charming than politeness and more likely to bind together [their] hearts."[39] These friends were calling for a society governed entirely through mutual choice.

Despite the upheaval that engulfed Paris in 1793, friendships flourished in the capital of revolution as well as the capital of empire. The Englishwoman Helen Maria Williams welcomed visitors to her salon in the winter of 1792–3. Sophie de Grouchy, the young wife of the Marquis de Condorcet and later the definitive translator of Adam Smith's *Theory of Moral Sentiments*, had long entertained the likes of Jacques-Pierre Brissot, Thomas Jefferson, Adam Smith, Madame de Staël, and Olympe de Gouges, author of the 1791 *Declaration of the Rights of Woman and Female Citizen*. Most important to Wollstonecraft and Imlay was Marie-Jeanne Roland de la Platière, the wife of prominent Girondin Jean-Marie Roland de la Platière. Madame Roland took pride in avoiding "high society," preferring "a studious life" away from "gossip" and "fools." She held dinners twice a week for political friends of her husband and afterwards they discussed what had transpired. Despite Roland's claim that women should listen to men rather than speak about politics, she talked to close friends about this "worthwhile" subject and mocked old men who thought she was incapable of understanding it. Meanwhile, frustrated by her "lack of equality" with her older husband, she cultivated a relationship with "the man who might be my lover." While she was unable to hide her feelings for her new friend, Roland dutifully "sacrificed" her desire in deference to her husband. Monsieur Roland, in turn, was deeply torn between his resentment of the relationship and his anguish over her refusal to act on her feelings. The Rolands enacted revolution as much as Imlay and Wollstonecraft.[40]

We can speculate at length about what Wollstonecraft was thinking and feeling because Imlay returned her letters and Godwin published versions of them in 1798. His contributions to their correspondence, however, disappeared with him. In a rare reversal of a gendered historical norm, we hear the woman who became famous and interpret the man whose significance lies mainly in his connection with her only through her response to his behaviour or something he wrote. We know nothing about Imlay's sexual and romantic history before he arrived in Paris in the spring of 1793 and very little about it after he left Wollstonecraft for a woman usually identified as an actress. But we can infer much from Imlay's only published novel.

The Emigrants suggests that Imlay has a different take on what exactly a culture of mixed-gender social commerce would look like. The novel narrates the migration of an English family named T____n recently arrived in the United States from Pennsylvania to the Illinois Country sometime after the War for Independence. As the two central characters – daughter Caroline and the American Captain James Arlington – fall in love, they seek to fashion a society in which people choose each other out of sympathy and self-interest and learn that autonomy and mutuality are complementary. In this sense, *The Emigrants* recapitulates the ideas of Wollstonecraft and others in an American setting, where, in theory, they will be more easily realized. But the book is also a defiant post-colonial denunciation of Great Britain by an angry American fixated on sexuality as the foundation of masculinity. Imlay, like many of his peers, shed his colonial insecurities by loudly proclaiming his national independence.

The degeneracy of British husbands reinforces the degeneracy of British governors. They are brutes whose authority rests on coercion, savages who must force their wives to obey them. British law makes romance (including adultery) illegal while it legitimizes domestic tyranny (marriage). The "*barbarous codes of a savage world, have continued to oppress and restrain the acts of volition on the part of women, when the most licentious bounds on the part of men, have found impunity from the prejudices of the world.*" Imlay makes his case by narrating the history of marriages in Great Britain in such detail that we can only suppose he spoke from personal experience. But where British radical intellectuals promoted a universal culture of mixed-gender sociability in the place of a universal regime of tyranny, the American identifies these regimes with specific nations. His criticism of Britain is criticism of British men who have selfishly exploited their power to pass laws for their "own immediate convenience" rather than the greater good. Because marriage was the means through which men maintained economic and social of women's property and their bodies, any discussion of divorce or alternative relationships ipso facto was subversive of their power.[41] Imlay advocates making divorce easier in Britain because it will benefit English women at the expense of English men. His assault on patriarchal privilege is not a call for mixed-gender mutuality so much as it is an assertion of American masculinity. Once free to choose their own destinies, sensible English women will prefer the company of romantic American men; together they will happily cuckold and ruin English husbands. Imlay's novel is a tale of male competition that is all about the sexual humiliation of British men, who are tyrants in private as well as public. American men do not have to rape or seduce English women. No, the latter recognize that a liaison with the former is natural and salutary. Marriage in Britain is a prison; marriage in America is the union of friends. In Britain, sex is rape, coerced and utilitarian; in America, sex is love, consensual and romantic.

Central to the meandering narrative of *The Emigrants* is the anti-social character of British marriages. In London, Caroline's older sister Eliza's husband Mr F____ ruins himself with unrestrained debauchery and reckless spending. Then he demands that Eliza prostitute herself to pay off his debts. It is a "cruel circumstance" that a woman must sacrifice her body to the will of a man so obviously "impotent." A good husband would respect his wife by restraining his desires and helping her to realize hers; he would never contemplate treating her like a slave or an animal. If divorce were easily accessible, Eliza could have rescued herself. Alas, she can only find "a refuge from brutality" in dependence on another man. What else could "a *woman*" do? Imlay presents adultery in Britain as a socially acceptable alternative to rape masquerading as marriage. Why should not "a woman of feeling" when she "has been imposed upon and insulted" find solace "in the tender solicitude of some friend or lover?" Adulterous women should be treated like human beings, not property. Conveniently, the suddenly ashamed (and still ruined) husband dies the death of a coward "by putting a loaded pistol to his head."[42] Imlay's point, however, is that neither Eliza nor her husband should have had to endure such misery in the first place, which is why British women ought to emigrate.

Civilized people could not move to the Ohio Valley and find happiness immediately, however. They had to develop a wilderness into a commercial society, something in between a complete state of nature (associated with Indians) and the artificiality of Europe. Mixed-gender social commerce would thrive in the Ohio Valley. Divorce will be legal and people will "obtain those gratifications" they need for their happiness without "recourse to … cunning and stratagem." What was wrong with women as well as men looking "abroad for those amusements which alone can compensate for domestic feuds?" Imlay lamented the "most inhuman" situation of "a woman of honour and delicacy ... driven to seek for some mitigation of the sufferings of an afflicted bosom, in the friendship of an ingenuous heart," suffering "when that friendship has led to more tender ties – ties which spring from the finest feelings, and which characterize the most humane and exalted souls," the horrible fate of being "branded with contempt, and condemned to live in poverty, unnoticed, and unpitied."[43] Sympathy for afflicted women aside, Imlay spends far more time contemplating how to end relationships than he does considering how to sustain them. As important, he justifies the sexual liberation of British wives as a political act. His logic is clear: British women are married to corrupt brutes; American men are empathetic; therefore, British women should leave British men for American men.

Like Wollstonecraft, Imlay believed human beings "are by nature social beings." People should share their "joys," "pains," and "comforts," in "cordial sympathy." American men, unlike their British counterparts, exercise legitimate dominion. They earn respect, even deference, because they pay attention to women and encourage them to embrace sexual as well domestic liberation. They are decisive as well as sympathetic. Arlington, "one of the most heroic soldiers in the American army," demonstrates "the greatest diffidence and distant politeness; except in those with whom he is very intimate, when he is occasionally highly facetious and entertaining." When he holds her hand, Caroline confides to her sister, "My whole soul appeared to be rebelling against the despotism of restraint, and it was not possible any longer for me to controul its emotions." She "felt that supreme bliss which flows from the banquet of pure love, in the genial hours of sentimental rapture."[44] Caroline, in short, does what Imlay thinks women should do: she accepts natural desire. Social commerce works: Caroline helps Arlington restrain his passions while he helps her to indulge hers.

At one point, Arlington flees from Kentucky across the Ohio River looking for peace of mind. Rejecting urban society, he "will live in this uncultivated, and uncivilized waste, until my person shall become as wild as my sense." The region, however, is no middle ground, no paradise of natural freedom. Caroline pursues Arlington across the river and is captured by Indians, whose lack of respect for persons and property testifies to their exclusion from the social compact that is the foundation of civilized life. Arlington quickly rescues her. Deprived of her freedom – and much of her clothing – Caroline incites intense sexual interest from her saviour. Catching sight of her, Arlington feels his "swelling heart beat with joy." He relishes "a glance from the brilliant eyes of the most divine woman upon earth, torn into shatters by the bushes and briars, with scarcely covering left to hide the transcendence of her beauty." "Embracing her," he is transported by "the divinity of feminine charms" until his servant Andrew covers her with a "surtoute" and puts her in the raft that will carry them back to civilization. "Her bosom disclosed the temple of bliss, while her lips distilled nectareous sweets." Arlington stares at her breasts, "more transparent than the effulgence of Aurora ... and now half naked." He had "to extinguish the light, to preserve [his] reason." Arlington does not act on his desire in the manner of British brute; nor does he, like the primitive, child-like Indians who cannot act on desires they do not have, ignore her.[45]

In the end, Caroline and Arlington find "mutual happiness" on a plantation north of the Ohio River. They will promote "the dignity of man" with a democratic government that will nurture "love, and harmony." In a division of labour gendered by nature and affirmed by choice, Caroline will be busy working with the wives of Arlington's "fellow soldiers." Together they will structure an environment that encourages education and exchange and thus autonomy and mutuality. In "small societies," people are more likely to become friends, to know "the human heart," to converse and imagine themselves in terms of their relationships with their neighbours, to nurture usefulness and discourage vulgar and vicious habits. The Arlingtons and their families and friends were lucky to live in the Ohio Valley, a place where "love seems to have gained absolute and unbounded empire."[46] Interestingly, Imlay says virtually nothing about the consequences of heterosexuality – children.

Beyond valorizing American masculinity at the expense of the British, Imlay qualifies assumptions about American liberty by emphasizing the importance of male agency in its development. Deliberate revolution as much as natural evolution had created the American republic and promoted the empire of love. Shaped and tempered by war, not only against the degenerate British but against the altogether too natural American Indians, Imlay puts a premium on decisive action. Caroline needs Arlington to do things she cannot do: engage in trade, transform forests into fields, preside over their small society, and rescue her from Indians. Like many Americans males, Arlington treasures his personal independence, or rather his freedom from dependence on dissolute English tyrants and European fops; his freedom has been naturalized by the informed consent of an educated woman fully capable of telling a good man from a bad men. Mixed-gender social commerce is in part a means to an end: the love of a beautiful, intelligent woman reflects well on her lover. Americans do not have to force women to have sex with them because women desire sex with them, just as other people of lesser position will defer to their judgment naturally, not because they are ordered to obey but because they benefit from that decision.[47] As American colonists had seceded from an abusive British Empire, so too wives ought to leave abusive relationships. A fine idea perhaps for young men roaming the Atlantic reinventing themselves as circumstances required, but hardly a good idea for women, especially when male fascination with their bodies left them pregnant and fascination with another woman's body left them alone.

Wollstonecraft had learned from her reading of her friend Jacques-Pierre Brissot's *Nouveau voyage dans les États-Unis* of "the simplicity conspicuous in the manners of every class [in the United States], particularly the innocent frankness that characterizes the American women, and the consequent friendly intercourse that subsists between the sexes, when gallantry and coquetry are equally out of the question."[48] By the time she wrote her unfinished novel, *Maria, or The Wrongs of Woman,* in the months after her final break with Imlay, she was less sanguine. Maria, a young married Englishwoman imprisoned for defying her tyrannical husband, makes friends with a sensible prisoner named Henry Darnford, who sends her books and letters, and eventually talks with her. Born in Britain, Darnford had bought a commission in a regiment raised "to subjugate America." Wounded and captured, he "traveled into the interior parts of the country, to lay out my money to advantage." Unfortunately, he discovered that while American minds were "enthusiastically enterprising," American hearts were full of "cold selfishness." Finding that the United States offered little in the way of refinement, that vice and trade dominated its towns, he left the "land of liberty and vulgar aristocracy, seated on her bags of dollars" and came back to Britain, only to end up in the asylum.[49] Wollstonecraft had obviously concluded that Americans were not what she had imagined them to be. As important, she seemed to have concluded that mixed-gender relationships could only flourish in isolation. Once Maria and Darnford escape into the real world, they cannot sustain their mutuality. But Wollstonecraft was nothing if not persistent. Just as she never completely gave up on Imlay, so too was she willing to try again with another man who might understand her better.

3

William Godwin was a "somewhat frail" man of medium build with a solemn demeanour dominated by large blue eyes and a similarly oversized nose.[50] He compensated for his shyness and sensitivity with a blunt manner that struck more than a few of his acquaintances as cold and unfeeling. An instinctive critic of power, he devoted most of his adult life to asserting the ability of educated human beings to organize societies around the principle of mutual consent.[51] His idiosyncratic juxtaposition of emotional reserve and brutal honesty won over as many people with "his obvious sincerity" as he offended with his "frankness." Women, including writers Mary Hays, Amelia Alderson, and Elizabeth Inchbald liked Godwin. A celibate man, he had no interest in flirting. Coquetry appalled him. Indeed, he took pride in falling in love with Wollstonecraft in 1796 while reading her recently published journal of a tour of Scandinavia she had undertaken at Imlay's request.[52]

Godwin and Wollstonecraft's relationship unfolded much more slowly than her affair with Imlay. Wollstonecraft admired Godwin for his "self-government" rather than his self-indulgence. Love with him was not uncontrolled passion, a defiant surrender to emotion. With Godwin she experienced "one of those moments, when the senses are exactly tuned by the rising tenderness of the heart, and according reason entices you to live in the present moment, regardless of the past or future – It is not rapture. – It is a sublime tranquility. I have felt it in your arms."[53] She reluctantly lowered her guard and restated her ideas about love. Long-term happiness was found in contentment, not ecstasy. A well-considered love was a dynamic relationship in which two individuals came to know themselves better through regular intercourse, that is, "social communication between individuals; frequent and habitual contact in conversation and action." Godwin and Wollstonecraft believed they succeeded as a couple because they lived in separate spaces, maintained different social circles and often went alone to dinners and the theatre.[54] After spending evenings in the same bed in Wollstonecraft's house at 29 The Polygon in Somers Town, Godwin would retreat to rented rooms at 17 Evesham Building in Chalton Street, some twenty doors away, to devote his days to work.[55] They quarrelled, of course. Wollstonecraft objected when he was away too much or when another woman paid him too much attention. Godwin, for his part, found her moodiness difficult to take.

Their conflicts seem less evidence of incompatibility, however, than of their commitment to manly mutuality. They believed, recalled Godwin, "that it was possible for two persons to be too uniformly in each other's society." Their arrangement avoided "satiety. We seemed to combine, in a considerable degree, the novelty and lively sensation of a visit, with the more delicious and heart-felt pleasures of a domestic life."[56] Wollstonecraft agreed. She wanted Godwin to "visit and dine out as formerly, and

I shall do the same; in short, I still mean to be independent." She had married, she told a friend, because she "wished, while fulfilling the duty of a mother, to have some person with similar pursuits, bound to me by affection" as well as "to resign a name which seemed to disgrace me."[57] Godwin occasionally wondered if she did not "find solitude infinitely superior to the company of a husband?"[58] Wollstonecraft assured him that he was "a tender, affectionate creature."[59] But she also enjoyed her independence. "A husband is a convenient part of the furniture of a house." While she wished Godwin "riveted in [her] heart," she did "not desire to have [him] always at [her] elbow."[60] The couple managed to affirm their autonomy through their union; they found independence in acknowledging their interdependence. Each thought the other necessary to her or his happiness.

Godwin was a better partner for Wollstonecraft for many reasons, one of which was his history. Godwin grew up in a variation on English culture that structured his alienation through membership in a pre-existing alternative community, a community that flourished ironically precisely because of the existence of powerful religious, political, and social institutions. As the son of a provincial Dissenting minister, Godwin imbibed a vocabulary through which he understood life as a permanent outsider. Every time he passed the parish church he was reminded that he was in a minority; he did not belong. His father, along with hundreds others like him, prepared his children for a life outside the structures of power by emphasizing the importance of books. Knowledge had long been a bulwark of dissent. Reading theological works allowed young men and women to discover a larger community of similar individuals and to learn the vocabulary – the code, if you will – through which they could become members. He devoted most of his adult life to asserting the ability of educated human beings to organize their own societies around the principle of mutual consent. He was no less committed to revising himself.[61] Godwin had the temperament of a modern intellectual. Unlike Imlay, he preferred the comfort of his study to the rough and tumble milieu of the Atlantic trade or the streets of Paris; he imagined rather than implemented; he observed rather than acted; he kept the world at bay even as he critiqued it. Long before he knew Wollstonecraft, William Godwin had outlined a world compatible with the vision she explained in *A Vindication of the Rights of Woman.*

Godwin's most influential book, *Essay concerning Political Justice,* excited large numbers of readers in the 1790s because it was the fullest expression of the vision of the class of literary radicals to which Godwin belonged.[62]

The work located revolution in consensual relationships among men and women. The "demise of government" and the concept of "human perfectibility" are major themes. They follow from his "belief that moral truth is objective, that men and women are capable of grasping this truth through the exercise of their reason and judgment, that perceiving this truth is sufficient to motivate the corresponding performance, and that our capacities for reasoning and our grasp of these truths have improved through history and will continue to improve."[63] *Political Justice* argued that revolution would come not through the reform of government but through its replacement by society. Godwin trusted educated reasonable individuals to do what was best through mutual association, through consent rather than coercion. Human nature was malleable, not intractable, and therefore susceptible to persuasion. To expect a law "to restore a corrupt and luxurious people to temperance and virtue" was no more realistic than to expect a command to get "a conflagration to cease or a tempest to be still." Change depended entirely on a series of secular conversion experiences. There was "no criterion of duty to any man but in the exercise of his private judgment." Any interference in this natural process was "an execrable tyranny." Individuals could only expect to succeed in achieving justice in face-to-face communities, that is, in variations on London literary circles. Friendship – "conversation and the intercourse of mind with mind" – were the means to the end. Friends yielded to other out of choice. "Mind without benevolence is a barren and a cold existence. It is in seeking the good of others, in embracing a great and expansive sphere of action, in forgetting our own individual interests, that we find our true element."[64]

Godwin's attitude towards marriage epitomized this philosophy. If all relationships were volitional, then men and women should choose lovers as well as friends on the basis of perceived merit not out of family or economic considerations. Requiring unhappy men and women to live together was to institutionalize "thwarting, bickering, and unhappiness." Marriage was "a system of fraud" and property, a monopoly. Human relationships ought to function as commerce. Anything else was tyranny. "So long as two human beings are forbidden by positive institution to follow the dictates of their own mind, prejudice is alive and vigorous. So long as I seek to engross one woman to myself, and to prohibit my neighbour from proving his superior desert and reaping the fruits of it, I am guilty of the most odious of all monopolies."[65]

Godwin had gone beyond rejecting the patriarchal household as the microcosm of a patriarchal state; he had embraced the idea that there was no legitimate form of social organization except that founded on a consent that was inherently conditional. Because human beings and their circumstances change over time, they cannot and should not be forever bound by a choice. Just as a person could end a friendship, change his or her residence, and leave one country for another, so too should he or she be free to come and go in all human relationships. No one would expect a rational person to endure a tyrant in politics or to continue a friendship that had become stale. So why expect something different from lovers? Why should the selection of a romantic and sexual partner in one's youth control the rest of one's life? The abolition of marriage was thus as critical as the abolition of monarchy, churches, and monopolies. In a new world, the "intercourse of the sexes will … fall under the same system as any other species of friendship." Men and women would choose each other. Sexual intercourse would occur only with "unforced consent."[66] Much more than the American Imlay, Godwin saw marriage as a universal institution to be challenged by a class of people all over the world. The problem was not British patriarchy but patriarchy in general and the answer lay in persuasion rather than defiance, education rather than secession, consent rather than coercion, and love among friends rather than marriages begotten in lust, passion, greed, and convenience.

Overwhelmed by grief when Wollstonecraft died from puerperal fever in September 1797, Godwin surrendered to enthusiasm. Written in haste and published alongside Wollstonecraft's letters to Imlay, *Memoirs of the Author of A Vindication of the Rights of Woman* was intended to cheat death by continuing the culture of social commerce through a different kind of biography. An experiment in genre, *Memoirs* was an attempt to fuse a historian's devotion to fact with a novelist's interest in psychological truth. To investigate human behaviour, authors needed to delineate "consistent, human character" through "a display of the manner in which such a character acts under successive circumstances."[67] Godwin wanted readers to know Wollstonecraft personally, to engage with her as a friend as well as an author. Sympathy (emotional identification) was the best antidote to "malignant misrepresentation." Surely, "the more fully we are presented with the picture and story" of influential individuals such as Wollstonecraft, "the more generally shall we feel in ourselves an attachment to their fate, and sympathy in their excellencies." Godwin contextualized *A Vindication of the Rights of Woman*, which he thought as important in content as it was "uneven" in composition, by taking readers into Wollstonecraft's "closet" to narrate moments that revealed her development over time. Godwin admired Wollstonecraft because she was an ordinary person disadvantaged by her sex and her own weaknesses, especially an acute sensibility that tended to make her "a female Werter," who had achieved greatness by learning, adapting, and above all cultivating herself through direct and sometimes painful social intercourse with people like her. It had been a two-way street.[68] Knowing Wollstonecraft had improved him, or so he claimed. Learning to respect "private and domestic affections," he had awakened to the possibilities of emotional connection, to the knowledge that people were "more the creatures of sentiment and affection, than of the understanding."[69] Godwin told all, in short, as evidence of the success of mixed-gender social commerce. He and Wollstonecraft had found happiness together. As important, they had become better people.

Outrage greeted the publication of *Memoirs of the Author of A Vindication of the Rights of Woman.* Readers recoiled from the book of personal revelations and used them to prove the folly of *Vindication.* Its author could not control her enthusiasm for romantic love. What was intended as a tribute was received as an exposé. Wollstonecraft's story became a variation on a familiar theme: a smart woman dismissed because she indulged personal desire at the expense of social duty, a charge supported in this case by the published testimony of a misguided husband. In a nineteenth-century world in which commerce connoted trade, not conversation; and intercourse was copulation, not engagement; in a world that promoted sharp distinctions between men and women, Europeans and Africans, not to mention history and literature, it was hard to read Godwin's hybrid attempt to trace the contingent history of a complex person – let alone Wollstonecraft's insistence that what we call gender was historically constructed and therefore susceptible to change through education – as anything other than an intellectual transgression by one of a community of people whose foolish idealism had led them to betray their bodies, their God, their nation, their race, their children, and, above all, themselves.

Cultural convergence and divergence in the Imlay–Wollstonecraft and Godwin–Wollstonecraft relationships suggest something more important than the problems of three people, one of whom matters mightily as a major progenitor of modern feminism. We might contemplate not only how a discourse to which Wollstonecraft contributed as much as anyone was understood and used in different ways by different men, including her own lovers, but how a radical discourse designed to globalize revolution had its own imperial dimension and provoked an equally powerful national response. Imlay and Godwin meant it when they said they loved Wollstonecraft. But they meant it in different ways (and she heard them differently) in no small part because one was an American and one was an Englishman. Wollstonecraft's lovers were variations on a late eighteenth-century radical theme. Nation and class, not to mention personality, inflected the performance of gender, simultaneously advancing and compromising the prospects of an imagined world organized around the idea that love is above all an affirmation of how much human beings need each other.

NOTES

1 Some parts of this essay were originally published in Andrew Cayton, *Love in the Time of Revolution: Transatlantic Literary Radicalism and Historical Change, 1793–1818* (Chapel Hill, 2013).

2 Alan Taylor, *The Civil War of 1812* (New York, 2010); Maya Jasanoff, *Liberty's Exiles: American Loyalists in a Revolutionary World* (New York, 2011); and in Gilbert Imlay's [hereafter GI] native New Jersey, David Hackett Fischer, *Washington's Crossing* (New York, 2004).

3 Wil Verhoeven, *Gilbert Imlay, Citizen of the World* (London, 2008), 18–26. Short biographies are Oliver Farrar Emerson, "Notes on Gilbert Imlay, Early American Writer," *PMLA* 39 (1924): 406–39; Ralph Leslie Rusk, "The Adventures of Gilbert Imlay," *Indiana University Studies* 10 (March 1923): 3–26; and W.M. Verhoeven and Amanda Gilroy, "Introduction," in GI, *The Emigrants*, ed. Verhoeven and Gilroy (New York, 1998), ix–lvi.

4 William St Clair, *The Godwins and the Shelleys: The Biography of a Family* (New York, 1989), 11. Marilyn Butler and Mark Philp, "Introduction," in *Collected Novels and Memoirs of William Godwin*, vol. 1: *Autobiography*, ed. Mark Philp (London, 1992), 7–46, is an excellent overview of Godwin's life. See also Julie A. Carlson, *England's First Family of Writers: Mary Wollstonecraft, William Godwin, Mary Shelley* (Baltimore, 2007).

5 Anna Clark, *Scandal: The Sexual Politics of the British Constitution* (Princeton, 2004); and E.J. Clery, *The Feminization Debate in Eighteenth-Century England: Literature, Commerce and Luxury* (New York, 2004).

6 Seth Cotlar, *Tom Paine's America: The Rise and Fall of Transatlantic Radicalism in the Early Republic* (Charlottesville, 2011). Susan E. Klepp and Roderick A. McDonald make a similar point in "Inscribing Experience: An American Working Woman and an English Gentlewoman Encounter Jamaica's Slave Society, 1801–1805," *William and Mary Quarterly*, 3rd ser., 58 (3) (2001): 637–60.

7 Mary Wollstonecraft [hereafter MW], *A Vindication of the Rights of Men in a Letter to the Right Honorable Edmund Burke* (2nd ed., London, 1789), in

Janet Todd and Marilyn Butler, eds, *The Works of Mary Wollstonecraft*, 7 vols. (New York, 1989), 5:57.

8 On the nature and varieties of radicalism, see the essays in Glenn Burgess and Matthew Festenstein, eds, *English Radicalism, 1550–1850* (Cambridge, 2007). See also E.P. Thompson, *The Making of the English Working Class* (New York, 1966 [1963]); Albert Goodwin, *The Friends of Liberty: The English Democratic Movement and the Age of the French Revolution* (Cambridge, MA, 1979); and Anna Clark, *The Struggles for the Breeches: Gender and the Making of the British Working Class* (Berkeley, CA, 1997).

9 Emma Rothschild, *The Inner Lives of Empires: An Eighteenth-Century History* (Princeton, 2011); Naomi Tadmor, *Family and Friends in Eighteenth-Century England* (Cambridge, 2001); and Ruth Perry, *Novel Relations: The Transformation of Kinship, Literature and Culture, 1748–1818* (Cambridge, 2004). See Daniel Cottom, *Social Figures: George Eliot, Social History, and Literary Representation* (Minneapolis, 1987).

10 Andrea A. Engstrom, "Joseph Johnson's Circle and the *Analytical Review*: A Study of English Radicals in the Late Eighteenth Century," PhD thesis (University of Southern California, 1986); Gerald P. Tyson, *Joseph Johnson: A Liberal Publisher* (Iowa City, 1979); and Helen Braithwaite, *Romanticism, Publishing and Dissent: Joseph Johnson and the Cause of Liberty* (New York, 2003); James Raven, "Location, Size, and Succession: The Bookshops of Paternoster Row before 1800," in Robin Myers, Michael Harris, and Giles Mandelbrote, eds, *The London Book Trade: Topographies of Print in the Metropolis from the Sixteenth Century* (London, 2003), 89–126; John Barrell, *The Spirit of Despotism: Invasions of Privacy in the 1790s* (New York, 2006), 72–74; and William Zachs, *The First John Murray and the Late Eighteenth-Century London Book Trade* (Oxford, 1998).

11 William Godwin [hereafter WG], *Morning Chronicle*, 21 December 1809.

12 [Joseph Johnson to WG], "A Few Facts," n.d., Abinger MSS, Dep. b. 210/3, in Pamela Clemit and Gina Luria Walker, eds, *Memoirs of the Author of A Vindication of the Rights of Woman* (Peterborough, ON, 2001), 162.

13 MW to Everina Wollstonecraft [c. November 1787], in *The Collected Letters of Mary Wollstonecraft*, ed. Janet Todd (New York, 2004 [2003]), 141. See Janet Todd, *Mary Wollstonecraft: A Revolutionary Life* (New York, 2000), 116–17.

14 MW to Joseph Johnson [1790], in Todd, ed., *Collected Letters*, 166.

15 MW to Johnson, late 1788–early 1789, in Todd, ed., *Collected Letters*, 159.

16 [Johnson to WG], in Clemit and Walker, eds, *Memoirs*, 163.

17 MW to Everina Wollstonecraft, 7 November [1787], in Todd, ed., *Collected Letters*, 140. See Todd, *Wollstonecraft*, 137, 124.

18 MW to Everina Wollstonecraft, 7 November [1787], ibid. See Todd, *Wollstonecraft*, 137, 124. See Janet Todd, "Prefatory Note" to Wollstonecraft, *Contributions to the Analytical Review, 1788–1797*, in Todd and Butler, eds, *Works of Wollstonecraft*, 7: 14–18.

19 Mary Hays, *Appeal to the Men of Great Britain in Behalf of Women*, intro. Gina Luria Walker (New York, 1974 [1798]), v, ii, iii, iv.

20 MW, *A Vindication of the Rights of Woman*, ed. Carol H. Poston (2nd ed., New York, 1988 [1975]), 112, 144, 150, 165, 192.

21 Roy Porter, "Mixed Feelings: The Enlightenment and Sexuality in Eighteenth-Century Britain," in Paul-Gabriel Boucé, ed., *Sexuality in Eighteenth-Century Britain* (Totowa, NJ, 1982), 4, 7; Robert Darnton, *The Forbidden Best-Sellers of Pre-Revolutionary France* (New York, 1996), 91.

22 Robert Darnton, *Bohemians before Bohemianism* (Wassenaar, Denmark, 2006), 36. See Thomas Laqueur, *Making Sex: Body and Gender from the Greeks to Freud* (Cambridge, MA, 1990); Cornelia Hughes Dayton, "Taking the Trade: Abortion and Gender Relations in an Eighteenth-Century New England Village," *William and Mary Quarterly*, 3rd ser., 48 (10) (January 1991): 19–49; Joan Cadden, *Meanings of Sex Difference in the Middle Ages: Medicine, Science, and Culture* (Cambridge, MA, 1993); Clare A. Lyons, *Sex among the Rabble: An Intimate History of Gender and Power in the Age of Revolution, Philadelphia, 1730–1830* (Chapel Hill, 2006); Vic Gatrell, *City of Laughter: Sex and Satire in Eighteenth-Century London* (New York, 2006); Sharon Block, *Rape and Sexual Power in Early America* (Chapel Hill, 2006), 16–52; and Erin Mackie, *Rakes, Highwaymen, and Pirates: The Making of the Modern Gentlemen in the Eighteenth Century* (Baltimore, 2009).

23 Thomas Paine, "Reflections on Unhappy Marriages" [1775], in Philip S. Foner, ed., *The Complete Writings of Thomas Paine* (2 vols., New York, 1945), 1: 1119, 1118, 1119, 1120. See Matthew McCormack, *The Independent Man: Citizenship and Gender Politics in Georgian England* (Manchester, 2005).

24 MW to Johnson, 5 December 1786, in Todd, ed., *Collected Letters*, 96; MW to Johnson, 13 September 1787, ibid., 134. See Cora Kaplan's smart if ahistorical analysis of MW's "combination of equal rights and self-abnegating sexuality" in "Wild Nights: Pleasure/Sexuality/Feminism," in Kaplan, *Sea Changes: Essays on Culture and Feminism* (New York, 1986), 50.

25 MW to GI, [c. August 1793], in Todd, ed., *Collected Letters*, 228.

26 MW, *An Historical and Moral View of the Origin and Progress of the French Revolution* (London, 1794), in Todd and Butler, eds, *Works of Wollstonecraft*, 6: 302, 13.

27 Thomas Holcroft, *Anna St. Ives*, ed. Peter Faulkner (London, 1970 [1792]), 292.

28 Susanne Desan, "Transatlantic Spaces of Revolution: The French Revolution, *Sciotomanie*, and American Lands," *Journal of Early Modern History* 12 (6) (2008): 467–505.

29 William Charvat, *Literary Publishing in America, 1790–1850* (Amherst, 1993 [1959]); Michael Davitt Bell, "Beginnings of Professionalism," in *Culture, Genre, and Literary Vocation: Essays on American Literature* (Chicago, 2001), 67–133; Michael T. Gilmore, "The Book Marketplace I," in Emory Elliott, ed., *The Columbia History of the American Novel* (New York, 1991), 54; Jeffrey Rubin-Dorsky, "The Early American Novel," in Elliott, ed., *Columbia History of the American Novel*, 11; *The History of the Book in America*, vol. 2: *An Extensive Republic: Print, Society, and Culture in the New Nation, 1790–1840*, ed. Robert A. Gross and Mary Kelley (Chapel Hill, 2010); and Andrew Cayton, "The Authority of the Imagination in an Age of Wonder," *Journal of the Early Republic* 33 (1) (2013): 1–27.

30 Peter Silver, *Our Savage Neighbors: How Indian War Transformed Early America* (New York, 2007). On the culture of sociability in America see Catherine Kaplan O'Donnell, *Men of Letters in the Early Republic: Cultivating Forums of Citizenship* (Chapel Hill, 2008); Sarah Knott, *Sensibility and the American Revolution* (Chapel Hill, 2009); and G.K. Barker-Benfield, *Abigail and John Adams: The Americanization of Sociability* (Chicago, 2010).

31 Ann Laura Stoler, "Intimidations of Empire: Predicaments of the Tactile and Unseen," in Stoler, ed., *Haunted by Empire: Geographies of Intimacy in North American History* (Durham, NC, 2006), 2.

32 Thomas A. Foster, ed., *New Men: Manliness in Early America* (New York, 2011).

33 Verhoeven, *Imlay*, 96, 124, 138.

34 Philipp Ziesche, *Cosmopolitan Patriots: Americans in Paris in the Age of Revolution* (Charlottesville, 2010), 64–87; David Hancock, *Citizens of the World: London Merchants and the Integration of the British Atlantic Community, 1735–1785* (Cambridge, 1995); P.J. Cain and A.G. Hopkins, *British Imperialism, 1688–2000* (2nd ed., Harlow, 2002 [1993]); and Sheryllynne Haggerty, *The British-Atlantic Trading Community, 1760–1810: Men, Women, and the Distribution of Goods* (Leiden, 2006), 41–6.

35 H.E. Scudder, ed., *Recollections of Samuel Breck, with Passages from His Note-Books (1771–1862)* (Philadelphia, 1877), 170, 171, 172. See Christopher Iannini, "'The Itinerant Man': Crèvecoeur's Caribbean, Raynal's Revolution, and the Fate of Atlantic Cosmopolitanism," *William and Mary Quarterly* 61 (2) (2004): 201–34; J.M. Opal, *Beyond the Farm: National Ambitions in Rural New England* (Philadelphia, 2008); and Edward G. Gray, *The Making of John Ledyard: Empire and Ambition in the Life of an Early American Traveler* (New Haven, 2007).

36 GI, *A Topographical Description of the Western Territory of North America*, 3rd ed. (London, 1797 [1792]), repr. (New York, 1969), 1, 179.

37 Thomas Paine, "Forgetfulness" (1794), in Foner, ed., *Writings of Paine*, 2: 1123. See Moncure Daniel Conway, *Life of Thomas Paine* (2 vols., New York, 1909), 2: 64–9.

38 I.B. Johnson [to WG], 13 November 1797, in Pamela Clemit and Gina Luria Walker, ed., *Memoirs of the Author of A Vindication of the Rights of Woman* (Peterborough, ON, 2001), 166.

39 Jean Jacques Rousseau, *Émile, or, On Education*, trans. Allan Bloom (New York, 1979 [1762]), 351, 352.

40 *Memoirs of Madame Roland*, ed. Evelyn Shuckburgh (Mount Kisco, NY, 1999), 61, 81, 246.

41 GI, *The Emigrants*, ed. Verhoeven and Gilroy, 114, 105. See Toby L. Ditz, "The New Men's History and the Peculiar Absence of Gendered Power: Some Remedies from Early American Gender History," *Gender & History* 16 (April 2004), 1–21.

42 Ibid., 239, 241, 252, 250.

43 Ibid., 47, 43, 32.

44 Ibid., 43, 41, 180.

45 Ibid., 186, 192–3, 198, 199, 200, 203.

46 Ibid., 231, 234, 235, 247. See Amanda Gilroy, "'Espousing the Cause of Oppressed Women': Cultural Captivities in Gilbert Imlay's *The Emigrants*," in W.M. Verhoeven and Beth Dolan Kautz, eds, *Revolutions & Watersheds: Transatlantic Dialogues, 1775–1815* (Amsterdam, 1999), 191–205.

47 See the essays by Barbara Taylor and Silvia Sebastiani in *Women, Gender and Enlightenment*, ed. Sarah Knott and Barbara Taylor (New York, 2005). Leonard Tannenhouse, "Libertine America," differences: A Journal of Feminist Cultural Studies 11 (5) (1999/2000): 1–28, notes the different roles of the libertine in American and British seduction stories. In "American stories," libertines tend to "break up the traditional patriarchal family in a way that ushered in a new family based on mutual consent" (4). As important, American seduction stories tend to be about male competition for women, and not, as so often was the case in Britain, with a young woman finding happiness with a wealthier and cultivated aristocrat (9). In America, libertines disrupt a British system of relationships to create an American one.

48 MW, review of Brissot's *New Travels*, in Todd and Butler, eds, *Works of Wollstonecraft*, 7: 391.

49 MW, *Maria, or, The Wrongs of Woman* (New York, 2004 [1798]), 75, 76.

50 St Clair, *Godwins and Shelleys*, 11; Butler and Philp, "Introduction," in Philp, ed., *Collected Novels*, 7–46.

51 St Clair, *Godwins and Shelleys*, 56.
52 Peter H. Marshall, *William Godwin* (New Haven, 1984), 172, 175. See St Clair, *Godwins and Shelleys*, 150.
53 MW to Godwin, 30 September 1796, in Todd, ed., *Collected Letters*, 369; MW to Godwin, 4 October 1796, ibid., 371.
54 Ibid., 406n.
55 Marshall, *Godwin*, 187; St Clair, *Godwins and Shelleys*, 173.
56 WG, *Memoirs*, quoted in *A Short Residence in Norway, Sweden and Denmark* and *Memoirs of the Author of A Vindication of the Rights of Woman*, ed. Richard Holmes (New York, 1987 [1796]), 263.
57 MW to Amelia Alderson, 11 April 1797, in Todd, ed., *Collected Letters*, 409.
58 Ibid., 416n.
59 MW to Godwin, 6 June 1797, in Todd, ed., *Collected Letters*, 417.
60 MW to Godwin, 6 June 1797, ibid., 418.
61 Pamela Clemit, "Holding Proteus: William Godwin in His Letters," in Heather Glen and Paul Hamilton, eds, *Repossessing the Romantic Past* (Cambridge, 2006), 100.
62 Mark Philp, *Godwin's Political Justice* (Ithaca, NY, 1986), 1; Isaac Kramnick, "On Anarchism and the Real World: William Godwin and Radical England," *American Political Science Review* 66 (1) (March 1972): 119.
63 Philp, *Godwin's Political Justice*, 2.
64 WG, *An Enquiry concerning Political Justice and Its Influence on General Virtues and Happiness* (Dublin, 1793), 135, 240, 271, 379, 387.
65 Ibid., 380, 381.
66 Ibid., 382, 383.
67 WG, "Essay of History and Romance," in Mark Philp, ed., *Political and Philosophical Writings of William Godwin*, 8 vols. (London, 1993 [1987]), vol. 5: *Educational and Literary Writings*, ed. Pamela Clemit, 291.
68 WG, *Memoirs of the Author of A Vindication of The Rights of Woman*, ed. Holmes, 204, 232, 242.
69 WG, *Thoughts occasioned by the perusal of Dr. Parr's Spital Sermon, preached at Christ Church, April 15, 1800* (London, 1801), 181, 182.

chapter five

Susanna Rowson's Antislavery and Feminist Ideals in Transatlantic Translation: A Tale of Three Cities

JENNA GIBBS

In a letter written on the eve of the War of 1812, Susanna Haswell Rowson lamented the resurgence of hostility between Great Britain and the United States: "For, though I am by birth a Briton, my heart always clings to dear America, and it would be with equal anxiety I should contemplate the misery of either country." She called on "the good angels of peace" to protect against "civil discord" between her two countries, "revered old England" and "beloved America."[1] The British-born but American-raised Rowson had dual transnational loyalties throughout her life.[2] Her declaration in 1812 was, however, not merely a product of her undoubtedly tense situation as a British-born American citizen in that fraught milieu of imminent war. For Rowson was a child of both worlds whose multifaceted career as an actress, playwright, poet, and educator spanned three decades and three Atlantic locales. She began her writing career in London, had a brief theatrical career in Philadelphia, and eventually founded and ran an academy of female education in early nineteenth-century Boston. Throughout her transatlantic life and in diverse cultural media – poetry, novels, plays, and pedagogical texts – Rowson repeatedly articulated antislavery and pro-feminist ideals. Yet, her transatlantic trajectory evidences the crucial importance of time and place in shaping and circumscribing an author's political advocacy, especially that of a female author with dual national loyalties in the volatile era of revolution and reaction unleashed by the American Revolution.

Rowson expressed her antislavery and pro-feminist prescriptions in contrasting terms and media in the three primary locations and phases of her writing career. In London in the late 1780s and early 1790s, she wrote and published several poems and four novels, including *The Invisible Rambler* (1788), in which she critiqued women's lack of property rights and condemned British West Indian slavery and the British slave trade. Her attack on slavery was full-frontal and resolute, but used the prevailing Christian and humanitarian arguments promoted by the newly formed London Society for the Abolition of Slavery rather than more radical democratic notions of rights. She resumed her Christian antislavery arguments as a respected schoolmistress in early nineteenth-century Boston in her textbook *An Abridgement to Universal Geography* (1805), albeit adding a biting indictment of slavery and slave owners in her "beloved America."

But Rowson's theatrical sojourn in 1790s Philadelphia arrestingly disrupts what might otherwise appear to be the continuity of her expression of pro-feminist and antislavery ideals. In Philadelphia, Rowson wrote *Slaves in Algiers; or, a Struggle for Freedom* for the New Street Theatre, and in the play – in which she performed a lead role – overtly used revolutionary and democratic discourses to call for women's marital and political rights through the allegory of enslavement in an Algerian harem. In marked contrast to her London and Boston works, however, she did not directly critique African slavery through the harem metaphor, which is why most literary critics argue for the play as pro-feminist but dismiss its antislavery message.[3] But rejecting outright the possibility that Rowson wrote *Slaves in Algiers* with both feminist and antislavery intent is tenable only if we divorce the play from her earlier British and later Boston antislavery writings. Moreover, textual analysis reveals that she embedded in the play an oblique critique of slavery by merging her Christian, humanitarian arguments with the rights-based parlance of 1790s Philadelphia. Yet, in the play Rowson retreated from open abolitionist commitment. She did so in the face of political furore over the French Revolution and acute fears galvanized by the Saint-Domingue slave uprising and the influx of refugees to Philadelphia. As a British-American with dual loyalties and as a female author of humble means she needed to err on the side of political caution to make a living and get ahead. To these ends, Rowson carefully tailored and re-tailored her antislavery and pro-feminist prescriptions to suit the political pressures and passions of three Atlantic cities in three discrete periods of the age of revolution and reaction: 1780s London, 1790s Philadelphia, and early nineteenth-century Boston.

Rowson's earliest engagement with the problem of slavery was a product of her experiences both in revolutionary America and in post-war Great Britain at pivotal periods of antislavery fervour. In both countries, she lived in geopolitical sites where she was exposed to prevailing antislavery discourse not only in society at large, but also in her own household.

Born in Portsmouth, England, she spent her formative years in 1760s and 1770s Massachusetts because her father was a tax collector for the British crown. With the Revolution the family was forcibly expelled to Great Britain. Educated in the colonies, she had access to her father's extensive library, where she voraciously read Dryden, Pope, Shakespeare, the classical philosophers, and key Enlightenment texts by, for example, Abbé Raynal and David Hume.[4] Through her father's precarious position she would have been fully aware of the colonists' revolutionary preparations and republican rhetoric of the mid-1770s. Moreover, in Massachusetts she was tutored by James Otis, a noted anti-slavery and pro-revolutionary patriot. Otis grounded his antislavery on precepts of natural rights and stressed the rhetorical contradiction between rejecting political enslavement to Great Britain's tyranny, on the one hand, while perpetuating black slavery in America, on the other. In a 1764 pamphlet, for example, Otis characterized slavery as "a shocking violation of the law of nature" and indicted American slaveholders protesting Britain's rule as "hypocritical tyrants ... who every day barter away other men's liberty."[5] Otis's views were prescient, as numerous pro-revolutionary and antislavery patriots persisted in this line of anti-slavery attack. Thomas Paine, for example, in *African Slavery in America,* published in the widely read *Pennsylvania Journal and Weekly Advertiser* in March 1775, denounced slavery as a horrible contradiction to the natural right to liberty, and fumed, "With what consistency or decency [can American slaveholders] complain so loudly of attempts to enslave them, while they hold so many hundred thousand in slavery? We have enslaved multitudes and shed much innocent blood in doing it, and now are threatened with the same."[6] In the 1770s, this daughter of a royal tax collector and pupil of a revolutionary patriot would surely have been aware of the prevalent denunciation of slavery as contradictory to American patriot ideals.

Rowson and her family were deported to England in 1778, and between 1778 and 1793 she was mostly based in London, another crucial time and site for the development of antislavery discourse. By then, her family was destitute and her father deeply in debt, as their Massachusetts property had been confiscated before their expulsion. Due to these reduced family circumstances, Rowson was forced to work as a governess for the Duchess of Devonshire, with whose financial patronage Rowson published her first novel, *Victoria,* in 1786.[7] That same year she married William Rowson. Little is known about Rowson's London years. But one might surmise that she was aware of the antislavery sentiments of her patroness, the duchess, and her Whig circle, which included abolitionist

Members of Parliament Charles Fox and Richard B. Sheridan, who went on to become key architects of the 1807 legislation banning the slave trade. Sheridan was one of the earliest parliamentary antislavery advocates.[8] He was also the manager of Drury Lane Theatre, and his antislavery sympathy had prompted abolitionist Hannah More to suggest in 1788 that he stage *Oroonoko*, a play featuring a blackface slave and antislavery commentary, as a means to reach three thousand people a night with an antislavery message.[9] As early as 1783, then Secretary of State Charles Fox, for his part, had refused, on antislavery grounds, to return former American slaves whom the British had promised their freedom in return for fighting on their side in the American Revolution, and by 1788 he was an avowed abolitionist member of parliament.[10]

Even if Rowson was not directly privy to discussions between these antislavery pioneers during her residence in the duchess's household, her keen awareness of antislavery discourse in 1780s London can be evidenced in her 1788 poem *Trip to Parnassus; or, the Judgment of Apollo on Dramatic Authors and Performers.* In this piece, Rowson also expressed her growing interest in the theatre and its potential for moral and political education, including pro-feminist and antislavery appeals. Thus, in *Trip to Parnassus* she praised several female playwrights for "speaking for the female sex with their pens."[11] But she reserved some of her highest praise for George Colman Jr and his musical comedy *Inkle and Yarico. Inkle and Yarico* is the story of an English merchant, Inkle, who was shipwrecked off the coast of Barbados and rescued from death by the native Yarico, whom he then sold into slavery. On the London stage, Yarico was originally played as Native American but, as antislavery gained momentum, the character was frequently portrayed as African. Frances Maria Kelly's recollections of playing the role in the late eighteenth and early nineteenth centuries indicate that the part became firmly linked to African-ness and, by extension, slavery. In her memoirs, Kelly recalled being asked by the manager of Covent Garden to play Yarico early in her career to generate sympathy for the "ill used African." Kelly then took pains to "carefully put on a Brown-Sherry complexion for Yarico" so as to be "excessively African."[12] *Inkle and Yarico* had been widely hailed by London theatre critics as an antislavery commentary, and Elizabeth Inchbald even claimed the play "was the bright forerunner of alleviation to the hardships of slavery."[13] In *Trip to Parnassus,* Rowson applauded the supposed antislavery sentiment of *Inkle and Yarico,* which she deemed "a soft tale of distress ... that teaches humanity, [of which] all must approve."[14]

But it was not in the theatre that Rowson first denounced slavery, but rather in an early novel, *The Inquisitor; or, Invisible Rambler.* Rowson wrote and published *The Invisible Rambler* in London in 1788, just as the British abolition movement was gathering force.[15] A picaresque novel, *The Invisible Rambler* is composed of vignettes of London life observed by a magically invisible voyeur who speaks forthrightly against slavery and also comments repeatedly on women's lack of property rights and education. Indeed, the entire novel is framed by gender in the preface, which features a fictive dialogue between Rowson and a friend. The invented friend asks, "But why do you make your Inquisitor a man?" to which the author replies, "For a very obvious reason … A man may be with propriety brought forward in many scenes where it would be the height of improbability to introduce a woman."[16] Rowson's pointed commentary on women's limited access to the social spaces into which men could freely wander underlined how women's behaviour and speech were circumscribed, while also implicitly claiming their right to speak out on political and social issues.

Rowson advocated for expanded rights for women in *The Invisible Rambler* and in several other novels she published in London, in which she decried women's lack of property and divorce rights. Thus, on the invisible rambler's excursions through London, he encounters an unmarried pregnant woman abandoned by her lover, and a wife whose husband had spent all her dowry on his mistress, a lack of fiscal control for women that the rambler laments. In similar ilk, *Charlotte Temple: A Tale of Truth* (1791) – commonly but erroneously dubbed as the first American best-selling novel on the grounds of its many later American editions[17] – is the story of a young British woman seduced by a soldier who persuaded her to elope with him to revolutionary America, where he thereafter abandons the pregnant Charlotte to die a pauper's death after he opportunistically marries an heiress. The novel thus illuminated how lack of legal and property rights left women defenceless against male lust and tyranny. Her subsequent novel, *Mentoria,* published in London in 1792, offered one antidote. Consisting of a series of tales told to young ladies by their governess, it illustrated the necessity of education both as a requisite for women's virtue and to ensure women a means to financially support themselves. Rowson, then, was not only already an accomplished writer before her return to North America, but was already an outspoken advocate of women's education and improved legal status who had claimed her right (and, by extension, the right of all women) to engage in public political commentary.

And one issue that Rowson repeatedly protested in *The Invisible Rambler* was the injustice of slavery. Rowson's London antislavery arguments in 1788 closely tallied with those put forth by the newly formed London Society for Effecting the Abolition of the Slave Trade, and those that Wilberforce would present in the first parliamentary debate about slavery in 1789. Both she and Wilberforce cast opposition to slavery as a moral and Christian obligation. Both argued that slavery and the slave trade were physically brutal, that slavery was unchristian, destroyed families through separation, and was at odds with enlightened humanitarian principles. Rowson further argued that slavery was antithetical to British "liberty," and supported this premise by referencing the abolitionist Granville Sharpe's legal victory in the Somerset case of 1772, namely, Lord Mansfield's influential ruling that slaves could not be sent out of England to the West Indian plantations. While his limited ruling did nothing to challenge the legal premises of slave owning and slave trading, antislavery advocates, poets, and novelists popularized the ruling with the boast that England's air was "too pure for slaves to breath in," a phrase used by Sergeant-at-law William Davy in his opening arguments on behalf of Somerset, which he grounded in seventeenth-century precedent.[18]

Thus, in one episode of *The Invisible Rambler*, the unseen reporter encounters a former slave and denounces slavery as shamefully un-Christian, unenlightened, and un-British:

> Why did I blush, why did I tremble, as I pronounced the word slave? It was because I was ashamed of the appellation; it is a word that should never be used between man and man – the negro on the burning sands of Africa was born as free as him who draws his first breath in Britain – and shall a Christian, a man whose mind is enlightened by education and religion … sell the freedom of this poor negro, only because he differs from him in complexion?

Rowson concluded this scene by asking her reader to imagine the tables were turned and consider the horror of being enslaved themselves: "What right has an European to sell an African? Do they leave their native land, and seek our coast … entice our countrymen away and make them slaves?"[19] This rhetorical tactic foreshadowed her later deployment in *Slaves in Algiers* of the analogy between American sailors held in Algerian captivity and African slavery in America.

A subsequent vignette voiced unequivocal condemnation of slavery, while embodying a tension between Rowson's universal humanism and her propensity to hierarchically rank human and cultural difference, a core paradox in the broader canvas of eighteenth-century Enlightenment thought. In this episode, the narrator's encounter with the former slave continues to haunt his thoughts. His meditations prompt him to graphically recount the horrors of the middle passage, the separation of a family at a Barbados slave sale, and the indignity of a slave dying and being "thrown into the grave … without one tear of affection or regret being shed." He rhetorically demands, "Had not that poor Negro a soul?" His reply concluded the piece: "Yes – and in futurity [his soul] shall appear white and spotless at the throne of Grace, to confound the man who called himself a Christian, and yet betrayed a fellow-creature into bondage." While Rowson, like many of her contemporaries, assumed that whiteness and Christianity stood at the pinnacle of moral purity, her vision of the "poor Negro" appearing at "the throne of Grace" also presupposed the spiritual worth of African souls and their equal potential to earn salvation.

Rowson's belief in the universal nature of humanity coupled with a hierarchy of cultural and religious difference are on display in her musical comedy *Slaves in Algiers; or, a Struggle for Freedom*, which debuted in Philadelphia in 1794. Financial need had driven Susanna Rowson and her husband, William, into the theatre after her husband's business failed in London. After performing briefly with a humble Edinburgh theatre troupe, she and William were recruited to join Philadelphia's aptly named New Theatre Company in 1793. There she wrote four plays, of which only *Slaves in Algiers* is extant. Set in the Orientalist setting of an Algerian harem, the plays tells the story of how white Christian captives teach Algerian Muslim captors and a stereotypically money-grubbing Jew, Ben Hassan, the meaning of liberty and the value of women's rights. Although couched in American revolutionary language, the plot itself fused British origins with American rhetoric, as Rowson created the play from a subplot in her London-penned novel *Mary; or, the Test of Honour* (London, 1789), in which England had served as her symbol of liberty.[20] In *Slaves in Algiers*, Rowson also embedded in the story a subtle critique of slavery by fusing Christian morals and precepts of British constitutional liberty to antislavery motifs prominent in 1790s Philadelphia: American republican rights and liberty; Mary Wollstonecraft's likening of women's position in marriage to slavery; and topical debate over American seamen captured for ransom by Algerian pirates between 1785 and 1793.[21] Rowson's explicit use of the seraglio metaphor and her choice of Algiers as setting suggests her implicit rejection of African slavery even though she never named it, a point to which we will return.

Rowson wrote her pro-feminist and antislavery musical comedy *Slaves in Algiers* just as Wollstonecraft's *Vindication of the Rights of Woman* had become the chief referent for women's political rights in Philadelphia and in the early republic at large. In the tract, Wollstonecraft argued for a "revolution in manners" and demanded women be educated and given political rights, such that they could be companionable and intellectual equals to men in marriage. The tract fundamentally altered the terms of debate over the nature of women's rights by suggesting that women were as equally capable of reason as men and shared the same natural rights.[22] Initially published in instalments in 1792 by the Philadelphia *Ladies Magazine*, the editor glowingly introduced Wollstonecraft as "employing her pen in behalf of her own sex."[23] William Gibbons in 1792 and Mathew Carey in 1794 published complete editions in Philadelphia. By 1795, Wollstonecraft's tract graced more private American libraries than did Paine's *The Rights of Man.*[24] Several women's periodicals embraced Wollstonecraft's ideas and took up her marriage-slavery analogy to advocate for women's political rights, legal rights within marriage, and female education.[25] One anonymous author who wrote an article in *Philadelphia Lady's Magazine* in 1792 under the pseudonym "Matrimonial Republican" even argued that the word "obey" should be taken out of the marriage vows because, the writer reasoned, "Where I have sworn or even promised to obey any man … I have bound myself to be a slave." Like Wollstonecraft, she concluded that marriage should be a "reciprocal union of interest, and implied partnership of interests, where all differences are accommodated by conference."[26]

Wollstonecraft's ideas thus resonated with the aspirations of some American women and a few sympathetic male radicals to expand education, legal rights, and political participation for women. Despite Abigail Adams's famous plea in 1776 to "remember the Ladies" and the active role the Daughters of Liberty had played in boycotts of British goods and as suppliers of provisions to revolutionary solders, the American Revolution had done little to change women's legally and politically dependent status. True, there had been a subtle expansion of women's rights in laws pertaining to legal *coverture* and divorce. But these were nuanced, incremental changes rather than fundamental alterations of women's legal and political status.[27] The common consensus, meanwhile, of most male Democratic Republicans and their Federalist opponents as well as many women was that women's rights were distinct and separate from those of men: men's were political and legal, while women's were non-political benefits dependent on their roles as wives and mothers.[28] Yet the radical talk of the American Revolution had nonetheless fomented debate about women's rights, and the multiple editions of *Rights of Woman* were published just as Abigail Adams, Judith Sargent Murray, playwright Mercy Otis Warren, and novelist Hannah Webster Foster – as well as Susanna Rowson – were challenging these constricted definitions of rights.[29]

Wollstonecraft's ideas also became part of Philadelphian antislavery discourse. She had, of course, sarcastically deprecated the dependent state of married women by calling, tongue in cheek, on the popular oriental trope of enslavement in the Turkish harem: "Surely, these weak beings are only fit for a seraglio!"[30] The marriage-slavery analogy had been in common currency with British and French authors throughout the seventeenth and eighteenth centuries, and predated contention over black slavery.[31] But Wollstonecraft *explicitly* referenced African slavery when she likened women to slaves.[32] When calling for women to be educated "to respect themselves as rational creatures," Wollstonecraft disparaged the uneducated wife who brings to marriage only "meekness and docility," as no better than a "house slave."[33] She unambiguously drove home her point that women's legal *coverture* made marriage akin to African slavery by demanding: "Is sugar always to be produced by vital blood? Is one half of the human species, like the poor African slaves, to be subject to prejudices that brutalize them?"[34] Wollstonecraft thus re-contextualized the marriage-slavery parallel to overtly reference African slavery.

When Rowson wrote *Slaves in Algiers*, the seraglio was already a popular antislavery metaphor. She lent it particular potency, however, by setting the seraglio in Algeria. Several playwrights before her had written popular transatlantic plays using the seraglio to negotiate abolitionist and feminist demands. Isaac Bickerstaffe's *The Sultan; or a Peep in the Seraglio* (London, 1775; Philadelphia, 1794), for example, tackled issues of gender and slavery, Elizabeth Inchbald's *Such Things Are* (London, 1787; Philadelphia, 1793) set feminist and antislavery narratives in an Asian harem; and in *A Day in Turkey; or the Russian Slaves* (London, 1791; Boston, 1797) Hannah Cowley explored slavery in a Turkish seraglio.[35] But when Rowson staged the seraglio in Algeria, she capitalized on widespread sympathy generated in the press for Americans enslaved by Barbary pirates.[36] Just two months before the play's debut, the New Theatre held charity performances to raise ransom money for the "American citizens [held] captive in Algiers."[37] The captives were also the subject of congressional debate.[38] Rowson thus naturalized the metaphor to Philadelphia political discourse.

More importantly, Philadelphian antislavery advocates were making strident use of the crisis to denounce African slavery. Rowson's Philadelphia publisher, Mathew Carey, drew upon the analogy to condemn slavery in his *Short Account of Algiers* (1794), in which he declared, "The Christians of Europe and America carry on this commerce an hundred times more extensively than the Algerines ... Before, therefore, we reprobate the Algerines, we should enquire whether it is not possible to find ... the systematic brutality [of African slavery] still more disgraceful?"[39] And just a few months before the play's debut, the first ever National Abolition Convention met in Philadelphia and in their published proceedings demanded that the United States "refrain immediately from ... African slavery" because it was "Algerian piracy in another form."[40] Similarly, Absalom Jones, pastor of the African Episcopal Church, petitioned Congress to protest African slavery by comparing it with "the deplorable ... situation of citizens of the United States captured and enslaved ... in Algiers."[41]

Given their prevalence in Philadelphian abolitionist rhetoric, one might expect Rowson to utilize the Algerian captivity/African slavery comparison and the seraglio trope to openly attack African slavery, but instead she veiled her critique in allegory. In the play, she gestured to her London arguments, but also couched Algerian captivity and the marriage/slavery analogy in American revolutionary theory to protest the shortcomings of its practice for women and, by inference, for slaves. Rowson's playful fantasy of the power of Christian, republican, and female virtue to depose antidemocratic despotism exposes the irony of the American Revolution's shortcomings. The American captives include Rebecca, Rebecca's long-lost British husband, Constant, and Rebecca and Constant's daughter, the British-American Olivia. In a plot that mirrors Rowson's life, Constant is a British loyalist soldier and he and Olivia are separated from Rebecca amidst the turmoil of the American Revolution before being improbably reunited in Algerian captivity fourteen years later. The captives also number the Muslim Algerian Selima, as well as Fetnah, the British-born daughter of Ben Hassan, an archetypal Shylock-like Jew who sells his own daughter to the Dey of Algiers. The Christian American and British captives teach the Muslim and Jewish Algerian captives about liberty, especially Rebecca, who, we learn early on, was a Daughter of Liberty in the American Revolution. When the American and British captives foment a revolt, they are assisted by Zoriana and Fetnah, new converts to democratic ideals of liberty. The revolt is betrayed by the Janus-faced Ben Hassan. The Dey of Algiers, however, undergoes an eleventh-hour conversion to democratic liberty in the final scene of the play. After witnessing the slaves' willingness to die for their liberty – an unmistakable echo of American revolutionaries' "Death or Liberty!" battle cry – he frees all his slaves.

For all Rowson's pronounced gestures in *Slaves in Algiers* to American revolutionary rhetoric, she also wove in British antislavery discourse, albeit without the directness of her outspoken admonitions of the 1780s. She did, however, reference British constitutional liberty – as she had in *The Invisible Rambler* – but reconciled it with American republican rights. Moreover, the uniquely British-American Rowson brought together her British and American antislavery arguments largely through the agency of British and American female characters: the American Revolutionary Daughter of Liberty, Rebecca; the British-born Fetnah; and Rebecca's daughter, the British-American Olivia. To be sure, Rowson's transatlantic translation of her feminist and abolitionist precepts was central to the relationship between the American Rebecca and British-born Fetnah. Thus, in Act 1, scene 1, we learn that Rebecca, a captive in the household of Ben Hassan, has taught Ben Hassan's daughter, Fetnah, the democratic ethos of the "sons and daughters of liberty." After the unscrupulous Ben Hassan sells his daughter, Fetnah, to the Dey, Rebecca's republican ideals inspire Fetnah to spurn slavery. Now the Dey's pet slave, Fetnah rejects his sexual advances and educates the Algerian female slaves to resist slavery and patriarchal tyranny on the grounds of natural rights. As Fetnah informs Selima, "My father brought home a female captive, [Rebecca.] It was she who nourished in my mind the love of liberty, and taught me woman was never formed to be the abject slave of man. Nature made us equal with them, and gave us the power to render ourselves superior." Rowson made clear, however, that Fetnah's receptivity to American republican liberty was dependent on her birth in Britain, where the air was (of course) too pure for slaves to breathe. When pushed by Selima, Fetnah further explains her love of liberty thus: "I was not born in Algiers; I drew my first breath in England ... I feel that I was born free."

Having brought together British liberty and American republican rights, Rowson reasserted women's rights to political participation and slaves' rights to be free in the final scene. The scene was the denouement of the revolt plot in which every decisive move was made by female characters educated in their republican rights. For example, when Ben Hassan betrays the plot, it is his daughter, Fetnah, who saves the day. She disguises herself as a man to enter the male quarters and warn the male conspirators. Once there, she asserts women's capability for political leadership and boasts, "A woman can face danger with as much spirit, and as little fear, as the bravest man." And when the Dey discovers the conspiracy and the slaves seem doomed, Olivia (Rebecca's daughter) agrees to marry him in exchange for the slaves' freedom. Olivia's offer, in turn, stirs Rebecca to proclaim that rather than remain enslaved, the rebels "will die together; for never shall Olivia, a daughter of Columbia and a Christian ... live [as] the slave of a despotic tyrant." Rebecca is thus the agent of the "Death or Liberty" cry that persuades the Dey to free the slaves.

In this final scene, Rowson championed women's political agency and echoed the religiously based arguments against slavery she had first made in London, while also insisting that slavery was an infringement of the democratic rights of man and woman. Rebecca repeated the wording in Rowson's *The Invisible Rambler* when she argued that "by the Christian law, no man should be a slave; it is a word so abject, that, but to speak it dyes the cheek with crimson." Rebecca then fused this with American revolutionary antislavery arguments when she pointedly proclaimed the injustice of demanding liberty for oneself while denying it to others: "Let us assert our own prerogative to be free, but let us not throw on another's neck, the chains we scorn to wear." The British-American Olivia, played by Rowson herself, closes the play with a plea: "May freedom spread her benign influence through every nation, till the bright Eagle, mixed with the dove and olive branch, waves high, the acknowledged standard of the world." Rowson evoked the ideal of American freedom to conclude her appeal for universal justice for American captives, African slaves, and women.

This encomium to American freedom was issued by the British-American Olivia, whose transnational identity twinned that of Rowson, and hence the monologue also served as an appeal for transnational reconciliation. When the British paternity of Olivia (and Rowson) was fused to American ideals and culture, the reconciliation was both autobiographical and ideological. Not coincidentally, Rowson wrote and performed *Slaves in Algiers* against the backdrop of mounting tension with Great Britain over the United States' insistence on neutrality in the war between revolutionary France and Great Britain. Perhaps this was why the theatre managers explicitly advertised *Slaves in Algiers* as part of an attempt to "form an American stage" and begged their audience to give this American play "a fair and full trial."[42] The advertisement's emphasis on the *American* stage is particularly striking because it was contrary to the theatre managers' pronounced tendency to stage and promote the merits of British-penned repertoire, and thus suggests the managers were trying to avoid political controversy by positioning Rowson as American. Rowson herself would, no doubt, have been painfully aware of Philadelphians' potentially negative perceptions of her British paternity, which could surely have served as inspiration for Rowson to end the play by delivering a patriotic appeal for freedom through her British-American doppelganger, Olivia. Through the British-American Olivia, Rowson espoused transnational reconciliation between Great Britain and the United States to call for slaves' liberty and the rights of women.

Rowson put the final touches on her antislavery and pro-feminist claims in the epilogue, which she wrote and performed herself. In it, she directly appealed to her female audience for women's rights:

Well, Ladies tell me – how d'ye like my play?
"The creature has some sense," methinks you say;
She says that we should have supreme dominion,
And in good truth, we're all of her opinion.
Women were born for universal sway;
Men to adore, be silent and obey.

Rowson's inversion of gender constructions in which women were expected to be silent and obey thus also staked her claim to speak as a woman. She then brought the audience's attention back to the analogy between Algerian captivity and slavery:

You who feel humanity's soft glow
What rapt'rous joy must the poor captive know;
Who, free'd from slavery's ignominious chain,
Views his dear native land, and friends again.

Rowson's sentimental appeal to the audience's humanity was, on its surface, a plea for the safe return of American sailors in Algerian captivity. But "slavery's chains" and separation from "native land" could be just as readily applied to Africans trapped in American slavery. Tellingly, when Rowson reduced the original three-act version to a much shorter two-act afterpiece, she wrote an announcement for the performance, printed in the *Baltimore Daily Telegraph*, in which she pointedly alluded to slavery as a universal wrong in any context. She proclaimed "Sweet Liberty" to be the "dearest, the first ardent wish of my heart" and demanded that "each and every fellow creature who languishes in slavery should [be permitted to] rejoice in the blessings of freedom."[43]

Yet, in contrast to her earlier London writings, Rowson never named *African* slavery in *Slaves in Algiers*. Why, when she had openly and cogently spoken against slavery and the slave trade in London as the antislavery movement gained momentum, would Rowson tackle the problem in Philadelphia, a hotbed of abolitionism, only under allegorical cover? And why would she refrain from direct condemnation of slavery even though the seraglio and Algerian captivity had become prevalent metaphorical analogies to African slavery in 1790s Philadelphia? As one scholar who has argued against an antislavery reading of the play has observed, "It seems odd that Rowson would leave an abolitionist argument unvoiced were it important to her."[44] Several interrelated factors explain her timidity. She was writing at a politically fraught moment when the unfolding revolution in Saint-Domingue, which had begun in 1792 as a slave revolt, made African slavery an incendiary issue; she was writing and performing in a theatre whose Federalist managers sought to keep overt politics off the stage in the hopes of tamping down the political factions of the French revolutionary years; and, as a female author, Rowson needed to walk a precarious line between propriety and provocation in order to make a living. Last but not least, the British-born Rowson, daughter of a British royal tax collector, had always to consider how best to represent herself as a loyal American given her duelling national attachments. Hence, the Federalist theatre managers' insistence on presenting her as an American playwright and Rowson's emphasis in *Slaves in Algiers* on transnational reconciliation, a point she reinforced in her preface to the published play, in which she insisted she "intended no sentiment, in the least prejudicial to the moral or political principles of the government under which I live."[45]

The onset of what became the Haitian Revolution goes a long way to explaining her retreat from direct attacks on slavery. Rowson was writing just after some two thousand white Saint Dominguan émigrés swarmed into Philadelphia (and other northern port cities) after the burning of the northern port of Le Cap Français in June 1793, telling tales of massacre.[46] Even before the refugees' arrival, lurid descriptions of savage violence in newspaper accounts and letters from Saint-Domingue had been translated and republished in Philadelphian newspapers, such as the report of the overseer who was found with "his body mangled, and marks of teeth on several parts," and of the women and children who were tied to wooden planks and sawed in half.[47] These sensational reports of carnage incited fears that the revolt would spread to the southern plantations.[48] More nightmarish still was the idea of revolt erupting on Philadelphians' doorsteps in the persons of Saint Dominguan slaves, whose exiled masters had brought them to the city in the mistaken belief they could evade Pennsylvania's gradual emancipation law, passed in 1780, which freed slaves brought into the state after six months' residence. The Saint Dominguan slaves were both French-speaking Creoles, who were born on the island and tended to be lighter-complexioned, and dark-complexioned Yoruba and Ibo born in Africa.[49] The newcomers, strikingly distinguishable from Philadelphian blacks, drew negative attention because they frequently appeared in the vagrancy docket for allegations of theft and of conspiring against or disobeying their masters.[50] Their "vagrancy" suggested that their presence in Philadelphia was the result of coercion by, rather than loyalty to, their owners. The presence of these rebellious Saint Dominguan immigrants provoked anxiety that they would instigate Philadelphia-born free blacks to engage in violent and rebellious behaviour.[51]

In this context of disrupted race relations and panic about the spread of violence to Philadelphia, theatre managers proved reluctant to stage the thorny subject of antislavery. The New Theatre's managers, Thomas Wignall and Alexander Reinagle, were Federalists – the party that tended to be more sympathetic to antislavery – and had previously imported and staged British plays about slavery. They had, however, a history of watering down their potential antislavery appeal through alteration and adaptation, perhaps in part because the Dramatic Association that had aided the theatre's founding in 1789 was composed of wealthy elites that included slaveholders like Robert Morris and William Bingham.[52] As stage manager Charles Durang noted in his memoirs, the managers could not afford to lose the support of their wealthy sponsors.[53] Theatre managers' tendency to dilute antislavery became more pronounced as the Saint Dominguan white émigrés, their sensational tales of bloodshed, and their troublesome slaves unsettled Philadelphian society.

A notable example of the managers' attenuation of theatrical antislavery sentiment was Colman's *Inkle and Yarico*, so widely hailed as an antislavery piece in London (including Rowson's ode to its humanitarian sentiments in *Trip to Parnassus*) but stripped of its antislavery message in Philadelphia against the backdrop of the arrival of the earliest refugees from Saint-Domingue in 1792. Evidence intimates that the play was popularized more as spectacle than as antislavery. The advertisement in the *Pennsylvania Packet* for the Southwark production promised "a military scene in the denouement of the play, far surpassing any thing of the kind that has appeared on this stage."[54] Later adaptations also identified the play as fantastic extravaganza rather than anti-slavery fable. Lailson's Circus, for example, boasted that its enduringly popular iteration was "a Grand Historic and Military Pantomime – Ornamented with military Evolutions and Fights."[55] Even more revealing clues can be gleaned from the play's titles. The most striking change evident in the titles was to Yarico's ethnic identity. While Yarico was commonly played as African in London, playbills indicate that in Philadelphia she was performed consistently as an "Indian" and *never* as African. In the *Pennsylvania Journal*, for example, the New Theatre's production was billed *The Indian Heroine; or, Inkle and Yarico.*[56] Lailson's Circus's version was titled *The American Heroine*, meanwhile, and listed Yarico as an "Indian savage maiden."[57] The published copy of the New Theatre's *The Indian Heroine; or Inkle and Yarico* not only confirms the shift of ethnic identities, but also reveals the textual alterations tailored to its American audience. One glaring change was the insertion of dialogue that blamed the slave trade on the British and in so doing diminished contention over American chattel slavery. As Durang would later recall of the New Theatre's production, "This very excellent piece was written about 1787 by George Colman … but it was very much altered for [Philadelphia] representation."[58]

Another motivation for Rowson to opt for political caution by expressing her antislavery allegorically was to avoid provoking the antagonistic political partisanship that the French revolutionary years had fostered. Durang summed up the managerial intent in this regard: "Political questions, where two large parties are neatly balanced, should be warily touched on the stage."[59] When *Slaves in Algiers* premiered in 1794 the theatre managers were exceptionally wary; Democratic Republican plebeians crowding the pits and galleries were fired up with French revolutionary calls for liberty, equality, and fraternity.[60] As Philadelphia journalist William McKoy would recall, "during the French revolutionary enthusiasm that prevailed here from '93 to '97 … the new French songs like the *Marseilles Hymn* … were sung between the acts … by the audience in full chorus."[61] Allegory (and comedy) permitted Rowson to tackle the question of slavery warily enough to satisfy the Federalist managers' dictate of avoiding political controversy, while also playing to the Democratic Republican everyman with crowd-pleasing talk of the Rights of Man.

Rowson also had a fiscal incentive to be savvy about the need for political caution. She did, after all, have to make a living. And amidst the plethora of shocking reports from Saint-Domingue and the visceral impact of the refugees, several plays featuring blackface African slaves and direct antislavery sentiment had fared dismally on the Philadelphia stage. In 1792, for example, just as the first Saint-Domingue refugees arrived, the New American Company, run by the Kenna Family, brought Thomas Southerne's *Oroonoko; or the Royal Slave,* to their Northern Liberties Theater. Featuring a blackface slave hero and a scene of slave revolt, Southerne's play, one of the most popular on the eighteenth-century London stage, had been embraced by London antislavery advocates like Thomas Clarkson, who eulogized Southerne as one "who inveigh[ed] both against the commerce and the slavery of the Africans."[62] But the play's graphic scene of slave uprising seemingly made it an unpopular choice in Philadelphia. Concurrent with the play's opening in 1792, the papers were saturated both with the rebellion on Saint-Domingue and the heated debate in Congress stimulated by the abolition motion put forward by Warner Mifflin, a member of the Pennsylvania Abolition Society. Press coverage of the two events was interrelated. The press reported that the motion was denounced by a pro-slavery congressman as "mischievous, disturbing to the harmony of the Union, and likely to precipitate insurrections among the slaves."[63] *Oroonoko,* with its slave revolt and abolitionist implications, received only one performance – clearly not the Kennas' original plan, as the *Daily Advertiser* playbill had advertised and promised more.[64] *Oroonoko* was not seen again in Philadelphia until 1840.[65]

In Rowson's case, the financial mandate to cleave to political caution was especially acute. Throughout her career she was the primary breadwinner for her entire family: her impoverished father; her financially irresponsible, alcoholic husband; their adopted daughter; his illegitimate son; and her husband's much younger sister.[66] Indeed, her husband sometimes spent the profits from her published works even before she earned them; her publisher, Mathew Carey, recorded issuing numerous financial advances to William.[67] Moreover, Rowson had to carefully operate within the very strictures for her gender that she sought to challenge.[68] Rowson acknowledged the need for a patina of feminine propriety in the preface to *Slaves in Algiers* when she claimed to be "fully sensible of the many disadvantages under which I labour from a confined education."[69] Rowson could thus risk a playful allusion to "women's universal sway" – which could have elicited chuckles – with less fear of reprobation than a strident demand for women's legal and property rights might have earned. Similarly, by confining herself to the safety of allegory in preference to direct antislavery commentary, Rowson could allude to the problem of slavery in *Slaves in Algiers* but still court the commercial success that had eluded *Oroonoko.* Her efforts were rewarded, as *Slaves in Algiers* was a crowd pleaser that became part of the New Theatre's repertoire, earning repeat performances in Philadelphia and in Baltimore, Boston, and New York.[70]

The paucity of theatrical reviews makes it difficult to gauge, much less pin down, audience reactions to and interpretations of *Slaves in Algiers*. Did audiences understand the play as pro-feminist and antislavery? Or did the fact that Rowson embedded both sets of arguments in allegory permit reviewers to tiptoe around direct commentary on the thorny issues of women's political rights, slavery, and slave revolt? Given Philadelphian abolitionists' pervasive use of the African/Algerian analogy, it seems likely that at least some of her New Theatre audience would have made the metaphorical leap from "slavery's chains" and separation from "native land" in Algeria to African slavery in America. Yet none of the reviews explicitly tackled African slavery. Perhaps, like Rowson herself, critics were unwilling to publicly commit themselves to a direct commentary on such an inflammatory issue. Certainly several applauded the play's humanitarian sentiments without stating to which subject matter or sentiments, exactly, they were referring. As one reviewer vaguely put it, "the subject" – left undefined – "was highly interesting to the finest feelings of the human character."[71]

When William Cobbett countered this praise with derision, his two-pronged thrust hinged not on slavery but on critiquing Rowson's pro-feminist ideals and challenging her national loyalty. In his 1794 *Kick for a Bite*, "a review on the roman-drama-poë-tic [*sic*] works of Mrs. S. Rowson," he took particular exception to the couplet in *Slaves in Algiers*'s epilogue, "Women were born for universal sway / Men to adore, be silent, and obey." If sentiments like these were pursued, Cobbett raged, the dreadful result would be a House of Representatives constituted entirely of women! Cobbett also lambasted the play's potential to rouse the plebeians "in the theatre's gallery ... the senate, the pulpit, the jail, the parlour, the kitchen, and the cradle." For Cobbett, Rowson emblematized an abhorrent feminist threat to hierarchy and deference. He then accused Rowson of speciously adopting republicanism not out of conviction, but rather for commercial gain.[72] Despite being an occasional attendee of the Philadelphia theatre, he completed his attack by trying to discredit her morality through an exposé of the adulterous lack of morals in the theatre.[73]

That Cobbett chose to ignore the issue of slavery in his review does not negate the antislavery allegory of Rowson's play. In the context of the French revolutionary contest, the issue may have seemed less an immediate threat to the arch-Federalist British immigrant than the spread of republican ideas. A subsequent theatrical review by Cobbett lends support to this idea. The following year, he again unleashed his ire on Rowson. In a 1795 review, he heaped scorn on her 1795 play *The Female Patriot; or, Nature's Rights*, which was based on Philip Massinger's *The Bondsman* (1624), the story of a slave revolt with a female heroine, and on John Murdock's 1795 abolitionist play "*Triumphs of Love* by a citizen of Philadelphia," which featured the first scene of slave emancipation on the early American stage and had survived only one night's performance. Both, Cobbett scornfully concluded, deserved to "go silently to the grave." Cobbett attacked the merits of Rowson's and Murdock's writing and politics, but he again left the question of slavery untouched despite the fact that the subject matter of both plays was pertinent to slavery and slave revolt, and that Murdock's play contained an overt critique of African slavery in America. Cobbett instead preferred to attack what he viewed as the republican sentiments of the two plays, and to again cast aspersions on the sincerity of Rowson's embrace of American republicanism.[74]

Rowson's response to Cobbett is instructive, as it reveals yet again her acute need to present herself as a British-American who was loyal to America and desirous of transnational reconciliation. In the preface to her subsequent 1795 novel, *Trials of the Human Heart*, she returned fire. After describing Cobbett as a "loathsome reptile … of the literary world who has lately crawled over the volumes, which I have had the temerity to submit to the public eye," she explained her political views in terms of her personal background. To this end, she defended her British father, proclaimed her devotion to the United States, but also asserted her own uniquely dual loyalties. Mirroring – whether consciously or otherwise – Thomas Paine's argument in *Common Sense* of the brotherly consanguinity of England and America, Rowson characterized the revolutionary war as a family quarrel between brothers "who are equally dear to my heart."[75] She poignantly recounted her emotional distress at seeing her "affectionate brothers … fighting against each other," and finished by noting that it was unfair of Cobbett to expect her to "be insensible to the fate of the vanquished." That Rowson was forced to defend her political and literary aesthetic by reasserting the strength of her affection for America adds further insight into why, in the tumultuous 1790s in Philadelphia, she simultaneously embraced American revolutionary rhetoric yet muted her critique of slavery.

While much of the immediate debate over Rowson's *Slaves in Algiers* was focused not on slavery but rather on her provocative argument for women's political participation, one hint that theatre audiences would have understood the Algerian-African analogy was that many subsequent imaginative writers, unlike Rowson, used the Algerian crisis to *directly* denounce African slavery. Novels like Royal Tyler's *The Algerine Captive* (1797) and the anonymous *Humanity in Algiers; or the Story of Azem* (1801) also blatantly compared the injustice of African slavery with Algerine captivity. And later overtly antislavery stage plays written after the storm of the Saint-Domingue Revolution had subsided and the independent republic of Haiti had been founded in 1804, like James Ellison's *The American Captive* (1811), and David Everett's *Slaves in Barbary* (1810), similarly used the Algerian example to critique African slavery in America. These imaginative antislavery comparisons suggest that contemporaries would have understood the analogy in *Slaves in Algiers*, even though Rowson had not taken the fiscally and politically risky step of explicitly denouncing African slavery.

In her later Boston writings, however, freed from the crisis of the Saint-Domingue Revolution and the violent partisan tempers of 1790s Philadelphia, Rowson resumed an overt attack on slavery after her career took her out of the theatre and into the classroom. After moving to Boston to briefly join the new Federal Theatre Judith Sargent Murray had helped found, Rowson, who had acquired modest financial stability through her writing, retired from the stage altogether after 1797. She then founded an Academy for girls whose curriculum closely tallied with the new ideas for republican female education being promoted by men like Philadelphian Benjamin Rush.[76] Indeed, Rush's well-publicized views on slavery, education, and reform may perhaps have even shaped Rowson's own.[77] Benjamin Rush's educational reform accorded closely with that of Noah Webster, who argued that "the education of females, like that of males, should be adapted to the principles of the government, and correspond with the stage of society [in which they live]."[78] Rush, Webster, and others argued that teaching females the aristocratic manners of French, music, drawing, and dancing was inadequate; their education should prepare them for republican motherhood. It was on this premise that John Poor founded an Academy for girls in Philadelphia in the mid-1780s. Rush, meanwhile, in *Thoughts upon Female Education* (1787), prescribed a female education of English, geography, history, science, and "figures and bookkeeping" such that she could manage her husband's property, and educate her children in civic polity: the skills of republican motherhood.[79] Rowson adopted and contributed to this agenda of republican female education after founding "Mrs. Rowson's Academy" in 1797.

After assuming the mantle of a schoolmistress in Congregationalist Boston Rowson bluntly critiqued slavery and commented on the position of women, but did not use the more radical language of rights she had embraced in *Slaves in Algiers*. No doubt keen to attract fee-paying students to her newly founded school and perhaps equally zealous to distance herself from her thespian past in a city in which Puritan anti-theatrical sentiment abounded, Rowson seems to have adopted a self-consciously more demure approach to her political aesthetic.[80] Her efforts were successful; she had begun her academy with just one pupil, but by 1808 she had sixty students, among them the daughters of some of the most well-respected Boston families.[81] Her later writings were educational tracts, a dictionary "for children and young persons," and textbooks "for the use of schools and academies in the United States," such as her *Universal Geography* and *Exercise in History*, which was a history of, as Rowson touchingly put it in the preface, "my dear adopted Country, America."[82] All told, in her Boston sojourn she wrote six textbooks and a volume of poetry, as well as several more novels. In these writings, Rowson denounced slavery but now solely in terms of the Christian, humanitarian arguments she had first made in London. Similarly, she persisted in commenting on the need for women's education, but did not repeat her call for women's political participation.

In her educational writings, Rowson remained consistent about articulating these concerns in a self-consciously British-American voice that acknowledged her British past but insisted on her present-day American loyalty as she sought to consolidate her reputation and living as a schoolmistress. Thus, in *An Abridgement to Universal Geography*, written in 1805, Rowson constructed a cognitive map of the United States as part of Western cartography in which she defined the Occident in opposition to the Orient. To this end, her entries on Turkey, Asia, Africa, and elsewhere compared these countries and regions unfavourably relative to both Great Britain and the United States. In fact, Rowson was adamant that the United States and Great Britain, with their shared past, stood at the pinnacle of Western civilization, and were superior culturally, politically, and religiously to places like Scandinavia, the Netherlands, and the German-speaking states. Borrowing from Hume's notion of stadial history and citing Abbé Raynal, Rowson commented on topographical and geographical features of a given region, but also assessed the relative progress of each society based on key Enlightenment indices, such as the extent of religious toleration, taxonomies of human difference, the position of women in the society, and "morality and good government."[83]

In this vein, she considered Tartary in Asia less advanced because "they consider women as very inferior to men."[84] The Turks, for their part, were "lazy" and suffer from a "native indolence" due to the torrid climate, and were also morally inferior because "they are allowed by law 4 wives but the great men are indulged in as many as they can afford to maintain."[85] The United States was, by contrast, more enlightened because the urban seaports of Philadelphia, New York, and Boston boasted "female academies, colleges, and schools" and charitable societies in which women were active. Great Britain, meanwhile, was "the most [religiously] tolerant in its principles" and was the "seat of learning and the muses."[86] In contrast to her earlier *Mentoria, Invisible Rambler,* and *Slaves in Algiers,* Rowson was, however, conspicuously quiet on the question of women's legal and political rights in Great Britain and the United States – even while engaging in a steady commentary on women's social status and property rights elsewhere in the world.

Rowson also positioned herself explicitly as a British-American to communicate her continued critique of slavery in *Universal Geography.* She borrowed heavily from Jeremiah Morse's textbook, also titled *Universal Geography,* even repeating whole passages verbatim.[87] But her antislavery commentary was all her own. In an entry on Sierra Leone, Rowson attacked under the same breath "the English together with the Americans for growing rich by the purchase, sale and enslavement of their fellow creatures." "Let LIBERTY blush and CHRISTIANITY hide her dishonored head!," she fulminated at the entry's end.[88] She indicted both American and British slavery repeatedly throughout *Universal Geography* in sections on Africa, the West Indies, North America, and Great Britain. In fact, she sprinkled *Universal Geography* with word-for-word extracts from her London novel *The Invisible Rambler.* For example, she again wrote that a slave-owner or slave-trader, "whose mind is enlightened by reason and religion, one who bears the sacred name of Christian ... is a disgrace to humanity."[89] But these *Invisible Rambler* passages were now amended to address American as well as British slavery. Rowson reiterated in *Universal Geography* that "the negro on the burning sands of Africa was born as free as him who draws his first breath in Britain," but now the republished passage tellingly ended, "draws his first breath in Britain or in America."[90] Rowson's antislavery critique now encompassed American slavery, while still phrased in the antislavery language she had first employed in London.

Rowson's convictions were a product as much of 1780s London discourse as the early American republic, but her expression of them was dictated by the political strictures peculiar to each of her geopolitical locales, as well as by her sometimes vulnerable position as a British-American female author. In 1780s London, under sway of the nascent abolitionist movement and the discursive influence of its key proponents, Rowson, like William Wilberforce, emphasized humanitarian, Christian arguments against slavery and its contradiction with British constitutional "liberty." She also was already a passionate advocate of female education and economic self-reliance, although without offering a prescriptive curriculum. In the 1790s, Rowson used American republican precepts and the language of Wollstonecraft to claim expanded political and legal rights for women, thus melding the available political discourse of that revolutionary moment in Philadelphia to her long-cherished beliefs in uplifting women through education. Against the backdrop of the Saint-Domingue revolution and its reverberations in 1790s Philadelphia, however, she timidly confined her antislavery sentiments to allegory. By her tenure in Boston, in keeping with her newly respectable role there as a female educator, she retreated from her 1790s rights-based feminist arguments in favour of civic rights for women, emphasizing instead republican education and civic virtue learned through history and geography. Nor did she apply democratic precepts of rights to her renewed open protest of slavery, but rather rephrased her earlier religiously driven protest of slavery to critique both her countries: Great Britain and the United States. The chameleon-like Rowson adapted to the disparate milieus of London, Philadelphia, and Boston by availing herself of the topical political parlance of each urban cosmopole to her own prescriptive ends, but her public prescriptions were also delimited by the geopolitical realities of each time and place. This adaptivity, however, does not belie her enduring opposition to slavery and advocacy of women's education and improved position in society, ever-evolving products of her transatlantic career as a British-American female author in an age of revolution and reaction.

NOTES

1 Letter to student, c. 1812, in Elias Nason, *Memoir of Susanna Rowson with Elegant and Illustrative Extracts from Her Writings in Prose and Poetry* (Albany, NY, 1870), 152–3.

2 Marion Rust, *Prodigal Daughters: Susanna Rowson's Early American Women* (Chapel Hill, 2008), 3.

3 Benilde Montgomery, "White Captives, African Slaves: A Drama of Abolition," *Eighteenth-Century Studies* 27 (4) (Summer, 1994): 615–30. Montgomery persuasively argues for the play as embedded in Philadelphian abolitionist discourse. Scholars who reject an antislavery interpretation of *Slaves in Algiers* include Jennifer Margulis and Karen Poremski, eds, Susanna Haswell Rowson, *Slaves in Algiers; or, A Struggle for Freedom* (Acton, MA, 2000); and Elizabeth Maddock Dillon, "Slaves in Algiers: Race Republican Genealogies and the Global Stage," *American Literary History* 16 (3) (2004): 408–36.

4 Nason, *Memoir of Susann Rowson*, 14.

5 James Otis, *The Rights of the British Colonies Asserted and Proved* (Boston, 1764).

6 Thomas Paine, *African Slavery in America* (1775), in Micheline Ishay, ed., *Human Rights Reader: Major Political Writings, Essays, Speeches and Documents from the Bible to the Present* (New York, 1997), 130–3.

7 Nason, *Memoir of Susanna Rowson*, 31–2.

8 Linda Kelly, *Richard Brinsley Sheridan: A Life* (London, 1997), 268–70.

9 Letter from Hannah More to Lady Middleton, Cowslip Green, 10 September [1788], Lady Georgiana Chatterton, Memorials Personal and Historical ... from family papers, by Georgiana, Lady Chatteron (London, 1861), 169. Quoted in Clare Midgley, *Women against Slavery: The British Campaigns 1780–1870* (London and New York, 1992), 32.

10 Christopher Leslie Brown, *Moral Capital: Foundations of British Abolitionism* (Chapel Hill, 1996), 296 and 300.

11 Susanna Haswell, *Trip to Parnassus; or, the Judgment of Apollo on Dramatic Authors and Performers. A poem* (London, 1788), 5–6.

12 British Library, Add MS 42920, ff. 120–210b.

13 Elizabeth Inchbald, *Remarks to Inkle and Yarico*, published with George Colman's Inkle and Yarico, an opera in three acts: as performed at the Covent-Garden, Hay-Market, and New-York (New York, 1806).

14 Haswell, *Trip to Parnassus*, 6.

15 Susanna Rowson, *The Inquisitor; or, Invisible Rambler*, 3 vols. (London, 1788), "The East Indian," 87–8; "The Slave," 88–90.

16 Rowson, *Invisible Rambler*, Preface.

17 *Charlotte: A Tale of Truth. By Mrs. Rowson of the New Theatre, Philadelphia; author of Victoria, The Inquisitor, Fille de chamber, etc; in two volumes* (Philadelphia, 1792). For a discussion of the novel's success in early America see R.W.G. Vail, "Susanna Haswell Rowson, the Author of Charlotte Temple: A Bibliographical Study," in *Proceedings of the American Antiquarian Society* 42 (April–October 1932), 72–6; see 78–80 for a complete listing of the novel's editions.

18 David Brion Davis, *The Problem of Slavery in the Age of Revolution, 1770–1823* (Ithaca and London, 1975), 471–2.

19 Ibid., 87–8.

20 Patricia L. Parker, *Susanna Rowson* (Boston, 1986), 69.

21 Robert J. Allison, *The Crescent Obscured: The United States and the Muslim World 1776–1815* (New York and Oxford, 1995), 87.

22 Rosemarie Zagarri, *Revolutionary Backlash: Women and Politics in the Early American Republic* (Philadelphia, 2007), 44.

23 *Ladies Magazine and Repository for Entertaining Knowledge*, June 1792.

24 Rosemary Zagarri, "The Rights of Man and Woman in Post-Revolutionary America," *William and Mary Quarterly* 55 (2) (April 1998): 203–30, 208.

25 Bertha M. Stearns, "Early New York Magazines for Ladies," *New York History* 14 (January 1933): 36–7; Eugene P. Link, *Democratic Republican Societies 1790–1800* (New York, 1942), 58n.

26 "On Matrimonial Obedience," *Ladies Magazine and Repository for Entertaining Knowledge*, July 1792, 64–6.

27 Linda Kerber, *Women of the Republic: Intellect and Ideology in Revolutionary America* (Chapel Hill, 1980).

28 Zagarri, "The Rights of Man and Woman," 203–30; Mary Ann Glendon, *Rights Talk: The Impoverishment of Political Discourse* (New York and Toronto, 1991); Carole Pateman, *The Disorder of Women: Democracy, Feminism and Political Theory* (Cambridge, 1989); Joan B. Landes, *Women and the Public Sphere in the Age of the French Revolution* (Ithaca, 1988).

29 Ruth H. Bloch, "The Gendered Meanings of Virtue in Revolutionary America," *Signs: Journal of Women in Culture and Society* 13 (198): 37–58; Jan Lewis, "The Republican Wife: Virtue and Seduction in the Early Republic," *William and Mary Quarterly* 64 (1987): 689–721; Kerber, *Women of the Republic*, esp. chap. 7, "Why Should Girls Be Intellectual and Wise? Education and Intellect in the Early Republic."

30 Mary Wollstonecraft, *A Vindication of the Rights of Woman*, ed. Anne K. Mellor and Noelle Chao (New York, 2007), 26.

31 Karen Offen, "How (and Why) the Analogy of Marriage with Slavery Provided the Springboard for Women's Rights Demands in France 1640–1848," in Kathryn Kish Sklar and James Brewer Steward, eds, *Women's Rights and Transatlantic Antislavery in the Era of Emancipation* (New Haven and London, 2007), 59.

32 Moira Ferguson, "Mary Wollstonecraft and the Problematic of Slavery," in Eileen Janes Yeo, ed., *Mary Wollstonecraft and 200 Years of Feminisms* (London and New York, 1997), 89–104; see esp. 89–90.

33 Wollstonecraft, *Vindication*, 120 and 121–2.

34 Ibid., 177.

35 John Daniel Collins, "American Drama in Antislavery Agitation," unpublished dissertation (State University of Iowa, 1963), 40. Collins gives the arrival of Cowley's *Day in Turkey* as 1794 and its performance date as the retitled *Liberty Restored* as 22 March 1797. He in turn references – with no volume or page number – George Seilhamer, *History of the American Theater* (Philadelphia, 1889). For the Philadelphia debuts of Isaac Bickerstaffe's *The Sultan* on 19 May 1794 and Elizabeth Inchbald's *Such Things Are* on 5 July 1793, see "Day Book of the Philadelphia Stage," in Thomas Clark Pollock, *The Philadelphia Theatre in the Eighteenth Century* (Philadelphia, 1933).

36 See, for example, *Pennsylvania Gazette*, 1 July 1789, for an article discussing whether or not Congress should negotiate a peace with Algiers (item #75893) and *Pennsylvania Gazette*, 13 October 1790, for a "list of Americans in slavery at Algiers," which were published semi-regularly.

37 *General Advertiser*, 24 March 1794.

38 See, for example, *General Advertiser*, 24 March 1794; *Pennsylvania Gazette*, 1 July 1789 and 13 October 1790.

39 *Mathew Carey, Short Account of Algiers, Containing a description of the climate of that country, of the manners and customs of the inhabitants and of their several wars against Spain, France, England, Holland, Venice, and other powers of Europe … with a concise view of the origin of the rupture between ALGIERS and the UNITED STATES* (Philadelphia, 1794), 18.

40 American Convention for the Promoting the Abolition of Slavery and Improving the Condition of the African Race, "Address of a Convention of Delegates from the Abolition Society to the Citizens of the United States" (New York, 1794), 7.

41 Quoted in Montgomery, "White Captives, African Slaves," 616.

42 *Aurora*, 30 June 1794.

43 *Baltimore Daily Telegraph*, 26 November 1795.

44 Dillon, "Slaves in Algiers," 431 n. 20.

45 Margulis and Poremski, eds, *Slaves in Algiers*, 6. All quotes from the play are from this edition.

46 *National Gazette*, 10 July 1793, 290–1; Carolyn E. Fick, *The Making of Haiti: The Saint Domingue Revolution from Below* (Knoxville, 1990), 158–9.

47 *General Advertiser*, 10 October 1791; *Pennsylvania Gazette*, 9 September 1791. For an in-depth account of the Philadelphian press coverage of the Haitian Revolution, see James Alexander Dun, "Dangerous Intelligence: Slavery, Race, and St. Domingue in the Early American Republic," unpublished dissertation (Princeton University, 2004).

48 Gary B. Nash, *Forging Freedom: The Formation of Philadelphia's Black Community, 1720–1840* (London and Cambridge, Massachusetts: Harvard University Press, 1988), 175.

49 Julie Winch, *A Gentleman of Color: The Life of James Forten* (Oxford, 2002), 134–5.

50 Gary B. Nash, "Reverberations of Haiti in the American North: Black Saint Dominguans in Philadelphia," *Explorations in Early American Culture* (supplement to *Pennsylvania History*), no. 64 (1998): 56–7.

51 Ibid., 52 and 60–2.

52 Heather Nathans, *Early American Theater from the Revolution to Thomas Jefferson: Into the Hands of the People* (New York and Cambridge, 2003), 64.

53 Charles Durang, *History of the Philadelphia Stage. From the Year 1749 to the Year 1855. Partly Compiled from the papers of his father, the late John Durang; with notes by the editors* [of the Philadelphia *Sunday Dispatch*] (Philadelphia, 1854), vol.1, chap. 15, f. 25.

54 Playbill, *Pennsylvania Packet*, Monday, 17 May 1790.

55 *Gazette of the United States*, June 1797; *Pennsylvania Daily Advertiser*, June 1797.

56 *Pennsylvania Journal*, 27 June 1792.

57 *Gazette of the United States*, June 1797; *Pennsylvania Daily Advertiser*, June 1797.

58 Durang, *History of the Philadelphia Stage*, vol. 3, f. 261.

59 Ibid., vol. 1, f. 75.

60 William McKoy, *Long Syne Papers for Poulson's Daily Advertiser*, vol. 2, 34. Charles Augustus Poulson's *Scrapbook of Philadelphia History*, vol. 4, 16. William McKoy published essays under the signature of "Long Syne" in Poulson's *Daily Advertiser*, and his essays, along with other material published in Poulson's *Daily Advertiser*, were republished in 1828 as Poulson's *Scrapbook of Philadelphia History*.

61 McKoy, Long Syne Papers for 21 March 1828. The quotation is excerpted from an essay originally published by McKoy in the 1790s, exact date unknown but published after the onset of the Terror.

62 Thomas Clarkson, *History of the* [...] *Abolition of the African Slave Trade*, vol. 1, 48.

63 Quoted in Dwight L. Dumond, *Antislavery: The Crusade for Freedom in America* (Ann Arbor: University of Michigan Press, 1961), 76.

64 Daily Advertiser, 29 April 1792.

65 See the listing for June 1840 at the Walnut Theater in "Annual Chronological Records," in Arthur Herman Wilson, *A History of the Philadelphia Theatre 1835–1855* (New York, 1968).

66 William Rowson played only bit roles, worked primarily as a poorly paid prompter, and had a reputation for heavy drinking and womanizing.

Margulis and Poremski, eds, *Slaves in Algiers*, xii–xii; Vail, "Susanna Haswell Rowson," 51–3.

67 Mathew Carey, Account books, Manuscript Department, American Antiquarian Society. For this citation and also for a discussion of William Rowson's financial irresponsibility, see Cathy N. Davidson, *Revolution and the Word: The Rise of the Novel in America* (Oxford, 2004), 65.

68 Rust, *Prodigal Daughters*, 9.

69 Margulis and Poremski, eds, *Slaves in Algiers*, 6.

70 Pollock, *Philadelphia Theater*, lists 1794 performances for 30 June and 22 December; for its Baltimore production see Parker, *Susanna Rowson*, 69, and Vail, "Susanna Haswell Rowson," 54–5; for its production in Boston and New York see Margulis and Poremski, eds, *Slaves in Algiers*, 5.

71 Review of a Philadelphia performance of *Slaves in Algiers*, *Columbian Herald, or Southern Star*, 4 August 1794.

72 William Cobbett, *A Kick for a bite; or, review upon review; with a critical essay, on the works of Mrs. S. Rowson; in a letter to the editor, or editors, of the American Monthly Review. By Peter Porcupine, author of the* Bone to Gnaw, for the Democrats (Philadelphia, 1795), 21–9.

73 For Cobbett's attendance at the theatre, see Parker, *Susanna Rowson*, 75.

74 William Cobbett, *A Bone to Gnaw*, vol. 2 (Philadelphia, 1795).

75 Susanna Rowson, *Trials of the Human Heart* (Boston, 1797), xviii–xix.

76 Janet Wilson James, *Changing Ideas about Women in the United States, 1776–1825* (New York, 1981), 76.

77 Ibid.

78 Noah Webster, *A Collection of Essays and Fugitiv* [*sic*] *Writings* (Boston, 1790), 27–8. Quoted in James, *Changing Ideas about Women*, 80.

79 James, *Changing Ideas about Women*, 78–80.

80 For a good discussion of anti-theatricalism in Boston and Philadelphia, see Nathans, *Early American Theatre*.

81 Nason, *Memoir of Susanna Rowson*, 90 and 143.

82 See, for example: Susanna Rowson, *An Abridgement of Universal Geography: together with sketches of history / designed for the use of schools and academies in the United States* (Boston, 1805); Susanna Rowson, *A Spelling Dictionary: divided into short lessons, for the easier committing to memory by children and young persons, and calculated to assist youth in comprehending what they read: selected from Johnson's Dictionary* (Boston, 1807); Susanna Rowson, A *Present for Young Ladies: containing poems, dialogues, addresses etc. as recited by the pupils of Mrs. Rowson's Academy at the annual exhibitions* (Boston, 1811).

83 Rowson, *Universal Geography*, iv.

84 Ibid., 110.

85 Ibid., 102 and 104.
86 Ibid., 43–4 and 176–7.
87 Rust, *Prodigal Daughters*, 14.
88 Rowson, *Universal Geography*, 150–1.
89 Ibid., 271.
90 Ibid., 272.

chapter six

Philippe Jacques de Loutherbourg's Romantic Retreat: Magic, Mesmerism, and Prophecy, 1776–1802

IAIN McCALMAN

In April 1789 Philippe de Loutherbourg, elite London artist, scenographer, and spectacle expert, became an early victim of Britain's counter-revolution. Much to his surprise and distress, he suddenly found himself the butt of a campaign of hostile newspaper reports, graphic satires, printed lampoons, jokes, ribald verses, public speeches, and even a derisive pantomime: all represented him as a once famous artist who'd fallen prey to "religious frenzy."[1] He had thrown down his pencil and abandoned his elite painting career to become a dangerous enthusiast and, Hannah More said, a practitioner of "demoniacal mummeries" designed to bewitch and derange the senses of innocent English women.[2] Specifically, Loutherbourg and his wife Lucy had opened a free healing clinic for the poor at their house in Hammersmith Terrace, where they were – the *Morning Post* claimed – performing "many miraculous cures upon all human infirmities ... without the least assistance from medicine."[3]

Towards the end of the same year a printed pamphlet from a plebeian prophetess, Mary Pratt of Marylebone, continued the story. Philippe and his wife Lucy had received "the gift of healing" from Jehovah in the form of an influx of "divine Manuductions." By a simple laying on of hands they were able to cast out evil spirits, cure abscesses and cancers, make the maimed whole, the crippled walk, and the blind see.[4] However, the Loutherbourgs had become victims of their own success. Despite curing more than two thousand patients in the first six months, the crowds had continued to swell.[5] Whether because of failed expectations or the sheer frustration of numbers, a mob outside their clinic had then turned nasty, pelting the windows with stones and even trying to tear down the house.

As well as frightening the Loutherbourgs, the riot outraged influential neighbours like Sir Clifton Wintringham, physician to the king, who petitioned local magistrates to act against this nuisance. The presence of a two-thousand-strong mob swirling around his house was evidently both a violation of respectability and an uncomfortable sign of the pulling power of unorthodox medical messiahs.[6] Shocked by the violence of London's crowd, the wave of social disapproval, and the savagery of the media attacks, the Loutherbourgs pre-empted the legal demand to close the clinic and fled to the country for several months. On returning to London in mid-November, Philippe announced he had stopped "working miracles" and returned to his painting.[7]

Until this time Philippe de Loutherbourg had been a darling of the London press, not least because he was an assiduous supplier of paid "puffs" advertising his artistic achievements. Since migrating to London from Paris in 1771 at the age of thirty-two, his career had been a glittering success. Already a celebrated double academician in France, who had been trained in the Paris salons of Carle Van Loo, Jean George Wille, and Francesco Casanova, he had flourished equally in England's social and commercial art milieux. By the mid-1780s he'd been elected to the Council of the Royal Academy of Art; accumulated a wealthy circle of patrons and friends, including Joshua Reynolds and Thomas Gainsborough; and built a brisk market at exhibitions and print shops for picturesque landscapes, comic social pieces, marine paintings, and book illustrations.[8]

At the same time, he had become the country's most celebrated scenographer, having been employed initially by David Garrick at an unprecedented salary to transform the dull orthodoxies of Drury Lane theatrical spectacle along the spectacular lines of the Parisian scenographic maestro Servandoni. Later he had also worked as chief designer under Sheridan, before launching his own innovative commercial spectacle, the *Eidophusikon* or moving picture show in Leicester Square in 1781. A former Paris associate claimed that Loutherbourg had migrated to England "in the hope of finding an occupation and filling his pockets with guineas," and the booming cultural entrepreneurship of Late Hanoverian Britain evidently suited him perfectly.[9]

As this career suggests, Philippe de Loutherbourg was no radical, not openly anyway, though he was definitely something of a physical and philosophical libertine. However, his fundamental pragmatism came to the fore when he experienced the unexpected public savaging in 1789 for engaging in enthusiastic public healing. He strongly disavowed any further connection with divine healing, occult science, or learned magic. And, like the one-time radical preacher Samuel Coleridge, who notoriously boasted of having broken his "squeaking child's trumpet of sedition," Philippe leaked the news that his wife had smashed his crucibles.[10]

Hereafter, healing missions, millenarian predictions, and alchemical experiments vanished from Philippe's public interests. He continued to practise mystical healing only for like-minded personal friends like Richard and Maria Cosway,[11] and always in secret. For the first time in his life he also began to avoid dangerous company. Though privately fascinated by the apocalyptic prophecies of a former naval lieutenant, Richard Brothers, during the mid-1790s, Loutherbourg kept his excitement quiet, especially when Brothers was locked in a madhouse at the instigation of the government.

At the same time, Loutherbourg worked feverishly to re-establish his social respectability. He persuaded the Prince of Wales to commission a series of picturesque landscapes and simultaneously won praise from George III for producing two massive paintings of early British victories against the French. To underscore his political rectitude these were produced in collaboration with the anti-Jacobin caricaturist James Gillray.[12] Finally, he contracted to produce book illustrations for a massive new publication of the Bible and a new patriotic edition of David Hume's *History of England.* Well before his death in 1812, then, Loutherbourg's lapse into dangerous enthusiasm had been entirely forgiven or forgotten. His tomb in Chiswick cemetery carried an epitaph written by clergyman Dr C.L. Moody, proclaiming:

> Here Loutherbourg! Repose thy laurel'd Head!
> While Art is cherish'd thou canst ne'er be dead!
> Salvator, Poussin, Claude, thy skill combines
> And beauteous Nature lives on in thy designs.[13]

In this chapter, I want to explore why this pragmatic artist and entrepreneur managed to get into such trouble in the first place. Why did the seemingly innocuous action of opening up a pious Christian faith-healing clinic generate such a torrent of conservative abuse, especially in the year 1789, when respectable English opinion was said to favour the French Revolution and the anti-Jacobin counter-revolution had not yet begun to rumble into action?

Second, I will argue that de Loutherbourg's forced retreat into political quietism after 1790 produced paradoxical outcomes. On the one hand, his abandonment of popular enthusiasm in the face of conservative attack is another sharp example of the still contested claims of radical historians about the rapidity and pervasiveness of the British anti-Jacobin terror, yet it was also the goad that led him to a new and creative phase of explicitly Romantic painting, possibly for the first and only time in his long artistic life.

1

Philippe de Loutherbourg's ill-fated lunge into mystical healing had a long, if largely secret, lineage. He was born in Strasbourg in 1740, and his Swiss parents appear to have encouraged the boy's fascination with mystical alchemy. Strasbourg University, where he undertook studies in engineering and theology up to the age of fifteen, was an established hub of mystical pietism, international freemasonry, and learned magic. Here he plunged into study of "the deepest and most abstruse of mystics."[14] It was likely here, too, that he acquired the questing experimental drive so typical of European mystical alchemists since the Renaissance.[15] By the time he left Strasbourg to take up an artistic apprenticeship in Paris, he was already what the aesthete William Beckford was later to dub him, a "mystagogue" – someone whose passion for technical, artistic, and scientific experiment was underpinned by ardent mystical aspirations to discover and harness God's celestial powers.[16]

His artistic, chemical, and esoteric studies had continued in Paris, where he befriended Giovanni Battista Torré, whose family of Italian entrepreneurs and craftsmen specialized in alchemy, bookselling, optical and scientific instrument making, and pyrotechnics.[17] Here, too, he joined several mystical freemasonic lodges where, according to friends, he engaged in outré initiations and seances.

Being an apprentice to successive painting masters also freed de Loutherbourg from parental control and allowed him – he later admitted – to become "a freethinker and a hot-head," indulging in "many singularities and extravagances."[18] His "freethinking" appears to have been more sexual than philosophical. Friends, male and female, thought him an accomplished libertine. Handsome and energetic with glittering eyes, he was always on the lookout for women and wealth.[19] Early in 1764 he married a black-eyed "widow *galante*" called Barbe Burlat,[20] who quickly initiated him into the arts of blackmail and extortion. Hailed by Diderot in the 1760s Academy Salons as a young artistic genius equal to the French and Dutch landscape masters Vernet, Berghem, and Wouwermans, Philippe's social reputation had nevertheless slumped by the end of the decade. He was accused by Diderot and others of a growing laziness in his art and of practising libertine criminality in his personal life.[21] After narrowly escaping conviction for bilking one of Barbe's elderly admirers, he had gained a reputation for sexual scandal, unpaid debts, and violent duels. By 1771, with the prospect of a fresh law case instigated by Barbe for theft and domestic violence confronting him, de Loutherbourg fled across the Channel, leaving her and five children to fend for themselves.

Though urgent, his migration was not unplanned. Loutherbourg and his friend Torré had hatched a scheme to exploit the burgeoning opportunities for foreign spectacle experts in commercial London. Despite a lack of theatre experience, Loutherbourg managed to use his artistic reputation and expatriate Paris connections to persuade David Garrick that he could revitalize Drury Lane scenography along the spectacular naturalistic lines of the Paris Opera. As well as assimilating some of Torre's theories of spectacle and displaying his own undoubted painterly abilities, he offered Garrick and his wife, Eva, the extra inducement of rare alchemical recipes to revitalize their minds and bodies,[22] for "there are sometimes things wich [*sic*] at first seem to be extraordinary, but you will find them to be right."[23] Along with these he also claimed to have developed technical innovations in the use of lacquers and varnishes that he referred to mysteriously as "*mon secret.*"[24]

Working with Garrick and then Sheridan as chief scenographer enabled Loutherbourg to create rich cross-pollinations between the practices of easel art, theatre spectacle, and technological magic. He was drawn especially to the popular theatrical form of adult pantomime, where formulaic plots centred on a lover's chase by Harlequin to rescue Columbine from an evil wizard enabled him to develop a rapid, almost cinematic, succession of illusions, transformations, and tricks. The result was a unique style of spectacular "magical realism" that did indeed revolutionize British theatrical special effects. He fabricated fantastic alternative worlds that crackled with occult forces and displayed the protean moods of nature, where man and God were working in sympathy, yet were presented through innovative and realist mechanical and optical simulations.[25]

2

In London Loutherbourg and Torré also joined a lively demi-monde of visionary émigrés, bohemian artists, and occult-minded shopkeepers and artisans. Their circle during the 1770s included émigré preachers like

Jacob Duché, medical men like Bernard Chastanier, artists like Richard and Maria Cosway, booksellers like John Dennis, sculptors like John Flaxman, musicians like François Barthelemon, and engraver-artists like William Sharpe and William Blake. Along with others in this milieu, Loutherbourg became a disciple of the Swedish engineer and mystic Emmanuel Swedenborg, whose portrait he painted, and whom he joined as a founding member of the London Theosophical Society. Here, in inner London lodges, taverns, and workshops, Philippe intoxicated himself and his friends with discussions of learned magic, dream visions, and alchemical experiments.[26] Rumour had it that some Swedenborgians also engaged in sexual experiment, including a bizarre form of testicular meditation designed to enhance sexual performance.[27] It was probably here that Philippe met Lucy Paget, a widow from Staffordshire – said to be the most beautiful woman in England – whom he married in 1774, despite his existing Parisian wife and family.

Loutherbourg immersed himself at the same time in the secretive world of freemasonry, joining both the respectable Grand Orient Lodge of London and a series of more fugitive occultist lodges in the East End presided over by a Polish alchemist and cabbalist named Dr Falk, known as the "Baal Shem of Grosvenor Square." After painting Falk's portrait, Loutherbourg was introduced into a shadowy international group of Illuminé mystics located in the occult hubs of Avignon, Paris, Lyon, and Strasbourg, including an influential Avignon mystic, Count Grabianka, who made several covert visits to London to recruit supporters. Loutherbourg's reciprocal Masonic mission to Strasbourg in 1783 put him in touch with an even shadier figure, the Egyptian Rite alchemist-freemason Count Alessandro de Cagliostro and his beautiful wife, Seraphina.[28]

Throughout the 1770s and 1780s Loutherbourg could thus be said to have lived a double life. A wealthy socialite artist in public, he privately cultivated émigré mystics, conducted alchemical experiments, and amassed one of the most extensive occult libraries in Europe. Numbering hundreds of volumes of "learned magic" in English, French, and German, his library included practical recipes for manufacturing the philosopher's stone to transmute base metals into gold and to regenerate fallen man. He also collected key works of Christian theosophy by Boehme, Bourignon, Guyon, Lee, Lead, and Lacy and the major philosophical treatises of the Renaissance hermetic tradition – Paracelsian, Rosicrucian, and Cabbalistic.[29]

This hybrid mix of ideas echoes a tradition usually assumed to be extinct by the eighteenth century. Historian Frances A. Yates famously traced the emergence in late-Renaissance Europe of a ferment of hermetic, Cabbalistic, Christian mystical and alchemical learning that she called the "Rosicrucian Enlightenment." In the aftermath of the religious wars, scholar-seekers like John Dee, Thomas Vaughan, Robert Fludd, and Nicholas Andreae – each conspicuous in Loutherbourg's library – had evolved a new "way of thinking" that combined practical alchemy with an ardent search for mystical illumination. This outlook was, Yates argued, compatible with, and productive of, both the spiritual and experiment-based researches of later Newtonian scientists. "Rosicrucian alchemy," she suggests, "expresses both the scientific outlook, penetrating into new worlds of discovery, and ... an attitude of religious expectation, of penetrating into new worlds of religious experience."[30]

When Loutherbourg used optics, mechanics, sound equipment, and chemical pigments to enhance his spectacles, the higher purpose of such tools was intended to surpass the real-life effects of nature and to grasp the divine. He sought to capture the invisible forces that animated the cosmos and connected man to God in a skein of secret sympathies. If such all-pervasive powers could only be harnessed, he believed, anything was possible: images could become realities; man could converse with the angels; bodies could throw off disease and impotence; and base metals could grow to their natural perfect state as silver or gold. Such a moment would usher in the millennium predicted in the Scriptures and fulfil the ancient Gnostic dream of becoming one with God. These visions – simultaneously idealist and materialist – impelled him to experiment ceaselessly with occult recipes, electrical machines, magnets, crucibles, magic lanterns, chemicals, and paints.

Rather than withering in the face of rational certainties, as is often assumed, this mystical-magical variant of Enlightenment seems to have evolved new forms consonant with the needs of Britain's commercial-industrial age. Historian of science Alan Debus finds one such incarnation in the writings and practices of the late-Georgian doctor Ebenezer Sibly, whose two most popular works also featured in Loutherbourg's library. Rather than being a "throwback," Debus contends, Sibly was "an early English representative of the vitalistic scientific and medical philosophies of the Romantic period."[31]

Religious historian Clarke Garrett points similarly to the survival of the modes of "mystical enlightenment" espoused by Swedenborg and his followers, a groundswell of men and women in Europe who "incorporated the traditions of prophecy and biblical millenarianism into the more widely held concerns for social improvement through human effort."[32]

Many of the energetic and occult-minded technicians, artists, and showmen who, with Loutherbourg, helped to shape the emerging popular visual cultures of late eighteenth-century London also fitted this profile of technomantic experimentation. They included mechanicians John Merlin and Henri-Louis Jacquet-Droz, wonder doctors James Graham and Gustavo Katterfelto, and mesmerists John Bonnoit de Mainauduc and John Bell.

3

In the early 1770s, when Loutherbourg first arrived in London, such "enthusiastic" individuals and groups were seen as harmless eccentrics, part of a larger spectrum of quacks, empirics, and projectors who worked within the city's booming medical and cultural marketplaces. The outbreak of the American war and its associated domestic crises, however, initiated a profound shift in attitude towards this enthusiastic public sphere among elements of the British establishment. Traditions of religious and political tolerance began to take a serious beating.

The immediate trigger was less the war itself than a moral panic that linked British Dissenters with democrats, pro-American radicals, and foreign spies. During the week of 5–10 June 1780, Loutherbourg's fellow mason and friend Lord George Gordon reignited ancient Anglican fears about the dangers of radical enthusiasm. Half a century of Enlightenment complacency collapsed when Gordon's neo-Covenanter rhetoric provoked the worst riots of the eighteenth century. Gordon claimed to be protesting against the British government's softening of anti-Catholic legislation so as to boost military recruitment among Highland Scots and Irish, but his denunciations of British tyranny and enslavement took on a revolutionary note. As London burned, commentators ransacked their memories for suitable parallels to describe the "mad dog" and "lunatic apostle" Gordon. Horace Walpole tried Kett, Masaniello, Jack of Leyden, and Lord George Macbeth before settling, like most, on examples derived from the Puritans of the Civil War.[33] To men of reason like Edmund Gibbon it seemed that forty thousand ferocious Puritan sectaries of Cromwell had risen up from their graves.[34] Not only Tories, but also anti-court Whigs like Edmund Burke traced the beginnings of their belief in a strong monarchical state to this week of "terror" when the mob ruled the city and more property was damaged in London than Paris experienced throughout the French Revolution.

Gordon's continued populist agitations after being acquitted of treason in 1781 kept sectarianism alight for the next decade by linking it to democratic politics. He set up correspondences with American and European liberals and revolutionaries, campaigned against the government at every opportunity, and even congratulated the lunatic prophetess Margaret Nicholson for attempting to assassinate George III. Gordon's reputation as a revolutionary and mad prophet was further confirmed when the inquiry into the riots found connections between prominent Protestant Association rioters and American spies, radicals, and millenarians.[35] William Blake was by no means the only artisan who wrote passionately in favour of American liberty and who exulted in the "Glad day" when the Bastille of Newgate burned to the ground.

Many leading British MPs were also quick to represent the riots as a failed pro-American conspiracy to overthrow the British constitution and monarchy. It was in the year of the riots, 1780, not a decade later as is usually thought, that Edmund Burke developed his fear of the "swinish" multitude and Dissenter radicalism. He never forgot the trauma of having to protect his house with drawn sword against an anti-Catholic crowd threatening to raze it to the ground. Nearly a decade before the French Revolution, British counter-revolution thus gained its most brilliant spokesman. Burke's famous Bristol speech of 1780 can be seen as its first manifesto,[36] and it included a call for the suppression of Dissenter enthusiasm. Neither was he alone. A post–American War backlash produced judicial attacks on liberal newspapers, government surveillance of Gordon's pro-American associates, the stifling of popular debating clubs, an increase in centralist law-and-order legislation, and attempted restrictions on Dissenting chapels. In 1787 Gordon himself was sentenced to jail within a rebuilt Newgate for preaching to male and female convicts that transportation to Botany Bay was against the laws of God.[37]

This conservative recoil also triggered bourgeois anxieties about aristocratic moral decadence and provoked the emergence of evangelical purity campaigns to reform morals and manners. Once again Loutherbourg chose his friends unwisely. In the Spring of 1781 the wealthy young aesthete William Beckford was excited to hear that his occult-minded friend and fellow Mason, Loutherbourg, had launched a moving-picture show, *The Eidophusikon,* that achieved "a sort of magical effect in art." After private demonstrations of Loutherbourg's "wonders," "experiments," and "deceptions," Beckford commissioned the artist to produce the special effects for a private party at Fonthill Splendens, his Wiltshire country house. He wanted "the mystagogue," as he called him, to prepare a saturnalian spectacle that would ravish the senses of his guests and transport them into a voluptuous world where normal sexual constraints could be thrown off. Within this ecstatic atmosphere, Beckford planned to pursue a triangular sexual tryst with his cousin's wife, Louisa, and his real love, a thirteen-year-old child aristocrat called William "Kitty" Courtenay.

To his Oriental theatre props and panoply of illusionist technology, Philippe added perfumed braziers, machine-operated banquet tables, and the haunting voices of Europe's three most celebrated castrati. For the next few days and nights Fonthill's vaulted Egyptian Hall became, Beckford later said, "a necromantic region ... one of those fairy realms ... those temples deep below the earth set apart for tremendous mysteries." The house's existing Turkish Room was also transformed into a seraglio or love palace where Beckford and his ménage reclined "like voluptuous Orientals on silken beds in the glow of the transparent curtains." And, according to Louisa Beckford's steamy letters, the event generated black-magical rituals, "iniquities," "sacrifices," and "young victims panting on the altar." Beckford summed up the weekend as "the realization of a romance in all its fervours, in all its extravagance. The delirium in which our fervid young bosoms were cast by such a combination of seductive influences may be conceived but too easily."[38]

In the aftermath, the party inspired two works of artistic genius. William Beckford drafted his brilliant Gothic-Oriental novel *Vathek*,[39] and de Loutherbourg pioneered a new spectral picture show based on Milton's diabolical Pandemonium scene, a spectacle that prefigured the later "phantasmagoria."[40] However, rumours of the black magic orgies at Fonthill also began to swirl through London's *haute monde.* "Kitty" Courtenay's family grew to suspect Beckford of a capital crime and Louisa's husband packed her off to the Continent. Even Beckford's swift tactical marriage and European honeymoon failed to stem the tide of gossip, eventually forcing him and his new wife into long-term Continental exile. His most remorseless opponent proved to be "Kitty" Courtenay's uncle, Lord Loughborough, a reactionary chief justice, who was baying for radical blood.[41] At Burke's instigation he had also launched a covert investigation of Gordon and his radical associates, which was eventually to lead to their imprisonment in Newgate.[42] To what extent Loutherbourg himself became a suspect is unclear, but the scandal undoubtedly tainted him socially and cemented a connection between mystical enthusiasm and sexual transgression.

4

Whether or not for this reason, Loutherbourg kept his mystical-magic activities relatively quiet for several years after the Beckford scandal. In 1784, however, he was among the first to embrace the new medical-occult fad of mesmerism that had wafted to England's shores from France. Viennese doctor Anton Mesmer claimed to have identified an invisible fluid that swirled through all matter in the universe, ebbing and flowing like a lunar tide in harmony with the planets. Blockages to its circulation within the human body supposedly engendered physical and mental illness. Trained mesmerists could, however, Mesmer said, stroke away these impediments and so regenerate their patients.

In France, mesmerism infiltrated freemasonry and many other realms of intellectual life until the official disapproval of the Parisian Royal Commission of 1784 forced the movement underground to take root among socially frustrated intellectuals as an ideology of revolution. Medical historian Roy Porter has argued, however, that, by contrast, mesmerism failed to establish a serious beachhead in Britain. Here it merely joined a spectrum of health cures and nostrums competing in a pluralistic medical market place where borderlines between respectable and unorthodox medical practitioners were already blurred.[43] Yet this interpretation overlooks the fact that mesmerism, too, ran afoul of the darkening mood of the British establishment during the mid-1780s, coming to be seen as an immoral French addition to an already suspect underworld of magic and enthusiasm.

Philippe and Lucy Loutherbourg, and their artist friends Richard and Maria Cosway, saw Mesmer's ideas as a long-awaited scientific confirmation of the elusive regenerative "quintessence" sought by alchemical philosophers. By the mid-1780s, declining physical and sexual vitality was preying on the minds of the two aging couples. Along with short sight and deafness, Loutherbourg had developed a marked body tremble. Both couples initially joined the crush of fashionables at the Temple of Hygeia, a magnetic sex clinic established in the Adelphi by a flamboyant Scottish-American medic, Dr James Graham, who advertised courses of sexual regeneration on a magnetically charged celestial bed. By July 1782, however, Graham had been driven by debts and newspaper attacks to flee to Scotland.[44] The following year the Cosways purchased Graham's vacated premises at Schomburg House and began group experiments with the new panacea of mesmerism. Presided over by "the magnetic muse" Maria Cosway and assisted by the Loutherbourgs, they held soirées that magnified the building's already outré sexual reputation.

A year later both couples enrolled in the lecture courses of London's newest animal-magnetist, John de Mainauduc, an Irish-born doctor with Parisian training, who claimed to be extending ancient esoteric knowledge. He sought to enhance his legitimacy by presenting animal magnetism as a spiritual science whose healing actions, though medical in nature, were enabled by divine assistance.[45] Loutherbourg was so impressed that he led a subscription campaign to fund a new "Hygeian Society" where de Mainauduc could administer magnetic healing to the London poor.[46] Within a year, however, de Mainauduc in turn found himself superseded by an even more charismatic European exponent of invisible powers and regenerative health, Count Alessandro di Cagliostro.

Cagliostro's arrival in London in 1786, fresh from a twelve-month spell in the Bastille, after his implication in the notorious Diamond Necklace affair,[47] coincided with quickening enthusiastic currents. By the late 1780s the rising social and political ferment in France was triggering corresponding anxieties and expectations among religious millenarians all over Europe. Men and women preachers began fomenting prophecies that aligned contemporary signs and portents with the scriptural prophecies of Daniel and Revelations to predict the advent of the millennium. Excited members of a mystic international network sent their envoys scurrying back and forth between occult groups in Strasbourg, Lyon, Avignon, Paris, and London to evangelize among Masonic lodges and theosophical groups. Loutherbourg linked himself to a small band of London literary mystics who had rediscovered the apocalyptic writings of the seventeenth-century English prophetess Jane Lead. He was thus already in a state of millennial intoxication when Cagliostro fled from Paris to London in 1786 to escape the wrath of the Bourbons.

The Masonic magus soon enrolled Philippe, Lucy, Lord George Gordon and others in a mission to establish a lodge of his Egyptian freemasonry in Britain. But both the French and British governments had Cagliostro under close surveillance from the moment of his arrival. His reputation as a Bastille agitator and revolutionary preceded him, not without good reason judging by an illustration that he produced in France of his enemy Marquis de Launay, governor of the Bastille, that shows the scowling figure with his severed head impaled on a pike.[48] Even though Loutherbourg and Cagliostro summoned meetings of would-be Masonic sympathizers and painted a series of vivid occult portraits to inspire potential male and female initiates, their mission was blighted by hostile publicity. Much of it was commissioned scuttlebutt from a wily émigré Parisian pressman, Theveneau de Morande, who was in the pay of the Bourbons, and the pungent graphic satire of James Gillray, who was receiving a British government pension. With his fraudulent past laid bare in the local press, Cagliostro had no choice but to flee to the mansion of wealthy supporters in Switzerland. Undaunted, Philippe and Lucy followed him, anxious to continue a newly arranged business partnership to exchange the artist's paintings for Cagliostro's regenerative recipes and treatments. After six months, however, the partnership foundered in a welter of sexual jealousies, quarrels, and litigations; and the Loutherbourgs were eventually forced to borrow money to return to London.

They returned poorer in pocket, but stronger in soul. Though disillusioned with their guru's behaviour, they continued to believe in his theosophical knowledge. In their absence, however, the political climate had become sharply less congenial to experiments in public enthusiasm. Loutherbourg's earlier association with Gordon and Cagliostro had already tainted his artistic reputation, and the timing of a new prophetic career could hardly have been worse. Just as Loutherbourg launched his healing clinic in 1789–90, Gordon was given a fresh sentence in Newgate for uttering subversive prophecies and Cagliostro was incarcerated in the Roman prison of Sant'Angelo for leading a supposed anti-papal conspiracy. Both men would ultimately die in prison.

Under the circumstances, it was hardly surprising that Philippe's millenarian-style healing mission should have brought such a harsh response from the political and social establishment. Given his notorious connections with Graham, de Mainauduc, and Cagliostro, Loutherbourg was an obvious target for those with a mounting animus against political enthusiasm and quackery. To many critics, he was simply the latest in a string of would-be medical messiahs. Enlightened radicals saw him as an advocate of exploded and superstitious epistemologies. Conservatives like Hannah More hammered "the demoniacal mummeries" of predatory mesmerists whose inflammatory methods sought to put susceptible women under sexual thrall.[49] She and others also began to catch the early currents of what would eventually become a full-blown anti-Masonic conspiracy theory fomented by émigré Catholic priests and featuring European-wide cells of republicans and freethinkers headed by the likes of Cagliostro and de Loutherbourg.

More orthodox and respectable medical individuals and institutions had a similar stake: like Sir Joshua Reynolds in the sphere of art, they were seeking to use the discourse of quackery to outlaw the lucrative practices of unsuitably credentialed practitioners and to instantiate their own. Even would-be medical reformers found the mesmeric and magical associations of men like Cagliostro a useful catch-all symbol for attacking generalized medical greed and ignorance.[50] In Britain, the former radical Robert Southey would soon write in his *Letters from England* of 1802, that mystics, magicians, and prophets were considered to be far more dangerous than irreligious *philosophes* like Voltaire and Holbach.[51]

5

At one level the collapse of Loutherbourg's ardent vision of achieving a spiritual and physical regeneration of the London poor seems a poignant example of how a conservative reaction triggered by the American Revolution and amplified by its French counterpart worked to snuff out the traditions of heterodox social prophecy and mysticism that found their greatest expression in figures like William Blake and Thomas Spence.

Yet Loutherbourg's expedient return to respectability in the 1790s was not exactly what it seemed. There are strong indications that his enthusiastic passions were driven underground rather than extinguished. Confronted by a tidal wave of loyalist abuse in 1789, the pragmatic artist seems to have displaced his apocalyptic social dreams back into his art, where they contributed to a last great surge of creativity. Ever conscious of his income and social position, Philippe chose to unleash a coded and aesthetic revolution within the genre of the biblical sublime, an interior illumination that gave expression to what we now call Romantic art.

During the 1790s the mystagogue's drive to grasp the occult forces linking God and man found new expression in a brilliant series of visionary paintings within the genre of the "the apocalyptic sublime." Deploying scriptural themes like "The Deluge" enabled Philippe to portend the coming millennium without arousing the political furore of his prophetic clinic of 1789. In 1801, too, while embarked on an ostensibly patriotic tour of the English county of Derbyshire, he also painted his one widely acknowledged masterpiece, *Coalbrookdale by Night.* Praised by modern critics as a pioneering expression of "the industrial sublime," it reveals the continuing power of visionary magic in Philippe's life. Examined closely, *Coalbrookdale* depicts a coded apocalyptic alchemical transmutation within a new technological age. The scarlet incandescence that lights up the sky from the giant Derbyshire steel forges represents a powerful new collaboration between man and God, a harnessing of the occult forces of nature for new social ends.[52]

As with so many other Romantics, large and small, Philippe de Loutherbourg's strategic political retreat had been replaced with transcendent revolutionary art.

NOTES

1 William Whitley, *Artists and Their Friends in England, 1700–1799*, 2 vols. (New York, 1928), 2: 354.

2 Austin Dobson, *At Prior Park and Other Papers* (London, 1912), vol. 2: 118.

3 *Morning Post*, 24 August 1789.

4 Mary Pratt, *A List of a Few Cures Performed by Mr. and Mrs. de Loutherbourg of Hammersmith Terrace, without medicine* (London, 1789), 5–7. On the mystical milieu of Pratt, see Thomas Faulkner, *The History and Antiquities of the Parish of Hammersmith* (London, 1839), 347–8; Desiree Hirst, *Hidden Riches: Traditional Symbolism, from the Renaissance to Blake* (London, 1964), 255–61, 276–81.

5 Letter 316 in R. Vernon Smith, ed., Horace Walpole, *Letters Addressed to the Countess of Ossary*, 2 vols. (London, 1848), 2: 342–5.

6 Faulkner, *Hammersmith*, 349–50.

7 Whitley, *Artists*, 2: 355.

8 See Iain McCalman, "Magic Spectacle, and the Art of de Loutherbourg's Eidophusikon," in Ann Bermingham, ed., *Sensation and Sensibility: Viewing Gainsborough's Cottage Door* (New Haven and London, 2005), 183–4.

9 Dobson, *Prior Park*, 100; Amy L. Walsh, "Pierre-Jean Mariette," in *Grove Art Online* (2004), http://www.oxfordartonline.com/public/;jsessionid=33918725D5AD55E68FC9CA12E992C532. See also Pont de Nemours to Margrave Caroline-Louise de Bade in 1773, Geneviève Levallet-Haug, "Philippe Jacques Loutherbourg," *Archives Alsaciennes* 16 (1948): 85–6.

10 Whitley, *Artists*, 2: 35; see also *The Times*, 4 August and 10, 16, and 24 September 1789.

11 See, for example, *Catalogue of the very curious, extensive and valuable library of Richard Cosway* … (London, 1821).

12 The two artists travelled for a month in 1793 through the crucifix-lined battlefields of Belgium, braving storms, illness, and whizzing bullets, to sketch the authentic details of the siege of Valenciennes. The following year, they visited Portsmouth, sketched ships, armaments, and riggings, and interviewed naval officers before completing a similar giant painting of

Admiral Howe's victory against the French on 1 June 1794. "Anecdotes of Mr Loutherbourg," *European Magazine* 1 (1782): 181.

13 Levallet-Haug, "Loutherbourg," 93–4.

14 *Morning Post*, n.d., Whitley Papers, 2, fol. 929; Levallet-Haug, "Loutherbourg," 77 n. 37.

15 Frances A. Yates, *The Rosicrucian Enlightenment* (London and New York, 1986), 226.

16 Guy Chapman, *Beckford* (London, 1937), 99ff.

17 Gavin Carver, "Torré, Giovanni Battista (*fl.* 1753–1776)," *Oxford Dictionary of National Biography* (Oxford, 2004), at http://www.oxforddnb.com/index/64/101064359/; Michael R. Lynn, "Sparks for Sale: The Culture and Commerce of Fireworks in Early Modern France," *Eighteenth-Century Life* 30 (2) (2006): 85–6; Alan St Hill Brock, *A History of Fireworks* (London, Sydney, 1949), 52, 58.

18 Joseph Farington, *Farington Diary*, ed. James Grieg, 8 vols. (London, 1922–8), 2: 222.

19 Johann Christian von Mannlich, *Mémoires du Chevalier Christian de Mannlich*, ed. Joseph Delage (Paris, 1949), 151–2.

20 André Girodie, "Notes biographiques sur les peintres Loutherbourg," *Archives Alsaciennes d'histoire de l'art* 14 (1935): 249–50.

21 Denis Diderot, *Salons*, ed. Jean Adhémar and Jean Seznec (Oxford, 1975), 3: 274, 4: 100–1; Levallet-Haug, "Loutherbourg," 78–9.

22 Torré had offered to teach Garrick the secrets of the Cabala and how to harvest "the celestial manna"; Frank A. Hedgecock, *David Garrick and His French Friends* (London, 1912), 394.

23 P.J. de Loutherbourg to Eva Maria Garrick, n.d. [1772], in Garrick Correspondence, 2, Folger Shakespeare Library, Washington, MS W.b. 486–9, fol. 44. The book he recommended was from the Cosmopolite, the name given to a seventeenth-century Scottish alchemist and adventurer called Seton. However, it might equally have come from the Polish alchemist Michael Sendivogius, with whom Seton was often confounded.

24 See especially, "Anecdotes of Mr Loutherbourg," *European Magazine*, 1 (1782), p. 181.

25 Iain McCalman, "Loutherbourg's Simulations. Reenactment and Realism in Late Georgian Britain," *Historical Reenactment*, eds Iain McCalman and Paul Pickering (Houndmills, Basingstoke, 2010), 200–17.

26 See, Whitley, *Artists*, 2: 113–19; Whitley Papers, 1, fols. 364, 368–73; Joscelyn Godwin, *The Theosophical Enlightenment* (Albany, NY, 1994), 100–33.

27 Marsha Keith Schuchard, *Why Mrs Blake Cried: William Blake and the Sexual Basis of Spiritual Vision* (London, 2006), 143–79.

28 Iain McCalman, *The Last Alchemist: Count Cagliostro, Master of Magic in the Age of Reason* (New York, 2003), 161–73.

29 Peter Coxe, *A Catalogue of all valuable drawings, sketches, sea-views and studies of that celebrated artist, Philip James de Loutherbourg* (London, 1812), passim. and Richard Cosway, *A Catalogue of the Pictures of Richard Cosway, Esq. R.A. Being the choice part of the very numerous collection made by him during the last fifty years ... to be sold by auction, by Mr. Stanely, at Mr. Cosway's late residence, No. 20, Stratford Place ... the 17th of May, 1821, and two following days, etc.* (London, 1821), passim.

30 Yates, *Rosicrucian*, 226; for an appreciative, if partially critical, assessment of Yate's theory, see Brian P. Copenhaver, "Natural Magic, Hermeticism, and Occultism in Early Modern Science," in D.C. Lindberg and R.S. Westman, eds, *Reappraisals of the Scientific Revolution* (Cambridge, 1990), 261–301.

31 Allen G. Debus, "Scientific Truth and Occult Tradition: The Medical World of Ebenezer Sibly (1751–1799)," *Medical History* 26 (1982): 278.

32 Clarke Garrett, "Swedenborg and the Mystical Enlightenment of Late Eighteenth-Century England," *Journal of the History of Ideas* 45 (January–March 1984): 67–81.

33 W.S. Lewis et al., *The Yale Edition of Horace Walpole's Correspondence*, 48 vols. (New Haven, 1937–83), 25: 11; 33: 197, 354.

34 Edward Gibbon to Dorothea Gibbon, 8 June 1780, in J.E. Norton, *The Letters of Edward Gibbon*, 48 vols. (London, 1956), 2: 245.

35 John Paul de Castro, *The Gordon Riots* (London, 1926), 216–37.

36 Iain McCalman, "Mad Lord George and Madame La Motte: Riot and Sexuality in the Genesis of Burke's Reflections on the Revolution in France," *Journal of British Studies* 35 (July 1996): 343–67.

37 Ibid., 359.

38 Iain McCalman, "The Virtual Infernal: Philippe de Loutherbourg, William Beckford and the Spectacle of the Sublime," *Romanticism on the Net, (Special issue) Romantic Spectacle* 46 (May 2007). Available from http://ravonjournal.org/.

39 See Roger Lonsdale, "Introduction," in *Vathek*, ed. Roger Lonsdale (Oxford, 1970), xii–xiv.

40 Richard D. Altick, *The Shows of London* (Cambridge, MA, 1978), 123, 217; Ralph G. Allen, "The Eidophusikon," *Theatre Design and Technology* 7 (1966): 14–15; Terry Castle, *The Female Thermometer: Eighteenth Century Culture and the Invention of the Uncanny* (New York, 1995), 120–67; Barbara Stafford, *Artful Science: Enlightenment Entertainment and the Eclipse of Visual Education* (Cambridge, MA, 1994), 14–16, 76–8, 288; C.W. Ceram, *Archaeology of the*

Cinema, trans. Richard Winston (New York, 1965), passim; Olive Cook, *Movement in Two Dimensions* (London, 1963), 19–22.

41 Timothy Mowl, *William Beckford: Composing for Mozart* (London, 1998), 123, 130, 211–12.

42 McCalman, "Mad Lord George," 355.

43 Roy Porter, "Under the Influence: Mesmerism in England," *History Today* 35 (September 1985): 22–9.

44 Roy Porter, *Health for Sale: Quackery in England 1660–1850* (Manchester and New York, 1989), 157; Roy Porter, "Sex and the Singular Man: The Seminal Ideas of James Graham," in H.T. Mason, ed., *Studies on Voltaire and the Eighteenth Century* (Oxford, 1984), 3–22; Roy Porter, "The Sexual Politics of James Graham," *British Journal for Eighteenth Century Studies* 5 (1982): 199–206.

45 Patricia Fara, "An Attractive Therapy: Animal Magnetism in Eighteenth-Century England," *History of Science* 32 (1995): 127–77.

46 *The Lectures of J.B. de Mainauduc, MD, Member of the Royal College of the Surgeons, Part the First* (London, 1798); G.E. Bentley, "Mainaduc [*sic*], Magic and Madness: George Cumberland and the Blake Connection," *Notes and Queries* 236 (September 1991): 296.

47 See McCalman, *Last Alchemist,* 105–42; Sara Maza, "The Diamond Necklace Affair Revisited," in Lynn Hunt, ed., *Eroticism and the Body Politic* (Baltimore, 1991), 65–70; Robert Darnton, *The Literary Underground of the Old Regime* (Cambridge, MA, 1982), 30–5.

48 Thanks to Professor John Barrell of the University of York for locating and presenting me with a copy of this rare and arresting work by Cagliostro, the only verified art work by him currently known to historians.

49 Dobson, *Prior Park,* 118.

50 Patricia Fara, "An Attractive Therapy: Animal Magnetism in Eighteenth Century England," *History of Science* 32 (1995): 148–56.

51 Robert Southey, *Letters from England by Don Manuel Alvarez Espriella,* 3 vols. (London, 1807), 293–348, 376–90, 406–42.

52 John Gage, "Loutherbourg: Mystagogue of the Sublime," *History Today* 13 (1963): 332–9, and his *Color in Turner: Poetry and Truth* (New York, 1969): 136–9, 181–2, 229; Stephen Daniels, "Loutherbourg's Chemical Theatre: *Coalbrookdale by Night,*" in John Barrell, ed., *Painting and the Politics of Culture: New Essays on British Art 1700–1850* (Oxford, 1992): 195–230.

chapter seven

From Radical Enthusiasm to Liberal Melancholia: Hugh Henry Brackenridge and *Modern Chivalry, Part 1 and 2*

ANTHONY GALLUZZO

Modern Chivalry, Hugh Henry Brackenridge's long and meandering life's work, is a picaresque epic with an obvious debt to Cervantes and the eighteenth-century quixotism that marked the early English novel. Brackenridge also borrows from his more immediate British predecessors, such as Fielding and Sterne, whose respective literary productions were enormously popular in the United States during the early republican period. An approximately eight-hundred-page narrative, published in instalments over a period of nearly twenty-five years stretching from 1792 to 1815, the novel recounts the self-consciously quixotic adventures of Captain John Farrago, an ineffectually elitist exponent of republican virtue, who sets off at the start of the novel with his illiterate Irish servant or "bogtrotter," Teague O'Regan, in order to "ride about the world a little" and "see how things were going on here and there, and to observe human nature."[1]

The fictional account that subsequently unfolds revolves around the misadventures of Teague, an illiterate Irish Catholic caricature, who is repeatedly drafted into a series of pursuits for which he is decidedly ill suited. He is, for example, at one point selected by a mob as a candidate for the Pennsylvania state legislature. Teague is also solicited for the ministry, courted by the American Philosophical Society, and pursued as a potential husband by a wealthy widow. While the Irishman is interested in all these alternative career paths, he is in each instance stymied by Farrago's outrageous misrepresentations of what such positions entail, so that, in the case of the Philosophical Society, the Captain persuades Teague that the amateur naturalists might want to "take the skin off you and pass you for an overgrown otter," frightening the bogtrotter away from the comic honour conferred upon him.[2]

Teague is similarly pursued by a conman, who after learning that Farrago's servant is a "speaker of the Irish language," hopes to use him in a scheme in which the Irishman would pose as a Kickapoo Indian chief at a treaty meeting with government officials so as to fraudulently procure treaty funds.[3] These officials are here understood as unable to distinguish an Indian from an Irishman. The Captain once again thwarts this plan, convincing Teague that these would-be Indians mean to scalp him for his red hair. Brackenridge here presents his reader with Teague's own speech for the first time. Up until this point in the novel, both narrator and Captain describe the servant's apparently incomprehensible brogue, while here Brackenridge transcribes his version of Irish speech: "Dear master, vid you trow me into ridicule, and the blessed shalvation of my life, and all dat I have in de vorld, to be trown like a dog to de savages, and have my flesh torn of my head to give to dese vild bastes"[4]

The bog-trotter's Irish dialect – featured prominently from this point onwards throughout the remainder of *Modern Chivalry, Part 1* alongside Brackenridge's transliterations of slave speech and early American versions of legalese, among other early American argots – has led critics to classify this largely unrecognized and undervalued novel as the first significant piece of dialect fiction in American literature.[5]

Modern Chivalry Part 1 demands that we readers widen the category of "voice" and "dialect" to encompass the late eighteenth-century political languages that command a central place in this narrative, including classical republicanism, nascent liberal individualism, and revolutionary Jacobinism itself. The novel resembles Benjamin Franklin's *Autobiography* as much as it does the aforementioned picaresque tradition, insofar as the text reflects, in fantastic form, both Brackenridge's picaresque public life and, by extension, the late eighteenth-century Anglo-American political arena in which the author-politician made his name.

This intertwining of text and context – whereby the biographical, political, and literary registers are collapsed into each other – represents a challenge for conventional literary criticism, and is potentially one reason why the novel itself is still largely neglected, even as Brackenridge the man is alternately praised or excoriated in several recent historical monographs on the Whiskey Rebellion and its place in the post-revolutionary period.[6] While this intersection of the political and literary spheres seemingly conforms to Jürgen Habermas's model of a public sphere and the specifically early American version of this paradigm, as envisioned by Michael Warner in narrowly national and appropriately republican terms, *Modern Chivalry* presents a significant conceptual problem for this influential theory.[7]

Rather than dramatize in fictional guise a series of disagreements that are resolved through a process of rational deliberation, Brackenridge's novel gives us a myriad of comic conflicts that are on the surface irresolvable, if only because the various parties speak different and incommensurate languages. The narrative in this way recalls Bakhtin's original theory,[8] according to which, the idiolects that distinguish the novel as a genre linguistically embody the different social groups from which they spring, lending credence to Ed White's recent interpretation of the novel as an idiosyncratic early American guide to " the dynamics of class struggle."[9]

I have in this introductory discussion confined my remarks to *Modern Chivalry, Part 1,* since, when Brackenridge resumed his literary work in 1804 with *Modern Chivalry, Part 2,* he abandoned the wildly imaginative and dialogical mode that marked the first part of his work. The later work displays an excess of political disquisition and polemic, which largely eclipses the narrative, and a remarkable set of reflections on the French revolution in particular and 1790s radicalism in general. Just as Brackenridge's ambivalent radical commitments assumed literary form as dialogical experimentation in the 1790s, so the repetitive and monologic rhetorical texture of the second part can and should be ascribed to what I will call radical melancholia. *Modern Chivalry, Part 2*'s often disparaged style and narrative strategy is not a product of either Brackenridge's declining powers or an older and more established figure's programmatic conservatism. Instead, the sequel's decidedly monologic character, as the narrator displaces the characters and their dialects while his narrative increasingly focuses in a self-reflexive, referential, and repetitive fashion on the revolutionary politics of the early 1790s, is a distinctively republican iteration of this melancholia.

Brackenridge's life and work testify to the incomplete character of the American Revolution and a post-revolutionary settlement that pitted the advocates of a more expansively democratic vision of the new polity against the sectional elites who sought, in the words of Terry Bouton, to "tame democracy."[10] Brackenridge identified with one or another of these factions at different times over his long public life, although always in an equivocating way. He was, over the course of his nearly forty year public career, an antifederalist Pennsylvania state representative and supporter of the Constitution; a pro-Jacobin antagonist to the Federalists under Alexander Hamilton – who pegged him as the ringleader of the Whiskey

Rebellion – and a moderate republican judge who wrote in favour of the common law and an independent judiciary against their radical democratic critics. These shifting identifications are, in turn, on view in *Modern Chivalry*, written in fits and starts over this same period, in which we can see Brackenridge, and the range of political positions with which he identified, in his narrator, the comically genteel Captain Farrago, and perhaps most of all, the ignorant but successful immigrant Teague O'Regan. It is because of these revealing equivocations that we can't easily assimilate Brackenridge to the radical democratic figures whom several recent neo-progressive historians of the early republic represent as a viable opposition to both Federalists and Jeffersonian Republicans alike; nor is he simply the opportunist turncoat other scholars of the Jeffersonian split between moderate and radical factions describe.[11]

Brackenridge's picaresque wandering from one ideological position to the next mirrored his movement from his humble immigrant beginnings to Princeton; from Philadelphia to the Pennsylvania backcountry; from minister to journalist; from journalist to lawyer and state representative, ambivalent rural insurgent, and finally State Supreme Court Justice. Brackenridge's unusually comprehensive life trajectory was accompanied by his long, serialized, composition of *Modern Chivalry*, which he finally revised and divided into parts 1 and 2 in 1815, when he published the text in its entirety. The two parts are in turn divided into volumes, all of which were published individually and split into books and chapters; the more widely read, topically relevant, and plot driven part 1 comprises four such volumes, written between 1792 and 1797, after which Brackenridge broke off his narrative, only to take it up again in 1804 with a more expository and monologic part 2.

Rather than writing to the moment, recording, or reflecting upon his public life, Brackenridge incorporates into his text the social idiolects and ideological vocabularies he used or overheard in the course of his travels in and through the 1790s American social body. Brackenridge's situation changed drastically with his appointment to the Pennsylvania state judiciary as a republican judge immediately in advance of Thomas Jefferson's 1800 presidential victor, when he brought his narrative to close, at least for several years. He resumed his novel, or what he would later deem its sequel, in1804. I therefore proceed here from biographical context to sprawling text, in order to trace the shift from the 1790s volume – the aesthetically ambitious product of that period's radicalism – to the post-1800 sequel – a work that is very much weighed down by the memory of the lost revolutionary moment.

1

Brackenridge's early life had several formative and contradictory aspects. Importantly, a rough-hewn upbringing on the rural margins of eastern Pennsylvania was followed by an elite education.[12] The precocious boy academically distinguished himself from an early age and was consequently taken up by the local clergy in what amounted to a scholarship; he attended the College of New Jersey (later Princeton), where he met Philip Freneau, with whom he authored "The Rising Glory of America."[13] This early combination of humble beginnings and proto-meritocratic social mobility offers one explanation for Brackenridge's ambiguous ideological commitments. He would, initially, use the classically republican political vocabulary he acquired at Princeton to at least initially argue for the disinterested rule of the same post-revolutionary elites among whom he was never accepted as an equal. But then he changed course in the 1790s and endorsed the radical republicanism of the French revolution and supported small backcountry farmers in their struggle with Treasury secretary Alexander Hamilton's economic policies – especially the hated excise tax on whiskey. Even more complicated, in both cases despite the rhetoric of disinterested virtue that recurs throughout much of Brackenridge's written output, there is a strong vein of opportunism that undergirds his contradictory political commitments.

In 1781, Brackenridge relocated to backcountry Pennsylvania in search of the national and international distinction unavailable to him in Philadelphia. As he subsequently confessed: "I saw no chance of being anything in that city, there were such great men before me, [so] I pushed my way to these woods where I thought I might emerge one day."[14] Brackenridge here acknowledges the opportunistic motives behind his flight to "the woods," as he sought to distinguish himself as a lawyer, politician, and man of letters. Indeed, Brackenridge's career embodied what Bryan Waterman calls the "competition among different kinds of intellectuals over newly significant knowledge industries, the management of public information, and representations of public opinion" in the post-revolutionary period.[15]

He accordingly took up the law and opened his own practice, while founding the *Pittsburgh Gazette.* He accompanied this venture in successfully running for state legislature. Brackenridge held office from 1786 to 1788, under the Articles of Confederation and concurrent with the Constitutional Convention. He was, in fact, the only western representative to support the new Federal plan, much to the chagrin of both fellow representatives, such as tailor-turned-politician William Findley, who appears in *Modern Chivalry* as Traddle the Weaver, and Brackenridge's own constituents.

By 1792, Brackenridge had rejected the Federalists and Hamilton's policies. He attacked the excise tax on whiskey, against which he successfully defended several local distillers in court. Historian Andrew Shankman links Brackenridge with erstwhile adversary Findley and Albert Gallatin as backcountry landowners and hence members of a rising local elite whose exclusion from the Federalist establishment provides the rationale for the common cause they made with the small distillers and marginal men behind the Whiskey Rebellion.[16] As Shankman puts it, "Resident speculators were different from absentee speculators such as George Washington. The president owned sixty-three thousand acres in western Pennsylvania. For a variety of reasons, including self-interest, he wanted a peaceful, even docile population. Rough behavior and political extremism had to be repressed. Bur Gallatin, Brackenridge, and rising strivers such as Findley had to live with their fellow westerners."[17]

The apparent unity of the democratic-republican movement in the 1790s concealed or at least forestalled emergent class conflict. Local elites, landowners, and masters united with plebeian journeyman, landless tenants, and journeymen under the open-ended rubric of democratic republicanism in order to oppose a semi-aristocratic Federalist order. This coalition fractured after Jefferson's victory in 1800, when these socio-economic divisions and their ideological correlates re-emerged in the form of factional splits within the republican party.[18]

Brackenridge's position in the 1790s was radical in these historically specific and often equivocating terms. He identified with the immigrant smallholders behind the anti-excise movement, despite Brackenridge's middling success as a lawyer and journalist. At the same time, he aspired to a position of informal cultural and political leadership as he linked the anti-excise activity in the west to the transnational republican movement. This transnational movement was, for him, apotheosized in the French Revolution in its Jacobin phase, the excesses of which he explains in a 1793 Fourth of July oration:

> The light kindled [in the United States] ... has been reflected to Britain, and a reform in the representation of the Commons is reflected. The light kindled here has been reflected to France, and a new order of things has arisen. Shall we blame the intemperature of the exertions? Was there ever enthusiasm without intemperance? and was there ever a great effect

> without enthusiasm? Thy principles, O! Liberty, are not violent or cruel: but, in the operation of thy efforts against tyranny, is it not always possible to keep within the limit of the vengeance necessary to defence.[19]

Brackenridge's Federalist opponents subsequently used the western émigrés nternationalist democratic sympathies to link him (incorrectly) to the most radical and violent elements of the Whiskey rebellion[20] But Brackenridge's republicanism is a peculiar and hybrid ideology. While Brackenridge remained within the orbit of classical republicanism with its keystone notion of disinterested virtue, he also emphasized interest. This perspective is best conveyed by an early set of observations on "Interest" that appeared in his *United States Magazine*, where we are told:

1. Interest speaks all languages, and acts all parts, even that of *disinterestedness* itself.
2. Interest, which blinds some people, enlightens others.
3. The name of virtue is as serviceable to interest as vice.
4. Interest puts in motion the virtues and vices.
5. Good-nature, that boaster of its great sensibility, is often stifled by its smallest interest.
6. We condemn vice, and extol virtue, merely through interest.
7. It is only in little interests that we usually venture to disbelieve appearances.[21]

Brackenridge's remarkable set of principles regarding interest emphatically demonstrates his scepticism, if not outright disdain, for at least a certain version of republican disinterestedness, whether in classical or radical republican form. The complex, and even dialectical, interplay between an awareness of real interests, such as those embodied in the grievances of his fellow westerners, and commitment to the radical republican ideal of "the people" animates Brackenridge's 1790s novel.

Modern Chivalry's greatest innovation is in its representation of real interests against the ideological fiction of a disinterested public sphere, even while the text holds out the *possibility of a utopian resolution* through its play of voices. It is within and among this play of these voices – the literary-aesthetic analogue of those various interests surveyed above – that we find both critique and aesthetic prefiguration. The juxtaposition of a classically republican narrator who aims to normalize American English and the polyglot dialects that parodically upend this goal functions like a meta-textual echo of Teague's victory over Farrago, even as the text depicts again and again the latter's manipulations of the former, against his disinterested pose. *Modern Chivalry* is *a* powerful representation of the idealized early American public sphere and of its failure to meet the ostensibly disinterested and formally egalitarian claims that underwrote it at the moment of its inception.

In this light, the importance of the novel's unnamed narrator comes into focus. The narrator opens the novel with a rhetorical question about "the best means to fix the English language" and surveys past solutions to this dilemma, such as "Dictionaries" or "Institutes," citing Swift even as he suggests Samuel Johnson. Against these Tory and emphatically British figures' linguistic solutions, our narrator offers another exemplary view: "It has always appeared to me, that if some great master of stile should arise, and without regarding sentiment, or subject, give an example of good language in his composition, which might serve as a model to future speakers and writers, it would do more to fix the orthography, choice of words, idiom of phrase, and structure of sentence, than all the Dictionaries and Institutes that have ever been made."[22] He immediately follows this declaration with the further – and in light of what follows – remarkable claim that *Modern Chivalry* is just such a model of "perfect style," although, like music, Brackenridge's novel should be evaluated according to the perfection of the sound or "melody," as opposed to "the matter of the work."[23]

But rather than providing a linguistic standard for American English, *Modern Chivalry* is very much a compendium of pastiched dialects, beginning with the heavily accented Irish patois of Teague O'Regan. But we should nonetheless take seriously the narrator's stated aim to establish a standard for language and literature in the new nation. I would first question in this regard the often-made identification between the narrator and Farrago – introduced as a "whimsical man, owing perhaps to his greater knowledge of books than of the world" – from which any satirical reading of the narrative voice must proceed.[24] There is indeed some rhetorical overlap between Farrago's classical republican posturing and the kind of narrative expostulation best exemplified in a reflection on Traddle the Weaver's apparently improper campaign for the legislature, in which the narrator echoes the protagonist's elitist arguments against commoners running for legislative office:

> DEMOCRACY is beyond all question the freest government: because under this, every man is protected by the laws, and equally has a voice in making them. But I do not say an equal voice; because some have stronger lungs

> than others, and can express more forcibly their opinions of public affairs. Others, though they do not speak very loud, yet have a faculty of saying more in a short time; and even in the case of others, who speak little or none at all, yet what they do say containing good sense, comes with greater weight; so that all things considered, every citizen, has not, in this sense of the word, an equal voice. But the right being equal, what great harm if is unequally exercised? Is it necessary that every man should be a statesman? No more than every man should be a poet or painter.[25]

On the one hand, this commentary echoes Farrago's own arguments against those labourers like Traddle, who, in assuming public office, usurp a role outside their proper sphere of knowledge. But what constitutes this properly political knowledge, apparently inaccessible to working men? The narrator provides one, provisional answer when he asserts that "a man's circumstances ought to be such as afford him leisure for study and reflection."[26] Politics, and the knowledge they require, is necessarily off-limits to the labourer exactly because he labours. This remark underlines the extent to which classical republicanism was, in the words of one intellectual historian, an "ideology of leisure. Its conception of citizenship privileges people who need not work, who have the time to devote themselves to civic life."[27] Republican leisure necessitates, even as it effaces, servitude in all its guises. The politically aware plebeian class who first asserted their political right during the era of the Atlantic revolutions threatened the propertied exponents of elite republicanism, who were forced, in a republic founded in some measure on popular consent, to devise baroquely complex institutional constraints on the "rage for paper money, for an abolition of debts, for an equal division of property, or for any other improper or wicked project."[28]

Brackenridge's novel anatomizes the anxieties of this customary leisure class in its depiction of master Farrago engaged in the most egregiously deceptive ploys as he strives to thwart his servant's aspirations in an increasingly democratic landscape dominated by common men. Farrago notably uses the language of disinterested republican virtue in order to accomplish these self-interested ends.

The narrator, by contrast, recognizes the ideologically distorted character of these rhetorical ploys and differentiates himself from his would-be protagonist, when he subsequently declares, "There is often wealth without taste or talent"; a sentiment he goes on to elaborate in contrasting the pride and arrogance" of those "who consider themselves first in a government" – Farrago and his peers – who deserve to be "checked by the populace" and "Genius and virtue," which are "independent of rank and fortune."[29]

These depictions represent the novel's most emphatic critique of early American political reality and the failure of the public sphere – institutionalized in the form of an officially representative republican state – to meet its own formally republican standards. In reading the narrator's impossibly normative linguistic goals alongside Brackenridge's political commitments, we can find a negative articulation of Brackenridge's sense that the unitary public sphere was absent from American political life. Moreover, it provides important clues for his initial and politically unpopular support of the federal union and his subsequent radical democratic enthusiasm for the French Revolution. Finally, it helps explain the writer's conflicted role as a mediator in the Whiskey Rebellion and his long novel's seemingly divided ideological investments.

The Janus-faced quality of this ideal is best captured in the narrator's rhetoric. His professed intention of standardizing American English is internally ridiculous in light of the book's collage of demotic dialects, a point brought home when we consider how it is his quest for a linguistic (social and political) norm, rather than Farrago's travels, that ultimately drives this nearly endless novel's discursive perambulations. In this way, Brackenridge's epic accords with wider currents in the radical Atlantic world during this period, as we can see in Kevin Gilmartin's suggestive account of English Jacobin culture, according to which, "political unity entered radical discourse as both stifling contemporary fact and utopian possibility: it was the narrow common ground of consensus, and the broad popular agreement that would generate reform and prevail in its aftermath."[30]

But unlike such radical exemplars as Leigh Hunt or the later William Cobbett, for whom universal suffrage and the end of patronage represented a utopian end-point after which radical opposition could dissolve itself, Brackenridge's utopia was written in the wake of a formally republican polity and its deficiencies. Brackenridge's critique is clear. His narrator's own utopian solution – the all-encompassing linguistic standard that would preserve the multiple dialects it must supersede – would, in keeping with the radical republic ideal type of "the people," necessitate a turn towards imagination. But this imagined people thereby would elide the emergent class differences that Brackenridge captures in the heteroglossic form of his novel.

I have until this point confined my remarks to *Modern Chivalry, Part 1.* Brackenridge resumed his literary work in 1804. The wildly imaginative

1790s text came to a halt with a fourth and final volume published in 1797, capping the several tumultuous years following the abortive Whiskey Rebellion, when Brackenridge was captured and held as an insurgent leader by Federal troops, personally interrogated by Alexander Hamilton, and ultimately exonerated. Brackenridge subsequently felt the need to write an account of the insurrection and his role in it, depicting himself as caught between the two extremes of backcountry radicalism and Federalist power. This moderation was belied by the ambivalent novelist-politician's written output, as we have seen.

When Brackenridge took up Teague and Farrago again in 1804, Brackenridge's situation had changed along with the political scene in the United States and the wider Atlantic world. Thomas Jefferson and the democratic-republicans had captured the presidency in 1800. Brackenridge had received his own appointment to the Pennsylvania state judiciary from republican governor Thomas McKean in 1799. This consolidation of republican power in the United States, accompanied by the failure of the French Revolution abroad marked the normalization of what had been an oppositional political movement in the 1790s. The early nineteenth century also witnessed the re-emergence of those inchoate class divisions subsumed by the united democratic-republican opposition to the Federalist administration during the 1790s. This transition was especially acute in Pennsylvania, where the state's relatively advanced degree of economic development brought with it recognizably capitalist social relations and a growing population of permanent wage labourers. It is against this background that historian Shankman views the split between moderate and radical Jeffersonians, or "Quids," and democrats in 1804 and 1805; their major point of disagreement was the independence of what, in the eyes of the radicals, was an "aristocratic" judiciary, even as the "Quid" moderates framed this assault on judicial independence – including unelected judicial appointments for life and a overreliance on English common law – as a threat to private property rights.[31]

Brackenridge's text evinces these tensions early on, so that while the second volume of the second part, published in 1805, ostensibly describes Farrago's sojourn into a backcountry settlement, this narrative falters as the narrator declares:

> I AM A DEMOCRAT. You, a man of some reading, one will say, and yet a democrat! Who put to death Socrates? The democracy of Athens. What of that? Democracy has slain her thousands; but aristocracy her ten thousands. There is this difference: with democracy, there is occasional tyranny, and

> horrid injustice. With aristocracy, there is ever-during oppression. I grant democracy is like the atmosphere, serene, or deforming the face of heaven with a hurricane and a whirlwind. Still, it is salubrious, and necessary to respiration.[32]

Whereas Brackenridge's narrator would often echo, or parody, Farrago in the 1790s text, there is in the sequel a noted discrepancy between the Captain's typically elitist republican pontificating and this full-throated defence of "democracy": a term typically used by the Federalists and their counter-revolutionary allies, united under the ministry of William Pitt in Great Britain, throughout the Atlantic world, to denote levelling schemes, Jacobinism, and the threat of the swinish multitude.

Before the election of 1800 and the subsequent open split between moderate and radical republican factions, both Thomas Jefferson and republican notables such as Alexander Dallas, Albert Gallatin, and Joseph Gales distanced themselves from the radical democratic constituency who predominated in northeastern coastal cities and their respective backcountries. The emergent Republican leadership recast these democratic activists as the party's Jacobin left flank, in effect appropriating the language of their "aristocratic" Federalist opponents to do so. This division largely reflected emergent class divisions, as the Jeffersonian coalition's incipient bourgeois elites and their planter allies became increasingly aware of the new threat from below. This ideological shift was muted before the election of 1800, since the radical vote was still needed to elect Jefferson. But Jefferson's inaugural address, in which he declared that "we are all republicans, we are all federalists," set the tone for things to come. As Seth Cotlar avers, "While the election of 1800 made 'democracy' a word that respectable leaders could use without apology, this transformation came at a cost. Together, leading Jeffersonians and Federalists sheared the word 'democracy' of its previously revolutionary and leveling implications."[33]

While our narrator's extended paean to democracy could be read as participating in this redefinition, Brackenridge's meditations are notable insofar as they depart from the emergent anti-Jacobin demonology. Take, for example, the case of the republican operative John Wood. Wood's attacks on New York's ruling Clinton faction included a diatribe against "United Irishmen" and "deists," all of whom he included in the ranks of the "Columbian Illuminati."[34] Unlike the radical political rhetoric of the 1790s, which pivoted on the division between aristocrats and the "people," the avatars of the new Jeffersonian dispensation equated a truncated "people" with the new middle class, who, after vanquishing the aristocratic threat, must draw the cordon sanitaire around a plebeian mob and its emphatically foreign ringleaders.

Brackenridge nonetheless maintains that democracy is always, and fundamentally, preferable to the "ever-during" tyranny of the old regime, despite democracy's own occasional "horrid injustices." Brackenridge treats these "horrid injustices" as almost natural, and presumably necessary, natural phenomena, such as the "whirlwind" or "hurricane," which help create a "salubrious" environment and the respiration it provides us. Brackenridge repeatedly analogizes democratic excess to various natural phenomena, undermining his own criticisms in tacitly asserting the foundational necessity of a revolutionary intemperance that must give way to a more moderate social order, in a teleological fashion.

To make matters more complex, many former radicals embraced the virtues of forgetting. Joseph Gales, for example, offers a revealing anecdote, in the course of his journalistic electioneering in the *Raleigh Register*, regarding Themistocles, who refused to learn the art of memory since he preferred the "art of forgetfulness," which helps us "look forward to prospects that may brighten."[35] *Modern Chivalry, Part 2* is as distinct from this successfully mournful species of forgetting – whereby the withdrawal and subsequent erasure of ideological investment is the precondition for those "prospects" – as it is from the theatrically anti-Jacobin gestures sketched above.

Modern Chivalry, Part 2 features a narrator who often and without irony speaks directly to his putative readers, much to the detriment of the narrative and those other, sub-literary, voices that distinguish the 1790s original. The text is for these reasons often read as an inferior, more monologic, and less formally inventive production, as Brackenridge himself writes in the conclusion to the second part's first volume: "My fancy is as cold as it was once warm. My inclination leads me to metaphysics, chiefly. But that subject is exhausted; or, so many have written well, that it is discouraging to come after them."[36] The metaphysics that preoccupy Brackenridge in his post-1800 volume are chiefly legalistic, as he by and large drops the character of the comic narrator who functioned as ironic foil and counterpoint to Farrago, in favour of long, topical, and technical disquisitions on the law against certain Pennsylvania republicans' assault on the judiciary.

This argument more often than not displaces the narrative, which, such as it is, recounts Farrago's return to his village with Teague. And Teague ultimately decides, at the Captain's urging, to compose an autobiographical account of his stint in revolutionary France and for this reason appears only now and then. The Captain, by contrast, decides to move west again in order to found a new community, accompanied by a group of comic figures new and old, by whom he is elected governor. This plot serves as an often transparent vehicle for Brackenridge's expostulations on governance, democracy, and the law. Ed White has more recently read the later work's tonal shift and seemingly single-minded focus on the law as reflective of a more profound change in Brackenridge's thinking. Brackenridge abandons the utopian possibility of a unified democratic-republican polity and public sphere, and with it the dialogic play of voices that distinguishes the 1790s text, only to adopt a personally significant if formally neutral legal proceduralism in which competing interests adjudicate their imperfect claims; this procedural pluralism is in turn implicitly underwritten by a disillusioned Brackenridge's acceptance of a fractured and necessarily imperfect body politic. I would contend that alongside this chastened and more recognizably liberal vision, we can also discern a melancholic impulse that separates Brackenridge from both the angry moderates and the forgetful former radicals in whose silence we can hear an attempt to erase the revolutionary past.

Brackenridge's reflections on the French Revolution in the first volume (1804) of the second part are exemplary instances of what we might call Brackenridge's melancholia. Walter Benjamin first adapted this long-standing model of psychological dis-ease for the purposes of political critique in a short critique of "left wing melancholy," which he identifies with a radical posture that "takes as much pride in the traces of former spiritual goods as the bourgeois do in their material goods."[37]

But melancholia has other affective, rhetorical, and ideological valences – melancholy as, for instance, first formulated by Freud and even as it is otherwise theorized by Benjamin himself. The long analyses of and apologias for the judiciary that occupy so much space in the later volumes do not signal a new procedural perspective on Brackenridge's part, or, insofar as they do, this new perspective is enabled by the disavowed lost object, which is, in this case, the radical democratic vision of the 1790s. This vision haunts the author's legal meditations, which are often and incongruously punctuated by extended discussions of the democratic-republicans or the status of justice and the rule of law under the French directory.

Freud, in his 1917 essay on the topic, defines melancholia as a pathological mode of desire in which the loss of the beloved object supersedes any urge to recover and proceed in the present, as in mourning; indeed, this loss is made the paradoxical object of attachment. Perhaps more significant for our purposes, "Melancholia is in some way related to the unconscious loss of a love object, in contradistinction to mourning, in which there is nothing unconscious about the loss."[38] Writing ten years later in his *The Origin of German Tragic Drama*, Benjamin redefines melancholia in rhetorical and epistemological terms, as he writes: " Melancholy betrays the world for the sake of knowledge. But in its tenacious self-absorption it embraces dead objects in order to redeem them."[39] Does liberal melancholia reify the revolution or its failure?

Thomas Pfau, in his recent monograph on *Romantic Moods*, synthesizes these models in his account of melancholia as both affective state and rhetorical construct, a model he then applies in an obliquely political manner to certain literary productions of the post–Waterloo Settlement, such as Keats's early lyric poetry. According to Pfau, "Whenever it is put to referential or expressive use, melancholy tends toward endless reflexivity, and it adopts a fundamentally metalingual stance … As such it "knows" (albeit in a strictly negative sense) that it cannot possess being and, burdened with that knowledge, must continually disavow being in articulate form."[40]

Melancholia, at least in this rhetorical iteration, represents the inverse of the picaresque, typified by Brackenridge's 1790s work, which is of course also characterized by allusive self-reflexivity. The latter's heteroglossic play, distinguished by the demotic incorporation of dialects, high and low, ethnic and vocational, gives way to the sequel's monomaniacal and repetitive inventory of allusion, anecdote, and reference. On the one hand, Brackenridge's radical picaresque literally enshrines many conflicting voices and in doing so, implicitly offers a resolution that, in its irreducibility to any one of the voices depicted, encompasses all of them, at least in negative form. On the other hand, the later, melancholic text baroquely accumulates allusion and rehearses a set of settled dilemmas as Brackenridge repeatedly tries and repeatedly fails to incorporate an earlier, more radical democratic republicanism – significantly depicted as the necessary but superseded foundation for the new liberal polity – into the body of the law.

For Brackenridge, the loss that haunts *Modern Chivalry, Part 2* is exactly the unfulfilled promise of a radical republican political vision to which the writer was once attached in a notably ambivalent, if unconscious, fashion commensurate with the melancholic's own equivocating attachment to the lost object.[41] While Brackenridge's ambivalent radical-democratic attachments animate the earlier volumes' dialogical literary form, this form is largely supplanted by the endless monologue and repetition that mark the later volumes as melancholic in form and substance.

The narrative is not simply minimized or displaced in the late volumes, so much as it is stillborn. Brackenridge hardly establishes a given comic episode before lapsing into his editorializing mode, in which he explains the issues confronting his characters by quickly dispensing with them in a way that is nearly antithetical to his earlier narrator's sometimes ironic and oftentimes bombastically parodic tone. This tendency is on view in one emblematic set-piece, which in turn leads the reader back to the 1790s and indeed the Jacobin republic.

This episode, which occurs in the first volume (1804) of the second part revolves around Farrago's return to his village, where he finds that one Peter Porcupine – William Cobbett's pseudonymous identity as editor of *Peter Porcupine's Gazette*, his virulently anti-Jacobin newspaper during the 1790s – has established a scurrilous press, after which he proceeds to malign the town's various inhabitants, only to encounter resistance in the form of one "Pole-cat," who sets up a skunk in a house adjoining Porcupine's headquarters in order to prove a point about libel and the problem of a degenerate public sphere.

The Captain ultimately drives Porcupine out by contriving to set up his own newspaper with Teague at its head, an idea Farrago abandons after defeating Cobbett. The narrator then jettisons this comic sketch, in order ostensibly to reflect upon freedom of publication and the revolutionary paper war of the 1790s. Brackenridge's evocation of this 1790s political debate and the polemical form in which he presents it to his readers, is notable for its anachronistic stridency, especially since it also functions as prologue to what might have appeared to contemporary readers as an even more dated set of observations on Robespierre, Marat, and the Jacobin phenomenon of 1792–4.

Brackenridge introduces the subject of Marat towards the end of the first volume of *Modern Chivalry, Part II*, when Farrago, after a series of semi-comic encounters with several, broadly drawn backcountry republicans, inexplicably adverts to the French Revolution: "I have no doubt, but that Marat meant well to the people; but he had not an understanding above the public, and judgment to correct the errors of occasional opinion. He was of the multitude himself, and did not overtop them *by having higher ground from whence to observe. He had not been a sage before he became a journalist.*"[42]

The Captain's critique of Marat proceeds from his unpleasant encounters with the various bumpkin republicans just mentioned. But, the elitist tenor of the Captain's disquisition on the French revolutionary government of 1792–3 reveals certain half-submerged sympathies – towards Marat's good intentions – and regrets regarding dashed radical republican hopes that are decidedly out of character.

Brackenridge's reflections on Jacobinism are likewise marked by the similarly conflicted and elegiac tone which distinguishes this late work as a whole. These "Observations" on Jacobinism explain and at least partially excuse the motives of the Jacobin leaders, while emphasizing the frequently disastrous consequences of good intentions, when he declares: "I never had a doubt with the Captain, but that the bulk of the jacobins [*sic*] in France meant well; even Marat and Robespierre considered themselves as denouncing, and trucidating only the enemies of the republic. What a delightful trait of virtue discovers itself in the behaviour of Peregrine, the brother of Robespierre, and proves that he thought his brother innocent. '*I am innocent; and my brother is as innocent as I am.*' Doubtless they were both innocent. Innocent of what? Why; of meaning ill."[43]

He first locates the root of both Marat's and Robespierre's error in their purely numerical conception of democracy, only to qualify this equivocating criticism in declaring that a "journalist of spirit is a desideratum in a revolution. But when the new island, or continent is thrown up from the bottom of the ocean; and the subterranean gass [*sic*] dissipated, why seek for a convulsion? But rather leave nature to renew herself with forests, and rivers, and perennial springs. But that activity which was useful in the first effort, is unwilling to be checked in the further employment; and under the idea of a *progressing reform*, turns upon the establishment which it has produced, and intending good, does harm."[44]

Brackenridge naturalizes revolution and revolutionary violence in analogizing historically novel acts of rupture and reorganization undertaken by a collective subject to volcanic eruption; in doing so, he effaces both the historical novelty of the late eighteenth-century democratic revolutions and the constituent power of the new revolutionary actors. Brackenridge here draws on a classical model of revolution whereby political history is rendered as a natural, and fundamentally cyclical, movement from one arrangement to another, precipitated by some excess "in need" of correction, or, in Aristotle's classic formulation, the disproportionate growth of one of the political body's parts.[45] In invoking this tradition, he at least partially exculpates alleged Jacobin excess, and with it, his own earlier career as a "journalist of spirit." This mixture of necessitarian and neoclassical rhetoric was also a central aspect of the Jacobins' own self-understanding, as one astute observer noted of the French revolutionaries in particular: "Just as they seem to be occupied with revolutionizing themselves and things, creating something that did not exist before, precisely in such epochs of revolutionary crisis they anxiously conjure up the spirits of the past to their service, borrowing from them names, battle slogans, and costumes in order to present this new scene in world history in time-honored disguise and borrowed language."[46]

Brackenridge's ambiguous verdict on the Jacobin legacy is continuous with his earlier celebrations of revolution, despite the older man's implicit aim of burying the revolutionary 1790s, as we see in reading the apologia excerpted above alongside Brackenridge's 1793 July Fourth oration, in which he argues, "Do we secure the air, or, the bastile [*sic*] of the mountain, when the rock is burnt, and the town engulphed ... Do we accuse the hurricane, when the mariner is tossed with the tempest, and is an incidental sufferer in the storm? The naturalist does not."[47]

Cataclysms are necessary, but apparently only up until the point when the post-revolutionary subject must temper the force of the hurricane in order to settle the continents cataclysmically thrown up by the revolutionary tumult. In other words, human beings are, somehow, in control of these tempests after all. Brackenridge accepts these implicitly extreme revolutionary "activities" as necessary and laments the persistence of a revolutionary urge. This melancholic vacillation attests to the incomplete character of the Atlantic revolutions, which shaped the trajectory of Brackenridge's life and work. We can more specifically see in these passages, and *Modern Chivalry, Part 2* as a whole, the author's inability to fully own or unequivocally disavow the revolutionary revenant that haunts his text.

In closing, I would like to offer Brackenridge's melancholia as one mode of political affect and literary discourse in the early nineteenth century. This period was characterized by reaction throughout the Atlantic world, as the revolutionary promise of the 1790s faded into the Napoleonic wars and national consolidation. Brackenridge's iteration of melancholia attests to the unhappy consciousness of the early nineteenth-century liberal in his unsuccessful attempts to inter a more substantively radical and democratic vision of the body politic in the then rising, formally representative, and legalistic edifice. This radical democratic vision, like the ghost of Marat or some other journalist of spirit, will not stay buried.

NOTES

1 Hugh Henry Brackenridge, *Modern Chivalry*, ed. with intro. by Ed White (Indianapolis, 2009), 4. All references to Brackenridge's novel are to this edition, unless otherwise specified.

2 The Captain goes on to argue, in a revealing manner: "Or if they should excuse you from such out of door services, they will rack and torture you with hard questions. You must tell them how long the rays of light are coming from the sun, how many drops of rain fall in a thunder gust; what makes the grasshopper chirp when the sun is hot; how mussel shells get up to the top of the mountains; how the Indians got over to America. You will have to prove absolutely that the negroes once were white." Farrago concludes his cautionary homily in noting how "many men have ruined themselves with their ambition, and made bad worse. There is another kind of philosophy, which lies more within your sphere; that is moral philosophy. Every hostler or hireling can study this." We should recall that much of Brackenridge's novel is dedicated to "moral philosophy": ethical and political rumination in a sincere and ironic vein. *MC*, 17.

3 Ibid., 150–4.

4 Ibid., 153.

5 *Modern Chivalry* was, until recently, relegated to the realm of frontier wit and the kind of "dialect writing" usually associated with nineteenth century regional literature, apotheosized in the work of Mark Twain. This older interpretation and assessment was first challenged by Cathy Davidson's revisionist reassessment of the early American novel, in a still neglected chapter on picaresque narrative. See See the Chapter, "The Picaresque and the Margins of Political Discourse" in Cathy Davidson, *Revolution and The Word: The Rise of the Novel in America* (Oxford: Oxford University Press, 1986), 151–211.

6 See Thomas Slaughter, *The Whiskey Rebellion: Frontier Epilogue to the American Revolution* (Oxford and New York, 1986); William Hogeland, *The Whiskey Rebellion: George Washington, Alexander Hamilton, and the Frontier Rebels Who Challenged America's Newfound Sovereignty* (New York, 2006); Patrick Griffin, *American Leviathan: Empire, Nation, and Revolutionary Frontier* (New York, 2007). All these historians of the Whiskey Rebellion rely on Brackenridge's own account of the rebellion that he mediated, albeit unsuccessfully, as he recounts in his own account-cum-apologia, *Incidents of the Insurrection in Western Pennsylvania in the Year 1794* (1795). Hogeland focuses extensively on Brackenridge, whom the historian takes to task for his elitism, and/or eastern allegiances, supposedly manifest

in the author-politician's ambiguous ideological sympathies during the conflict. It should be noted here that it was this same ambiguity that engendered Alexander Hamilton's very different characterization of Brackenridge as an insurgent ringleader and Jacobin at the time. Larry Tise sees the Whiskey Rebellion and the Federalist administration's largely unfounded characterization of Brackenridge as a ringleader as having effected an ideological transformation on his part: from revolutionary enthusiast to conservative defender of a nascent American elite order. See Larry E. Tise, *The American Counterrevolution: A Retreat from Liberty, 1783–1800* (Mechanicsburg, PA, 1998). Finally, Andrew Shankman offers the most compelling account of the Pennsylvania Democratic-Republican movement, including such backcountry exemplars as Brackenridge, which temporarily subsumed emergent class differences as rising men made common cause with a nascent wage-earning stratum in their struggle with a semi-aristocratic Federalist establishment during the 1790s, under the banner of "democracy," only to see these differences re-emerge with the Jeffersonian victory of 1800, when, for example, the republican movement in Pennsylvania split into more radical and conservative factions. For Andrew Shankman, it was Brackenridge's appointment to the Pennsylvania state supreme court in 1799 by republican governor Thomas McKean that accounts for the more "conservative" tenor of *Modern Chivalry, Part 2,* as the writer-politician joined the ranks of the new political establishment. While I agree with much of Shankman's account, he tends to flatten and simplify Brackenridge's ideological ambivalences, which I discuss below. See Shankman, *The Crucible of American Democracy: The Struggle to Fuse Egalitarianism and Capitalism in Jeffersonian Pennsylvania* (Lawrence, KS, 2004).

7 Michael Warner renders this pithy verdict on the novel as "an exercise in republican theory for a freeholder public" in the course of outlining his model of an early American public sphere characterized by transparency, anonymity, and an emphatic dedication to the promulgation of knowledge useful and rational. Warner presents a picture of Americans' desire to "maintain an identity between publication and public discourse." Warner, *The Letters of the Republic: Publication and the Public Sphere in Eighteenth-Century America* (Cambridge, MA, 1990), 175.

8 Mikhail Bakhtin presents "heteroglossia" – or the "play of voices" – as the distinguishing characteristic of the novel as genre, in two distinctive but complementary senses, the first of which involves the novel's relationship to previously canonized classical literary genres, such as poetry and drama. According to the Russian theorist, the novel incorporates these prior

and generically closed or rigid forms; and, while this new literary mode most resembles the epic in the grandiose sweep of its earliest exemplary narratives, such as *Don Quixote, Tom Jones,* and *Clarissa,* it nonetheless does so in a characteristically modern fashion. These texts opportunistically appropriate their literary precursors, even as they simultaneously depict their respective historical situations. In fact, the "quixotic" plot – as evinced by Cervantes's novel and the various eighteenth-century English-language picaresque fictions that follow in its wake, including *Modern Chivalry* – pivot on the comic juxtaposition of one such literary tradition in the form of those chivalric prose romances that preoccupy its bumbling protagonists, and the everyday realities for which these same protagonists are completely ill equipped due to their reading practices. These early novelists dramatize the aesthetic and epistemological superiority of the novel over and above its precursors insofar as they explicitly underline how absurd an account of the actual world we are given in these prose romances; this new literary form, in anatomizing this absurdity, is implicitly more attuned to those realities that escape romance and therefore defeat the respective "quixotes" shaped by this defective literary genre, now triumphantly subsumed in and by the novel. This generic inclusiveness is demonstrated by the second, and for our purposes, even more significant formal feature of the genre according to Bakhtin: namely, the way in which novels incorporate different voices and dialects, into the narrative; these voices acquire a seeming autonomy, often in the face of the dominant or normative narrative voice. Here is the key to both "heteroglossia" and Bahktin's second significant term – "dialogism" – since, like that drama the novel supposedly supplants and absorbs, *different voices and the various social groups represented thereby* are at least given their due, despite any given narrative's stated moral, allowing for a variety of readings, against the grain or otherwise. This linguistic diversity functions for Bakhktin as an analogue for the various social and political groups found in the novelist's milieu, even as this prototypically modern literary form resists any monologic perspective or even a synthetic conclusion drawn from the various voices depicted in the text and significantly akin to consensus. See, for example, Bakhtin's "Discourse in the Novel," in which he writes: "The novel orchestrates all its themes, the totality of the world of objects and ideas expressed in it, by means of the social diversity of speech types and by the differing individual voices that flourish under such conditions. Authorial speech, the speech of narrators, inserted genres, the speech of characters are merely those fundamental compositional unities with whose help heteroglossia can enter the novel; each of them permits a multiplicity of social voices and a wide variety of their links and interrelationships."

Bakhtin, "Discourse in the Novel," in *The Dialogic Imagination: Four Essays*, trans. with intro. by Michael Holquist (Austin, 1981).

9 White elaborates on this suggestive point in terms of the novel's title: "'Modern chivalry' seems to refer to the elaborate ideological gymnastics whereby class antagonisms are reconciled and rationalized. In this sense, *Modern Chivalry*, far from being just a satire directed at the frontier multitude, is an exploration of the complex class dynamics ranging from elite institutions to popular responses." Ed White, "Introduction," in Brackenridge, *Modern Chivalry*, xi, xii.

10 Terry Bouton argues that the American revolution unleashed a wave of democratic political and social activism on the part of common people, ranging from democratic state constitutions to publicly owned land banks and a widespread movement for debt forgiveness. This movement precipitated the notably antidemocratic Federal Constitution of 1787, as early national elites sought to "tame democracy." See Bouton, *Taming Democracy: The "People," The Founders, and The Troubled Ending of the American Revolution* (Oxford and New York, 2007).

11 In addition to the secondary works listed in notes 6 and 10, the neo-progressive rehabilitation of 1790s radical democracy – as distinct from and opposed to an American liberal tradition predicated on possessive individualism and deeply entangled in a nascent capitalist political economy – is best exemplified in Seth Cotlar's recent work. See, for instance, Seth Cotlar, *Tom Paine's America: The Rise and Fall of Transatlantic Radicalism in the Early Republic* (Charlottesville, 2011). The neo-progressive turn was anticipated by earlier, pathbreaking work in legal and labour history, which includes two monographs that have deeply influenced my current thinking about the early republic and the turn to what Ed White calls "legal proceduralism" (see below) in the early nineteenth century, as a liberal ideology organized around property right displaced radical democratic republicanism in tandem with the market revolution, which transformed the United States, even as its ideologues retained the rhetoric of democracy. See, for instance, Christopher Tomlins, *Law, Labor, and Ideology in the Early American Republic* (Cambridge, 1993); Jennifer Nedelsky, *Private Property and the Limits of American Constitutionalism: The Madisonian Framework and Its Legacy* (Chicago, 1990).

12 Much of this information comes from Brackenridge's own writings, including his account of the Whiskey Rebellion, in addition to Claude Newlin's admittedly insufficient biography of Brackenridge, *The Life and Writings of Hugh Henry Brackenridge* (Mamaroneck, 1932, 1971), 84. Newlin's anecdotal biography – one of only two written in the twentieth century –

established the standard narrative of Brackenridge's career and political development, whereby his earlier "Federalist" support for the Constitution is followed by subsequent alienation from the Hamiltonian Federalists and a French revolutionary mania, of which he is disabused by the Whiskey Rebellion.

13 *A Poem, on the Rising Glory of America* (Philadelphia, 1772).

14 Quoted in Newlin, *Life and Writings of Brackenridge*, 57.

15 Bryan Waterman, "Arthur Mervyn's Medical Repository and the Early Republic's Knowledge Industries," *American Literary History* 15 (2) (2003): 215, 220.

16 Shankman classifies Brackenridge, alongside Gallatin, as "entrepreneurs," a claim he substantiates through the size of land purchases: "1, 386 acres and 7,000 acres, respectively." While it is true that Brackenridge's emigration from Federalist Philadelphia to western Pennsylvania was motivated by failure – as a journalist and a lawyer – the intellectual, cultural, or even proto-professional nature of the distinction he sought on the frontier is certainly not "entrepreneurial" in the conventional sense, as is indicated by the meagre size of his land holdings as compared to his elite peers. Shankman, *Crucible of American Democracy*, 54.

17 Ibid.

18 Shankman alternately ascribes this alliance to opportunism on the part of these various "new men" excluded from the Federalist elite or, more suggestively, the limitations of radical republican ideology with its expansive ideal-type of a unified and unitary people arrayed against an aristocratic clique. See Shankman, *Crucible of American Democracy*, 16–73.

19 Brackenridge subsequently outlines the proper relationship between the new United States and revolutionary France, in posing the question "Is it the duty of these states to assist France? That we are bound by treaty, and how far, I will not say: because it is not necessary. We are bound by a higher principle, if our assistance could avail. The great law of humanity." This 1793 Fourth of July oration, unlike so many other radical texts produced during the 1790s, could be justifiably classified as "Jacobin, " was excerpted in Philip Freneau's *National Gazette* on Saturday, 27 July 1793. Brackenridge was one of the few self-described "friends of liberty" who still supported the French Revolution in the wake of Robespierre's rise to power and the Terror, as attested by this Fourth of July oration, which was delivered before the Pittsburgh chapter of the Philadelphia Democratic-republican society. It is interesting to consider Shankman's account of Albert Gallatin's response to the Federalist accusations of Jacobin sympathies, among western insurrectionaries as one, telling contrast: "Revolution and Jacobinism were

reactions to hierarchy, obnoxious arrogance, and the violation of individual liberty – behavior the Jeffersonians sought to eradicate. If the United States wished to avoid Jacobinism, it needed to defeat the Federalist Party that provoked violent reactions." Ibid., 58.

20 Alexander Hamilton – in a series of letters that he published pseudonymously as "Tully" in the *American Daily Advertiser* during the summer of 1794 – connects the western Pennsylvania insurrection, in addition to the several other "regulator" movements that wracked the early American frontier, with a wider revolutionary challenge to the post-constitutional American state. Tully addresses "the People of the United States, in the last of these somewhat overblown epistles: "Fresh symptoms every moment appear of a dark conspiracy, hostile to your government, to your peace abroad, to your tranquility at home." "Tully" doesn't so much delineate the contours of this "dark conspiracy" as he manufactures the darkness ascribed to the western insurgents' project. He depicts the rebels gathered around Pittsburgh, and their critique of the excise in overly general and notably *obscure* terms, as when he evokes "plotters of mischief" who at best underestimate the people they only pretend to champion, since they "derive what they mistake for [the people's] image, from an original in their own heated and crooked imaginations," while they "mould a wise, reflecting and dispassionate people, to purposes which presuppose an ignorant unthinking and turbulent herd." Alexander Hamilton, "Tully No. IV," in Harold C. Syrett and Jacob E. Cooke, eds, *The Papers of Alexander Hamilton*, vol. 17, August 1794–December 1794 (New York, 1957), 175–7.

21 *United States Magazine*, January 1779, 42. These observations appeared in the inaugural issue of Brackenridge's first stab at a specifically American periodical, launched in the midst of the American Revolution.

22 Brackenridge, *MC*, 3.

23 *MC*, 2–3.

24 Ibid.

25 *MC*, 21.

26 Ibid.

27 Isaac Kramnick, *Republicanism and Bourgeois Revolution: Political Ideology in Late Eighteenth-Century England and America* (Ithaca, 1978),1.

28 [James Madison], The Federalist Papers, no. 10.

29 Brackenridge, *MC*, 21.

30 Kevin Gilmartin, *Print Politics: The Press and Radical Opposition in Early Nineteenth-Century England* (Cambridge, 1996), 12.

31 See Shankman, *Crucible of American Democracy*, and Richard E. Ellis, *The Jeffersonian Crisis: Courts and Politics in the Young Republic* (New York, 1971).

32 *MC*, 373.

33 See Seth Cotlar, "Joseph Gales and the Making of the Jeffersonian Middle Class" in *The Revolution of 1800: Democracy, Race, and the New Republic* (Charlottesville, 2002), 355.

34 John Wood, a Scottish immigrant and sometime Aaron Burr partisan, who in a significantly republican reprise of William Cobbett's version of the previous United Irishmen conspiracy starring James Reynolds, linked radical deist Elihu Palmer and his movement to a conspiracy of "Columbian Illuminati." Wood's motivations were cynical ones, since he sought to smear the rival New York republican faction of DeWitt Clinton by association, as, for instance, when he writes: "This is no tale, no visionary dream or artful fabrication … [Sceptics] will have no occasion to write to foreign professors to obtain information as to the reality of the Illuminati – he will only have to write to the Mayor of New-York, to inform him whether such men as Elihu Palmer, a blind preacher, and David Denison, an editor of the American Citizen, are in existence, and it will be proved by me that the same Elihu Palmer and David Denison, with many other zealous Clintonians, have been members of a society, first termed the philosophical, and afterwards the Theistical, for the avowed purpose of propagating deism and opposing the Christian religion." John Wood, *A Full Exposition of the Clintonian Faction, and the Society of the Columbian Illuminati; With an Account of the Writer of the Narrative, and the Characters of his Certificate Men, and also Remarks on Warren's Pamphlet* (Newark, 1802), 43.

35 Quoted in Cotlar, "Joseph Gales," 351.

36 *MC*, 326.

37 Benjamin does not offer his reader anything like a systematic definition of "left wing melancholy" in the short 1931 essay of the same name, which is largely dedicated to abusing Ernst Kästner, a popular German social democratic poet of the Weimar era. Benjamin concludes his review by likening this attitude to petty bourgeois hot air, having "more to do with flatulence than subversion. Constipation and melancholy have always gone together. But since the juices began to dry up in the body social, stuffiness meets us at every turn." Benjamin understandably takes those radicals fixated on the past and its glorious lost causes rather than the present and its concrete possibilities to task here; but this indictment is nonetheless strange when we consider the thinker's other reflections on melancholia, as evinced in his *The Origin of German Tragic Drama* (see below), and his writings on Baudelaire, for whom melancholy was an extremely productive and potentially radical mode of feeling and perception, at least according to Benjamin. And, of course, Benjamin famously rejects the "empty

homogeneous time" of progress, as envisioned in standard liberal and orthodox Marxist models of history, in favour of a Messianic leap into the future that also, significantly, redeems the past, as outlined in his *Theses on the Philosophy of History*. Benjamin, *Selected Writings*: vol. 2, part 2, *1931–1934*, trans. Rodney Livingstone et al. (Cambridge, MA, 1999), 425, 426.

38 Freud, "Mourning and Melancholia," in *General Psychological Theory: Papers on Metapsychology* (New York, 1991), 164.

39 Benjamin ascribes the "persistent" – or what we might alternately call the obsessive – character of melancholia to this "loyalty to the world of things." Melancholy plays a pivotal role, as exemplified by the chapter on "Trauerspiel and Tragedy," in Benjamin's *The Origin of German Tragic Drama*, and it is this account of melancholy that animates contemporary critical analyses of the phenomenon, rather than Benjamin's dismissive treatment of "left-wing" melancholy in the short essay of the same name. Benjamin, *The Origin of German Tragic Drama*, trans. John Osborne (London, 2009), 157.

40 Thomas Pfau, *Romantic Moods: Paranoia, Trauma, and Melancholy, 1790–1840* (Baltimore, 2005), 325.

41 We might recall here Freud's own inclusion of political investments in his initial outline of mourning and melancholia, in which he writes: "Mourning is regularly the reaction to the loss of a loved person, or to the loss of some abstraction which has taken the place of one, such as one's country, liberty, an ideal, and so on. In some people the same influences produce melancholia instead of mourning and we consequently suspect them of a pathological disposition." Freud went on to significantly revise his first model of melancholia in his *Ego and the Id* (1923), in which he recasts this pathology as the very foundation of the ego, which Judith Butler renders as "constitutive melancholia, an emphatic and irreversible loss" that forms the basis of "being." Butler builds on this latter model of melancholia, which she synthesizes with Foucault's theories of power, subjection, and subjectivity. In fact, the disavowal upon which heterosexual, and by extension, racial and even national identity is predicated in Butler's reading of Freud's later revision of melancholia could be applied to the early nineteenth-century consolidation of English and American national identity, which I argue is exactly a reaction-formation arising from and against the promiscuous cosmopolitanism of the 1790s radical republican moment. And yet, as I argue here and elsewhere, Brackenridge's melancholia cannot be assimilated to the national romance, in either substantive or formal terms; radical melancholia in this way should be seen as a distinctive mode of political affect throughout the Napoleonic and post-Napoleonic periods

as manifest in certain, formally distinctive, narratives, such as *Modern Chivalry, Part 2.*

42 *MC,* 297.

43 Ibid., 298.

44 Ibid., 298–9.

45 Aristotle famously compares the polis to the body: "The body consists of parts, and all growth must be in proportion, lest the proper balance of the whole be upset, since otherwise the body becomes useless; as it would if feet a yard long grew on a body a foot high, or when a part of the body grows its bone or tissue like those of some other animal." Aristotle, *The Politics,* trans. T.A. Sinclair (London: Penguin Classics, 1964), 194. Aristotle understands this process as a natural corrective to some disequilibrium. He notably emphasizes the excesses of oligarchy and democracy. Ibid., 189.

46 As Marx elaborates: "Thus Luther put on the mask of the Apostle Paul, the Revolution of 1789–1814 draped itself alternately in the guise of the Roman Republic and the Roman Empire, and the Revolution of 1848 knew nothing better to do than to parody, now 1789, now the revolutionary tradition of 1793–95. In like manner, the beginner who has learned a new language always translates it back into his mother tongue, but he assimilates the spirit of the new language and expresses himself freely in it only when he moves in it without recalling the old and when he forgets his native tongue. When we think about this conjuring up of the dead of world history, a salient difference reveals itself. Camille Desmoulins, Danton, Robespierre, St. Just, Napoleon, the heroes as well as the parties and the masses of the old French Revolution, performed the task of their time – that of unchaining and establishing modern bourgeois society – in Roman costumes and with Roman phrases. The first one destroyed the feudal foundation and cut off the feudal heads that had grown on it. The other created inside France the only conditions under which free competition could be developed, parceled-out land properly used, and the unfettered productive power of the nation employed; and beyond the French borders it swept away feudal institutions everywhere, to provide, as far as necessary, bourgeois society in France with an appropriate up-to-date environment on the European continent. Once the new social formation was established, the antediluvian colossi disappeared and with them also the resurrected Romanism – the Brutuses, the Gracchi, the publicolas, the tribunes, the senators, and Caesar himself. Bourgeois society in its sober reality bred its own true interpreters and spokesmen in the Says, Cousins, Royer-Collards, Benjamin Constants, and Guizots; its real military leaders sat behind the office desk and the hog-headed Louis XVIII was its political chief. Entirely absorbed in the

production of wealth and in peaceful competitive struggle, it no longer remembered that the ghosts of the Roman period had watched over its cradle. But unheroic though bourgeois society is, it nevertheless needed heroism, sacrifice, terror, civil war, and national wars to bring it into being. And in the austere classical traditions of the Roman Republic the bourgeois gladiators found the ideals and the art forms, the self-deceptions, that they needed to conceal from themselves the bourgeois-limited content of their struggles and to keep their passion on the high plane of great historic tragedy." Karl Marx, "The Eighteenth Brumaire of Louis Bonaparte," in Robert C. Tucker, ed., *The Marx-Engels Reader*, 2nd ed. (New York, 1978), 575.

47 Brackenridge in *National Gazette*, Saturday, 27 July 1793.

chapter eight

Penal Reform and Politics in Early Nineteenth-Century England: "A Prison Must Be a Prison"

RANDALL McGOWEN

Politics in the Atlantic world, in the years around 1800, were shaped by the ideological contests that followed in the wake of the American and French Revolutions. This period saw fierce struggle between proponents of liberal, radical, or utopian principles, on the one hand, and conservative defenders of the established order, on the other. The lines were sharply drawn and the stakes were clear. While reformers dreamed of new beginnings, reactionary politicians feared that even modest change would undermine all authority. Among the various causes that stirred the passions of the advocates of change, one that attracted particular attention in almost every state was the condition of prisons. On the face of it, the existing operation of confinement represented to reformers in Britain and America the epitome of the abuses which they charged the existing order with perpetuating. Investigators such as John Howard discovered in prisons the existence of corruption, casual brutality, neglect, and moral disorder. The remedies these men proposed, as with the political program they pressed, struck at the heart of the old regime.

Yet while the story of penal reform conforms in some respects to the portrait of political conflict in the age of revolutions, in more subtle ways it departs from this narrative. This departure, moreover, has important implications for how we understand the currents flowing through this period. For unlike so many of the causes the reformers embraced during these years, penal reform experienced a considerable measure of success. In doing so it secured the support of people who vigorously resisted almost all other proposals for institutional change. In this essay I want to explore a brief, seemingly inconsequential, episode, the renewal of parliamentary debate over the prison in 1810. The discussions that followed from this event, both in Parliament and in the political journals of the day, offer a confusing spectacle; penal reform drew upon both radical and conservative impulses. The imagined prison offered a new vision of social order even as it sought to preserve the existing order of things. Far from being an instance of ideological incoherence, however, the controversies over the nature of confinement helped to constitute a new politics, one whose importance lies in the way in which it reconfigured and displaced the terms of class struggle and ideological conflict. The resolution of this controversy lay less in institutional changes than in the way the prison took shape as an idea and became experienced as a necessity.

In the standard histories of the development of the prison in England the motion offered by Sir Samuel Romilly in May 1810 to revive the Penitentiary Act of 1779 seldom receives a mention. No doubt there are good reasons for this omission. Historians preoccupied with the onward rush towards the rise of the "modern" prison find this glance back to an earlier measure disconcerting. There also seems nothing surprising about a motion for penal reform being offered by the great champion of amelioration of the severe criminal code. Besides, the debate was inconclusive and his measure failed. There appears to be little about this occasion that contributes to our understanding of penal developments in the early nineteenth century.

Yet there are good reasons why we should pay more attention to this episode. It was neither so transparent nor as insignificant as its neglect might lead one to believe. For Romilly's motion was the occasion for a renewal of interest in prison reform, both in Parliament and among the wider public. The last three decades of the eighteenth century had seen a remarkable alteration in both the conception and practice of confinement in England. The Penitentiary Act itself was one monument to this transformation. Though never implemented, the act inspired a number of provincial magistrates to persuade their counties to undertake an expensive program of prison construction. "In the 20 years between 1775 and 1795," Robin Evans has written, "a wholesale rebuilding of the country's gaols and bridewells was accomplished." Although the reconstruction of local prisons produced a peculiar patchwork of change, the effort spoke of the extent to which the traditional ruling class had been converted to the need to attend to penal questions. Further evidence of this alteration in penal attitudes was manifested in the shift in sentencing practices on the part of both magistrates and judges. The increased use of incarceration was already under way even before John Howard launched his investigation of local prisons.[1] By the later 1790s, however, this wave of reform had run its course. The ever-increasing cost of war combined with the mounting burden of the poor rates sapped the resources of local government. The ideological struggle with France also meant that most proposals for reform were greeted with suspicion or hostility.[2]

The political and economic state of the nation scarcely seemed more promising for penal reform in 1810 when Romilly offered his proposal. Nonetheless, against all expectation, his motion inaugurated a decisive period of penal discussion. While his call to revive the Penitentiary Act failed, the debate that followed led directly to the appointment of a parliamentary committee, chaired by George Holford, which conducted an important review of penal experiments. One outcome of this committee's deliberations was the decision to build the country's first national penitentiary. When it opened in 1816, at a cost of £458,000, it was the largest prison in Europe. Even more impressive than this achievement was the explosion of philanthropic interest in the state of prisons. James Neild, in imitation of John Howard's investigations of the previous century, offered the first of several surveys of prison conditions throughout the country. *The Philanthropist*, a journal created in 1811 by the Quaker William Allen, promoted penal reform as one of its central concerns. To further publicize the issue, Allen, in 1816, joined with Thomas Fowell Buxton and others to launch the Society for the Improvement of Prison Discipline and for the Reformation of Juvenile Offenders. The issue commanded the attention of the press and of influential periodicals like the *Edinburgh Review*. One author, moved by the publicity afforded the cause, congratulated his readers that "public feeling" had "at last been powerfully excited" in support of penal reform.[3] The efforts of Elizabeth Fry to instruct the female prisoners in Newgate were widely reported. Optimism among the advocates of penal change ran high. "Never was a time more happily adapted than the present," wrote one reviewer in 1819, "for the prosecution of benevolent undertakings," and prison improvement led the list of approved causes.[4] Parliament returned repeatedly to the issue. An author for the generally conservative *Quarterly Review* remarked in an 1824 essay that he lived in an "age of prison improvements." Looking back over the previous decade he felt compelled to acknowledge that profound changes had "been made" in penal administration and that "liberal views ... have gained ground in this country upon every thing connected with prisons within a few years."[5] It was, in short, a decade full of activity and full of promise.

Still, there is more to the story of Romilly's motion than its serving as the occasion for launching a new wave of agitation over prisons. The episode, as well as what followed from it, casts new light on a seldom observed dimension of the "origin of the prison." While scholars have sought to expose the interests served by prison reform or to trace the motives of the key actors, other aspects of the penal debates have been neglected. In particular, we need to pay more attention to how the prison question appeared to politicians and the public at this moment. It was precisely in relation to what we might call the logic of the prison that crucial developments occurred during the decade. Novelty lay less with changes in architecture, administration, or the design of particular regimes, than in the growing conviction about what a prison had to be. One clue to this elusive but insistent transformation of the penal question can be detected in the confusing politics of prison reform in the 1810s. The issue was pressed by a coalition of advanced Whigs and evangelically inspired philanthropists. It belonged to a list of causes, some of which made headway during this period, and many of which failed to advance.[6] What was it about the prison as a reform project that permitted it to succeed in a period more often hostile to innovation? Why, in particular, did penal change advance during a decade which saw reform of the criminal law stall? Advocates of reform often argued that their proposals represented a new kind of concern, one that was different from and superior to the issues that marked normal political contests. They pressed this theory even as some of them made little effort to disguise the political advantage they hoped to gain from its acceptance. When it came to the prison, however, the issue did indeed cut across the familiar political lines. What we note, particularly during these years, is that penal reform gave birth to a new politics, taken up with debates over the meaning and purposes of confinement. Parties formed around penal questions that bore little relationship to traditional political alliances. This development might well appear to bear out the claim that the penal question was apolitical. Yet we must be careful to analyse what this development represented and how the politics of the prison actually worked.

This chapter charts a transition that no one intended, but which we can, nonetheless, see taking place in the 1810s. The controversies around the prison created an impression that the institution was in flux and the outcome far from clear. The often passionate debates in pamphlets and journals over competing schemes for organizing confinement suggest a dynamic situation with few certainties. Viewed from another angle, however, we see that what this seeming tempest testifies to and helped to create was the necessity of the prison as the place of punishment. In fact, the actual course of the debates produced a narrowing of the conception of the prison. The attempts to invest the institution with a more utopian impulse were deflected, while the weight of the prison came to be felt more powerfully in shaping the argument.[7] When we ask what the discourse about confinement produced, the answer is, the prison itself, along with everything that notion involved in terms of characterizations of criminality, philosophical debates about human nature, and questions about the direction of social policy. The substitution of a new politics for the traditional party contests worked in turn to conceal the developing consensus about the inevitability of the prison as the essential form of punishment. The effect was to deepen and strengthen the grip of the prison upon politics, but more particularly upon the public imagination.

1

Romilly's turn to the prison question occurred at a time when he was much occupied with his campaign to reform the criminal law. Indeed, it probably makes sense to see his proposal to revive the Penitentiary Act as a manoeuvre in support of that struggle. During these years Romilly emerged as a leading voice among the advanced Whigs. To his beleaguered party the cause of law reform mingled principle with political advantage. It bundled together constitutional, utilitarian, and humanitarian concerns. It also divided Parliament, offering the opposition, and particularly its more progressive wing, a popular cause, one that incidentally struck at the heart of Tory principles of governance.[8] In February 1810 he proposed a bill that would abolish the death penalty for privately stealing in shops. His goal, he said, was "to lessen the severity and increase the certainty of punishment." He was convinced that existing penalties were far too severe, and that they discouraged people from prosecuting crimes, which in turn acted as an incentive to criminals to break the law. He believed that no other step would do so much to deter crime. In March he summarized his views in a pamphlet entitled "Observations on the Criminal Law," a work drawn from his speeches on behalf of law reform. In May he called for a return of convicts for the last five years in the belief that the results would support his contention that the too frequent reliance on the gallows hobbled criminal justice. In these very deliberate actions we see Romilly attempting to lead Parliament step by step to a sweeping transformation of the criminal law. The rejection of his bill to restrict the gallows suggested his struggle would be a long one.[9]

In this context, Romilly's proposal to "carry into execution" the Penitentiary Act of 1779 was both clever and provocative. His motion answered the charge of his critics who said his efforts to ameliorate the criminal law offered no alternative punishment. He also in this instance confounded their accusation that he promoted dangerous innovation. He pointed to the act's illustrious pedigree. It was the work of the "celebrated Mr. Howard" and his distinguished collaborators, William Eden, Lord Auckland, and William Blackstone. By the turn of the century Howard had been canonized as a kind of secular saint whose story condensed and propagated a particular portrait of penal change. An author in the *Edinburgh Review,* in 1814, called to mind "the memorable time when Howard achieved the painful and perilous adventure of visiting those dens of corruption, infection, guilt and misery, and astonished his countrymen with the plain unexaggerated narrative of the horrors he had seen."[10] The lengthy and detailed statute associated with his name presented an influential vision of how to organize a prison. It called for the construction, Romilly noted, of two penitentiaries near London where prisoners from all over the country would be subjected to a regime consisting of both solitary confinement with religious instruction and "well-regulated labour." The work would be of a "most servile kind," while the prison fare was to be uniform and simple. The prisons were never built, as first a dispute over their location and then the resumption of transportation intervened. The failure, Romilly charged, represented a stain on the nation. "For 36 years," he explained, a law framed upon correct principles of penal discipline "remained a dead letter on the statute book, although it was a monument of eternal praise to those who had framed it."[11]

This note of accusation dominated the speeches Romilly made in support of his proposal. Despite referring in passing to the "correct principles of penal discipline," he had little to say about them.[12] In his speeches in support of his measure he did not mention the schemes to reform offenders that so interested his Quaker and Evangelical allies. He never mentioned the name of his friend, Jeremy Bentham. What he chose to emphasize instead were what he spoke of as the failures of penal policy in his day. If the government, Romilly argued, was culpable for its omissions with respect to the Penitentiary Act, it was even more deserving of blame for the policies it pursued. Much of the passion in his speech was reserved for a description of what he characterized as scandals of penal administration. His main targets were the hulks and transportation to Australia. The hulks, ships moored in the Thames, emerged as a temporary expedient for dealing with the swelling number of prisoners retained in English prisons as a result of the disruption of transportation to the American colonies. According to Romilly, they brought to a horrible perfection all the evils associated with the old penal regime. They mingled together all kinds of offenders under lax supervision and with no effort made to restrain abuses of power. Instead of reforming prisoners, the hulks had become "schools of vice." The government compounded the folly of this arrangement by restoring transportation. "While the [penitentiary] law so lay dormant," Romilly charged, "a project was unhappily proposed to government, of sending the convicts to New South Wales to establish a colony there. It was, perhaps, the boldest and most unpromising project which was ever held out to any administration, to establish a new colony which should consist entirely of the outcasts of society, and the refuse of mankind."[13] Romilly's portrait of the government's penal policy painted it as a product of ill-considered expedients that were expensive, needlessly cruel to the prisoners, and did nothing to address the causes of crime.

In the face of this stinging indictment of its policies, and in sharp contrast to their reaction to Romilly's proposals to mitigate the capital code, the response of the government and its supporters was tepid to say the least. Romilly's bills to modify the criminal law aroused long debates and bitter denunciations of what were seen as misguided or mischievous attacks upon the English constitution. His call to revive the 1779 act produced a short discussion with little acrimony. Supporters of the government might experience some discomfort at Romilly's description of the hulks and transportation. Their responses were more awkward and hesitant than one might have expected. Still, no one challenged Romilly's main contention about the desirability of prison reform. Home Secretary Richard Ryder was content to argue that the hulks were at present not as bad as they once had been. He conceded, however, that he "agreed with many of the general observations" that Romilly had offered. Even more surprising, William Frankland, a particularly spirited opponent of criminal law reform, spoke of "agreeing as he did with him in most of the principles he laid down" with respect to prisons. William Windham was a bit more restrained in his praise for Romilly, but he admitted that the subject deserved more study.[14] While the Whigs had stressed the shortcomings of existing arrangements, the Tories responded that things were not as dark as their opponents claimed, and that caution should be observed in charting a new course. Still, there was little real disagreement over the characterization of the problems with the hulks and transportation. "Undoubtedly the mode of punishment now almost universally adopted," Solicitor General Thomas Plumer conceded, "is not calculated to produce on the mind of the offender, any sense of his disgraceful situation, or to amend his habits." As the discussion drew to a close, Plumer confessed that he was "extremely happy to find, that we differ only in the mode in which we shall carry into execution a plan, the principle of which is admitted to be good." Even as he counselled delay, asking only that the measure be put off to the following year, Ryder pronounced himself satisfied "with the general principles laid down" and said that he felt "so friendly to the measure" that his "cordial support" would not be wanting in the next session.[15]

Romilly no doubt experienced some disappointment at the outcome of the debate. To his mind the two issues of the gallows and the prison were inextricably linked. What the discussion of the prison revealed is that for conservatives they were not necessarily connected. This is all the more surprising because in terms of the sweeping indictment of existing practice and the scope of the proposed reform, Romilly's effort on behalf of prison reform paralleled the tone and ambition of his unsuccessful campaign to alter the criminal law. He presented each cause as part of the same general advance of humanity. In addition, he had many of the same allies in both campaigns. Yet the contrast in the response of the administration and its supporters could not have been greater. Romilly's repeated attempts after an early success to circumscribe the use of the gallows met with fierce resistance. His measures, modest as they appeared, were seen as a prelude to a more radical transformation of justice. They challenged the discretion vested in the judges and were said to diminish the majesty associated with the supreme penalty of the law. Romilly was condemned for advancing radical principles which threatened to overturn the settled customs of the constitution.[16] Criminal law reform spoke too directly of the legitimacy of government and of the representation of authority to be tolerated.

If the political lines around the gallows were clear, they were much less so when it came to the prison. The advocates of reform were happy to score political points off the issue, but they had only limited success in doing so. They preached to an audience that had already been converted by the message. What both the appeal to the 1779 act and the invocation of John Howard proposed was that the decisive break in the understanding of punishment had already occurred. "Is it likely," one of Romilly's allies, James Abercromby, remarked, "that any new facts could be disclosed, or any new principles be suggested which were not known to, or considered by the House at the time the law, to which it is now wished to give effect, was passed?"[17] Prison reform advanced not only within the framework of ideas established by Howard and his confederates, but perhaps more importantly under the sign and with the sanction of his name. The decisive event in the revival of the penal question, moreover, turned out to be not Romilly's motion but the government's response to it.

2

Romilly did not carry the day with his proposal. The government won the argument for delay. It did, however, deliver on its promise to appoint a committee to review the state of the nation's penal arrangements. This committee, in its composition and deliberations, reinforces the impression created by the debate over Romilly's motion that prison reform did not really divide parties. It came to carry the name of its forceful chair, George Holford. Despite the presence of several leading advocates for penal reform such as Abercromby, William Wilberforce, and Charles Bunbury, the committee as a whole reflected the interests of the current administration. Romilly was appointed to the committee, but he scarcely attended its meetings.[18] Thus, it cannot be said that the opposition drove the agenda. Rather, Holford exercised the decisive influence over the course of the committee's work. He himself had been brought into Parliament by Addington, and he had proved a regular supporter of the government. Though a man of deep religious conviction, he was not an ally of the Quakers, who were playing a leading part in pressing penal reform.[19] Under Holford's direction, the committee moved quickly to carry out an investigation with a clear goal in view. Its report began with what appeared to be an endorsement of Romilly's motion. It resolved that "the system of Penitentiary Imprisonment upon the general principles of the 19th Geo. III cap. 74 is calculated to reform offenders, and ought to be pursued." It summarized this act as calling for "a system of imprisonment, not confined to the safe custody of the person, but extending to the reformation and improvement of the mind, and operating by seclusion, employment, and religious instruction." It concluded by urging the construction of a penitentiary for London and Middlesex "without delay."[20] In doing so it gave no hint of moving beyond the penal principles articulated thirty years earlier.

Furthermore, the way in which the committee went about gathering evidence supports a similar conclusion. The committee proceeded in a very deliberate fashion and made little pretence of neutrality in its collection of testimony. The witness list was surprisingly short. A significant proportion of the evidence was provided by two men with deep experience of local penal arrangements, G.O. Paul and the Rev. John Becher.[21] Paul and Becher represented the dominant features of the penal regime of the previous three decades. During this period local notables like Samuel Whitbread in Bedfordshire, Thomas Butterworth Bayley in Lancashire, and William Morton Pitt in Dorset took the lead in prodding the county magistracy to look into the state of the prisons under their control and to undertake significant construction of new facilities. They did so with little support or encouragement from the national government, though notably with the acquiescence of their neighbours. Thus, Paul at Gloucester and Becher more recently at the house of correction in Southwell demonstrated how much could be achieved by an active magistrate.[22] Holford drew upon the experience of such men while turning their testimony to his own purposes. His ambition was not exhausted by the resolution to build a new prison. Nor was he content to compile a compendium of the knowledge acquired by previous generations. As he said at a later date, reflecting back on the achievements of the period after 1779, "much good has been done, but it has been done upon no regular system or principle."[23] Holford and his committee were single-minded in pressing this point. There was much to praise about earlier efforts to improve confinement. However, it was no longer enough to see that prison keepers observed basic rules or that prisons haphazardly employed some measure of separation and work. Holford committed himself to a search for a plan of prison organization that would unify the operation of prisons across the country.

For the most part, Paul and Becher lent themselves to Holford's purposes. They not only praised the 1779 act, they invested it with precisely the ambition that now guided Holford's efforts. Paul said that "by this Act we first created a legal system of punishment, by *mode* of confinement – by labour and seclusion," as an alternative to death and transportation. Becher added that "the fundamental principles laid down in the Penitentiary Act" appeared to him "incontrovertible."[24] Yet the testimony that Paul and Becher offered showed that they differed in fundamental ways about the best regime for the prison. Each argued for reformation as the principal goal of punishment, but they disagreed about how to achieve it. Paul was an adherent of the view that solitude was the most effective way to inspire offenders to amend their lives. He accepted that prisoners might be given work to do in their cells, but he opposed allowing them to gain any reward or benefit for their labour. Employment was simply a useful means to increase the effect of solitude.[25] Becher, by contrast, argued that the goal of punishment was to make prisoners "industrious." Solitude or separation was only to be employed "to bring men to a sense of obedience and of duty." "We treat mankind as constituted of habits," he said, "and our principle is to eradicate those which are bad, and to implant others that are better."[26] For the purposes of the committee these differences were not significant, even though they would soon become markers of a struggle between competing penal regimes.

What made it easier to ignore these differences was the fact that the committee was bent upon making another distinction, and this one emphatically. In some respects the definitive act of the committee was the rejection of the scheme of prison reform offered by Jeremy Bentham. If half the committee's efforts went to establish the idea that imprisonment should be based on a system, the other half went to demonstrate that some systems were completely unacceptable. Bentham became the all-too-real straw man, the necessary opponent, exploited by Holford to support his own views. There is something ironic about Bentham meeting this fate, for there can have been no more inventive creator of a system of imprisonment than him. Yet it may have been precisely this feature of his thought that made him so useful a target. The Holford committee accorded his plan an extensive hearing, but the questioning was sceptical, while Bentham's responses were combative. One might have expected a different result. Bentham's scheme, after all, promised to save the public a great deal of money. He explained that the prison population represented wasted potential which he would put to profitable use. His goal was to promote industrious habits that would prepare offenders to return to the world with useful skills and recognition of the rewards of honest labour. And, above all, Bentham offered the most elaborate system of confinement, one that was bold in ambition and detailed in its design. The committee responded positively to none of these features. The members could scarcely conceal their distaste for most aspects of the plan.[27]

There were simply too many points at which Bentham's panopticon conflicted with both the common sense and the idealism that guided the members of the committee. They singled out the entrepreneurial principle as particularly worthy of condemnation. "Is there not danger," the committee asked provocatively, "that the prisoners should be valued, and consequently indulged, rather in proportion to their work, than in proportion to their contrition and reformation?" "Pecuniary advantage" was given too large a role as an incentive to proper conduct on the part of both administrators and prisoners. Religiously inspired reformers disliked the role given to the financial motive, while conservatives resented the disrespect shown to the traditional social elite that governed local society. His scheme, most feared, proposed too little oversight of the contractor who undertook to manage the prison. Both Paul and Becher were invited to deliver their negative opinions of Bentham's plan. They saw his idea of opening up the prison to inspection by the public as flying in the face of their concern to contain the contagion of immoral sociability and to cut off the offender from communication with the outside world. It was as well entirely too democratic a principle of accountability. Above all, it was Bentham's limited interest in reformation that doomed his project. "Indulgence and treatment of every sort," he famously responded, "must be governed by appearances: there may be apparent contrition where this is not real." "I am no searcher of hearts; I can only judge from appearances."[28] This was too much for the committee to stomach. In its conclusion the committee delivered a damning judgment on Bentham's plan: "The reformation of the offender, instead of being a secondary concern, which must be the case if all power and influence within the prison were lodged in the hands of persons contracting for the manual labour of the prisoners, is contemplated as the primary object, to the accomplishment of which every regulation and arrangement is to be made subservient."[29] The complete rejection of Bentham's panopticon is revealing. Bentham, in his way, had gone further to oppose the emerging consensus about the organization of the prison than any other reformer. His defeat sealed the triumph of that consensus.

The most immediate consequence of the Holford committee's deliberations was the creation of a prison for London and Middlesex at Millbank. The speed with which Parliament acted on the committee's recommendation confirms the peculiar status of the prison issue for the political nation. The prison was not a question that divided political parties. Holford, in presenting his motion, remarked that "he was happy to find a general disposition throughout the House to accede to this proposition."[30] Millbank represented the triumph of the Penitentiary Act. For the new prison conformed to the basic features of the model laid down by that act.[31] The novelty in this measure lay in the fact that Parliament took the initiative and provided the huge sums needed to complete the undertaking. It signalled that the prison issue was becoming increasingly a national matter, much less subject to local direction and control.[32] Still, if Millbank was one achievement of the Holford committee, another was more enduring, the idea of system itself. The report offered a model of how to conduct a debate between different schemes and principles of imprisonment. It established the parameters of what could be introduced into the debate and what would be taken seriously. It set forth the notion that whatever problems were discovered in the operation of particular places of confinement, the solution lay in the discovery of a better system of punishment and its more consistent implementation.

3

If the Holford committee represented an important moment when the reform of prisons was reshaped as a debate over system, the ensuing controversy over penal reform in pamphlets, major journals, and the press consolidated this impression. As an author for the *Quarterly Review* noted in 1823, the prison question was "a matter of universal interest."[33] In often lengthy essays the journals presented extensive summaries of pamphlets and parliamentary reports. The urgency of the cause was felt well beyond the small circle of Quakers and Evangelicals who devoted considerable effort to promoting interest in the topic. The public had first been alerted to the problem of the prison through the work of people like Howard. It appeared as an issue involving abuse and neglect. But the essays and pamphlets of the 1810s demonstrated the triumph of system as the basic way of organizing the penal field.[34] To some authors this development represented the growth of a new area of political life that operated on different principles from the kind of struggle for power that characterized normal politics. This argument was developed by Francis Jeffrey in an article in the *Edinburgh Review* in 1818. He undertook this assignment at the request of the Quaker William Allen, who asked him to review pamphlets written by Bennet and Buxton.[35] Jeffrey opened his essay by suggesting that there were "two classes of subjects which naturally engage the attention of public men, and divide the interest which society takes in their proceedings." The one was "party politics," while the other Jeffrey called "Civil or domestic Administration." The former concerned political rights and the constitution, along with relations with foreign powers. It involved the struggle for office as well. The latter category encompassed trade and taxation, as well as "the care of the Poor," matters of education and morality, and "the protection of Prisoners." Jeffrey admitted that the division was inexact, because "in certain circumstances" an issue could become "an occasion for party contention." He denied, however, that such an outcome was a "natural" development. Party issues promoted friction and contests. In the civil sphere, Jeffrey argued, statesmen should work "to discover the best means of carrying into effect ends which all agree to be desirable."[36] Jeffrey presented this distinction as obvious and natural, yet the politicians and the public failed, he charged, to see the difference. The good of the nation was sacrificed "to the mere gladiatorship of the parties." He expressed sorrow that those whom he called the benefactors of humanity, the inventors and improvers, got less recognition than generals and politicians.[37] Prisons, Jeffrey implied, formed one of those causes so vital to the interests of humanity that it should not be the victim of normal political calculation.[38]

The journals, however, soon offered evidence that penal reform, if not the stuff of normal political conflict, could produce a new politics every bit as intense as traditional politics. The debate over competing systems rapidly emerged as a different kind of contest. This struggle soon evolved along a new axis, one characterized by a contributor as a choice between what he called "the vigorous system and the ameliorating system" of imprisonment.[39] One of the most dramatic instances of this transformation comes in the pages of the *Edinburgh Review* in an essay written by Sydney Smith, a Whig and one of the founders of that journal. Smith turned to the topic of prisons in 1821. He began his essay with a familiar portrait of the political divide between the government and its opponents. The latter proposed useful reforms which the former resisted in a fretful and self-interested fashion. He offered a scathing attack on the administration, portraying it as composed of "the plunderers of the public, the jealous jobbers, and those who sell themselves to some great man, who sells himself to a greater, all scent, from afar, the danger of political change – are sensible that the correction of one abuse may lead to that of another – feel uneasy at any visible operation of public spirit and justice – hate and tremble at a man who exposes and rectifies abuses from a sense of duty – and think, if such things are suffered to be, that their candle-ends and cheese-parings are no longer safe."[40]

After this perfunctory introduction, however, Smith struck a new note. In announcing this new line he exposed a crucial ambiguity in the meaning of the idea of reform. As he wrote in 1822, it was "a mistake, and a very serious and fundamental mistake, to suppose that the principal object in jails is the reformation of the offender."[41] Suddenly for Smith the enemy was no longer the administration but rather the proponents of naive reform. The energy of his essay shifted. The reformers, he feared, were fundamentally misguided about what a prison was for. "A jail," he wrote, "should be a place of punishment, from which men recoil with horror – a place of real suffering, painful to the memory, terrible to the imagination." He was frightened of the vision offered by the reformers of orderly workshops, healthy and well-fed prisoners, the mood of quiet contentment that suffused the institution. If prisons were places of luxury and ease, it was no wonder that offenders faced the prospect of returning to them with so little anxiety. In a witty aside he warned that under current conditions people were more likely to break into rather than out of prison. Smith attacked the Bury gaol, which had won Buxton's praise. "We have no doubt," he wrote, "it is well meant; but is it punishment?" "The first object," he argued, "should be, the discomfort and discontent of their prisoners; that they should become a warning, feel unhappy, and resolve never to act so again as to put themselves in the same predicament." Only after this goal had been achieved should society think about the reformation of the offender. And he could not hide his doubts that such an outcome was possible.[42] In this bold and decisive fashion Smith summoned up a new dimension to the prison debates, though one that had operated just below the surface in earlier plans to reform prisoners but seldom found such bald expression. Even as he supported the general goal of transforming penal establishments, he announced that more effective retribution was a legitimate object of reform. Earlier proponents of reform argued that it necessarily included the project of reforming offenders and that an appropriate system was the way to bring it about. Smith challenged this equation and proposed that system could serve another end, one more retributive in spirit, though he insisted it might still be called reform.

It is hard to exaggerate the importance of this development. Smith's sarcasm scored points off the advocates of the reformation of offenders. And one figure, that of Elizabeth Fry, attracted his particular attention. Fry's stature by 1820 rivalled that of Howard. The single most dramatic action that played through this decade, one that echoed the earlier conduct of Howard, was the decision of Elizabeth Fry to visit the female side of Newgate to minister to those confined there. Fry initially entered the prison in 1813, but more publicity greeted her return to the place in 1816. This act became a symbol whose significance exceeded the limits of time and place. Fry became a celebrity. The rich and powerful rushed to the prison to watch her speak to the prisoners. Where Howard had visited the prison to expose evils, Fry went in order to bring in what she saw as a healing influence. Hers was a more sharply defined example of how personal piety could touch and transform the fallen. The power she sought to exercise over the prisoners was illustrative of how social institutions and personal charity should work together to reduce social friction and class distance.[43] Newspapers amply covered her endeavours, with stories from the London press repeated widely in the provincial papers. The *Royal Cornwall Gazette*, for instance, in 1819, wrote approvingly of Fry's impact upon the female offenders. It described in moving terms how she addressed them as friends, read them the Bible, and brought them comfort and encouragement. She spoke of a different kind of system. "I have nothing that ought to astonish you," she explained to one well-wisher: "I have no other merit than that of having hazarded a moral experiment, which was indeed new – of having tried the influences of a system of mildness and kindness on souls quite strange to these impressions."[44] Here were the notes she struck time and again when she talked about what a prison should be. She upheld a model of a prison regime built upon personal influence. "I believe," she wrote, "kindness does more in turning them from the error of their ways than harsh treatment, and that many a poor creature claims a compassion and a tenderness that is little known, but to those who visit prisons."[45] What Fry offered was less a program than a narrative of reform. It highlighted the pitiable state of the prisoners while detailing the gift of kindness and comfort the philanthropic visitor brought to them. It represented the utopian ideal for how the prison might create relationships that could transform society. The spirit of benevolence, Fry's actions suggested, could mitigate and redeem the operation of regulation required to make an effective penal regime. "The story, we think," wrote Jeffrey, "is as affecting as it is instructive; and unites, in our estimation, the pathetic and the marvellous of the boldest work of fancy, with the sanctity of truth, and the utility of a great moral lesson."[46]

Smith would have none of it. Fry was deeply and dangerously misguided. "Mrs. Fry," he charged, "is an amiable excellent woman, and ten thousand times better than the infamous neglect that preceded her." "But hers is not the method to stop crimes." He doubted all talk of "sudden conversions." He attacked her proposed regime of mildness and sympathy. He cried out for rigour instead. "In prisons which are really meant to keep the multitude in order, and to be a terror to evil doers, there must be no sharing of profits – no visiting of friends – no education but religious education – no freedom of diet – no weavers' looms or carpenters' benches. There must be a great deal of solitude; coarse food; a dress of shame; hard, incessant, irksome, eternal labour; a planned and regulated and unrelenting exclusion of happiness and comfort."[47] As this passage shows, Smith was in no doubt about what features should characterize a proper prison regime. Indeed, Smith had little trouble in proposing the correct way to run a prison. It was less a matter of discovering new practices than of reversing the way in which one described the effect of measures the reformers themselves had proposed. "We would," he wrote, "in most cases, give as much of solitary confinement as would not injure men's minds, and as much of bread and water diet as would not injure their bodies. A return to prison should be contemplated with horror – horror, not excited by the ancient filth, disease, and extortion of jails; but calm, well-regulated, well-watched austerity." The mistake, according to Smith, made by the reformers was the tale they told of punishment and its conclusion. "Our general system then is," he explained, "that a prison should be a place of real punishment; but of known, enacted, measurable, and measured punishment." "A prison," he concluded soberly, "must be a prison."[48] Fry served for Smith much as Bentham had for Holford, as the practice too far, the system too impractical, the goal that was offensive to the desire for retribution. The rejection of Fry marked as important a moment as the earlier dismissal of Bentham had. It was a moment when the vision of the prison narrowed decisively.

Other journals took up Smith's complaint about "soft" prisons. An essayist in the *Quarterly Review*, the Tory rival to the *Edinburgh Review*, argued that the primary task of the prison was "to be a place of terror to those without, of punishment to those within." "Let us reform criminals if we can," the author added; "it is a great and glorious object, uncertain in the result, but imperative in the obligation." Still, he concluded, "punishment … is certain."[49] Once again the author contended that the desirable features of punishment included regulation, control, inspection, humanity but only as a modest limit on austerity, suffering but not pain. Yet there was no more unanimity among those who argued for severity than among reformers. Smith had made Holford, the chief defender of Millbank, one of his chief targets in complaining of the wrong principles at work in prisons. The reviewer for the *Quarterly*, by contrast, found more to admire in the place. "There is no appearance of severity," he wrote, "none of merely compulsory discipline; at the same time the prison is not made a place of ease and comfort; every thing is done in the first instance to make the individual feel that he has degraded himself in society, and that he must go through suffering and restraint before he can rise to his former level." "Hope of restoration," he added, was "never withheld from him."[50] Smith and the author in the *Quarterly* shared a great deal in their ambition for punishment. Yet their divergence over Millbank demonstrated how suddenly they could come to verbal blows over the differences.[51]

Even as the journals offered a glimpse of what the politics of the prison might look like, they also exposed how confusing the positions could become. The contradictions, however, far from discrediting the entire idea of the autonomy of the penal field, more deeply entrenched the notion. The advocates of penal reform, most famously, differed sharply over the necessity and character of labour for prisoners. "We all agree," Holford wrote, "in the advantage of their being employed, but we do not concur in the mode of effecting that object, or in the sacrifice to be made for its attainment."[52] By the second decade of the century work had replaced solitude as the subject that inspired the most intense debate. Disagreements could be stark and bitter. Holford took issue with Buxton's argument that prisoners should be paid for their work, and should be free to use a portion of that money for their immediate needs. Buxton, Holford charged, "is mistaken in supposing that to produce cheerful industry is the object of imprisonment." Holford applauded the advocates of the penitentiary who "contemplated for this purpose" ("the creation of a better disposition in the criminal") "an establishment of a sterner aspect, and of a more severe character than a manufactory." It was to take "a low tone in morals, to measure the amendment of the heart by the amount or value of the work produced by the hands." There were too many "occasions on which work, which is to produce profit, will run counter to discipline and moral improvement."[53] The ironic result of his conclusion was that Holford became an advocate of hard labour so that the principles of the "manufactory" did not invade and corrupt the prison. He came to endorse a position not far removed from that adopted by sceptics like Sydney Smith and C.C. Western, despite the fact that both men heaped scorn on his plans for using religious influences to reform offenders. "In short," Holford concluded, "prisons should be considered as places of punishment, and not as scenes of cheerful industry."[54] Western, by contrast, desired punishment to be retributive, but he opposed extended solitude, except for "refractory conduct," as a punishment too cruel for general use. He was a strong proponent of "hard labour," not for profit or to educate the offender, but simply to make punishment feared. He was convinced that "nothing ever was contrived so admirably adopted to the application of corrective labour, as the tread-wheel."[55]

Here is the kind of debate over the direction of confinement that we so often encounter during this decade. They argued about the same short list of penal expedients, though they differed in how they characterized their operation and outcome. Each side accused the other of being the greater dupe, the one in believing the pious hypocrisy of the old offender, the other in mistaking simple industry for monetary reward as true reformation. They circled around each other, each insisting on the absolute correctness of a particular scheme for dealing with offenders. What went unquestioned was the fundamental conviction that a prison properly organized and run would secure the desired goal. The Quaker J.J. Gurney, after setting forth his program for penal reform, expressed his conviction that "a prison so built and so regulated, would indeed fulfill the ends designed for it."[56] From a quite different direction, Western wrote that he was "more and more convinced of the advantages to be derived from the adoption of a good system of prison discipline."[57] This conviction was untroubled by the evidence of inconsistency. Rather there was a tendency for the various schemes to converge, using the idea of distinct stages as a way to accommodate opposed practices. One author who applauded Western's pamphlet yet wondered "why, in the quaint and whimsical language of the [*Edinburgh*] *Reviewer*, the tread-wheel and Mrs. Fry should not go on together."[58] The proponents of labour accepted that a brief spell of solitary confinement might be useful, even as they warned against being duped by the claims of reformation. The advocates of isolation granted the value of work, though they fought against making this central to the organization of the prison. What they all focused on was what the prisoner confined in a cell deserved or needed, and on how a properly constructed prison regime might address this requirement.[59]

4

The fate of Romilly's proposal to revive the Penitentiary Act of 1779 illustrates the peculiar status of the prison question during the second decade of the nineteenth century. His initiative failed as a manoeuvre to advance the cause of criminal law reform precisely because the prison did not inspire the same political passions as the gallows. Rather, the debate over his motion, brief as it was, demonstrated how little opposition there was in the political nation to the idea that penal administration stood in need of decisive reform. Indeed, what is striking about the discussions in this period is how widely shared was the conviction that confinement should be remodelled and that the general principles to guide this reform were well understood. It was the potential for this space that captivated the attention of politicians and the public. "The more the subject is considered," wrote Western, "the more apparent will be the practicability of establishing a system of prison discipline so effective, and at the same time so justly humane, that it shall realize all the benefits we can rationally expect to derive from the infliction of any punishment."[60] Yet as public debate broadened through pamphlets, newspaper coverage, and lengthy essays in major journals, new political lines formed around a debate over system. The prison question might appear apolitical in relation to traditional political divisions, but this did not mean it was an issue without politics. It spawned a different politics, as we have seen, one that only imperfectly overlapped with more familiar political lines. This debate would provide much of the drama over the course of penal change for the next several decades. It centred on the question of what the prisoner deserved. As the controversies unfolded, they suggested that there were real differences of opinion about what should or could be done to or for offenders. Yet these disputes never undermined belief in the prison as the appropriate and necessary location for dealing with the law-breaker.

One of the great challenges in the existing scholarship on the "rise" of the prison has been to account for the place of humanitarian reform in the development of this penal institution. It is precisely in this period that we see the challenge so clearly. As we have seen, there was no real opposition to penal reform. Rather there was an intense debate over how best to achieve the goal. The participants accepted the necessity of confinement, that a prison was the proper place to confine criminals; it was the natural and inevitable institution for dealing with crime. An enthusiastic reviewer of Buxton's pamphlet for *The Philanthropist*, in 1818, well expressed this conviction. Whenever it was shown, he announced, that "crime and misery" were produced by "our social or political institutions," no moment should be lost "in doing whatever is necessary to be done to effect a change." He thought Buxton had produced a devastating case for the failure of current penal policy. The solution was clear. He presented one set of facts "which prove the production of crime and misery within the walls of our horrid prisons," and another set "which prove that crime and misery may be prevented within the walls of prisons, when they are conducted upon principles of humanity and wisdom."[61] Sydney Smith did not disagree. During this turbulent decade, dominated by reaction and repression, penal reform advanced because it appeared to reconcile opposing ambitions. What the prison offered was containment. This was the reassuring idea that made it possible for the prison to excite both those who advocated the reformation of offenders and those who saw the need for greater severity. Some might see the prison as an opportunity to remodel social relations; others saw it as an important instrument for overawing a turbulent population. The prison promised order even as the debate around its constitution spoke of different visions of how that order was to be secured. The walls, however, were not neutral. They weighed upon the debate and the imagination. If they sustained hope, they more often aroused fear. The prison walls constituted the moment when the realm of possibility collided with the zone of necessity. This collision could not be an even contest. The weight of the walls and the spectre of what they contained produced a feeling of unease that inclined politicians and the public to more sombre thoughts of what a prison must be.

NOTES

1 Robin Evans, *The Fabrication of Virtue: English Prison Architecture, 1759–1840* (Cambridge, 1982), 239, 249, 94; Michael Ignatieff, *A Just Measure of Pain: The Penitentiary in the Industrial Revolution 1750–1850* (London, 1989), esp. chap. 6; David Eastwood, *Governing Rural England* (Oxford, 1994), 244–50; Margaret DeLacy, *Prison Reform in Lancashire, 1700–1850* (Stanford, 1986), 66–9; J.M. Beattie, *Crime and the Courts in England, 1660–1800* (Princeton, 1986), 556–7, 563, 601, 606; Peter King, *Crime, Justice and Discretion in England, 1740–1820* (Cambridge, 2000), 266–72.

2 As Romilly famously noted in his journal in 1808: "If any person be desirous of having an adequate idea of the mischievous effects which have been produced in this country by the French Revolution and all its attendant horrors, he should attempt some legislative reform, on humane and liberal principles. He will then find, not only what a stupid dread of innovation, but what a savage spirit it has infused into the minds of many of his countrymen." *Memoirs of the Life of Sir Samuel Romilly* (London, 1840; reprint, Shannon, 1971), 2: 253.

3 "Gurney's Notes on Prisons," *The Philanthropist* 27 (1819): 345; Evans, *Fabrication*, 239, 249; Ignatieff, *A Just Measure*, esp. chap. 6.

4 *Monthly Review* 89 (1819): 200.

5 "Prisons and Penitentiaries," *Quarterly Review* 30 (1823–4): 425, 440.

6 For a valuable discussion of the history of the word "reform" in this period, see Joanna Innes, "'Reform' in English Public Life: The Fortunes of a Word," in Arthur Burns and Joanna Innes, eds, *Rethinking the Age of Reform* (Cambridge, 2003), 71–97. For a slightly different perspective, see my "Cruel Inflictions and the Claims of Humanity in Early Nineteenth-Century England," in Katherine D. Watson, ed., *Assaulting the Past: Violence and Civilization in Historical Context* (Newcastle, 2007), 38–57.

7 For a parallel effort to trace the displacements and misrecognitions that formed a crucial aspect of the development of the prison, see Michael Meranze, *Laboratories of Virtue: Punishment, Revolution, and Authority in Philadelphia, 1760–1835* (Chapel Hill, 1996), 12–16.

8 See my "The Image of Justice and Reform of the Criminal Law in Early Nineteenth-Century England," *Buffalo Law Review* 32 (1983): 89–125; A.D. Harvey, *Britain in the Early Nineteenth Century* (New York, 1978), 264–84.

9 Romilly, *Memoirs*, 2: 289, 309–10, 324, 325–6.

10 "Nield on Prisons," *Edinburgh Review* 22 (1814): 388. See the long essay on Howard which was serialized in *The Philanthropist* starting in 1812. When H.G. Bennet published a pamphlet that sought to expose the failings of Newgate, he began with the description Howard offered of the prison several decades earlier. H.G. Bennet, "A Letter on the Abuses Existing in Newgate," *Pamphleteer* 11 (1818): 279. Most authors, in introducing the subject of penal reform, usually began with Howard, all lauding his actions. See "Prisons," *Quarterly Review* 30 (1824): 425–7. These portraits "omitted all sense of ambiguity" in describing his activities, and overstated his originality and uniqueness. Evans, *Fabrication*, 93, and more generally 91–3; Ignatieff, *Just Measure*, 47–60; Eastwood, *Governing*, 244–50; Sean McConville, *A History of English Prison Administration* (London, 1981), 88–98; DeLacy, *Prison Reform*, 18–19; Robert Alan Cooper, "Ideas and Their Execution: English Prison Reform," *Eighteenth-Century Studies* 10 (1976): 73–93.

11 *Parliamentary Debates*, 1810, 16: 944–6; *PD*, 1810, 17: 322–3; Beattie, *Crime and the Courts*, 573–6; Evans, *Fabrication*, 119–21.

12 The penal philosophy to which Romilly appealed in May was so general as to inspire little controversy. The purpose of punishment, he explained, was "the prevention of crimes." It had three facets: "the principle of the first was, that the punishment should operate in the way of terror." The second goal was to put it out of the power of the person offending to commit crimes in the future, either for the term of the sentence or forever. The third principle was "the reformation of the offending party." "This third mode," he suggested, "had been much neglected of late years." This bland statement of general principles scarcely sounded like a clarion call to a fresh wave of penal reform. *PD*, 1810, 16: 944.

13 *PD*, 1810, 16: 944–6. There is an irony in the fact that Romilly proposed the Penitentiary Act as a corrective for the policy of transportation, since, as Simon Devereaux has shown, that act made room for the return to transportation. "The Making of the Penitentiary Act, 1775–1779," *The Historical Journal* 42 (1999): 405–33.

14 *PD*, 1810, 16: 947–50.

15 *PD*, 1810, 17: 340–1, 331–2.

16 For Tory views on criminal justice reform, see my "Image of Justice," particularly 101–5. William Windham, in challenging Romilly's initiatives, said "he could not help looking with an eye of jealousy on all such visionary schemes, which had humanity and justice for their ostensible causes. What had we witnessed within the last twenty years? Had not the French Revolution begun with the abolition of capital punishments in every case; but not till they had sacrificed their sovereign, whom they had thus made the grand finale to this species of punishment." *PD*, 1810, 16:768.

17 *PD*, 1810, 17: 333.

18 Preoccupied as he was with criminal law reform, and giving more of his time to a committee on reform of the Court of Chancery, Romilly noted in his journal that he would "not be able to attend it [the penitentiary committee], or at least very rarely." *Memoirs*, 2: 289, 373, 400.

19 Janet Semple, *Bentham's Prison* (Oxford, 1993), 265–6.

20 *Parliamentary Papers*, 1810–11, 3: 3–4, 8.

21 Romilly, in his speech advancing his motion, mentioned both Paul and Becher favourably. *PD*, 1810, 17: 324. The committee also interviewed John Addison Newman, the keeper of Newgate, in order to present a brief survey of the widely acknowledged evils to be found there. The interview with Newman was perfunctory. Far from defending his prison, he admitted that there was too much association, that the picking of pockets went on without hindrance, and that liquor was smuggled into the prison. He offered no hint that anyone's morals or conduct was improved by a term there. *PP*, 1810–11, 3: 50–3.

22 E.A.L. Moir, "Sir George Onesiphorous Paul," in H.P. Finberg, ed., *Gloucestershire Studies* (Leicester, 1957), 205–8; J.R.S. Whiting, *Prison Reform in Gloucestershire 1776–1820* (London, 1975), 6–12. Paul was proud of his achievement. "Whilst I acknowledge," he told the committee, "regarding the whole of the system of imprisonment, that (like other ardent theorists) I imagined more than has been done, or than perhaps could be brought into practice and effect, I am sure I am justified in saying that the Penitentiary House has succeeded in its effect beyond the theory imagined by the original projectors of the system." *PP*, 1810–11, 3: 29.

23 George Holford, "Thoughts on Criminal Prisons," *Pamphleteer* 18 (1821): 157. Another committee member, William Morton Pitt, had made a similar point in 1804. "All places of confinement for offenders should be governed according to one general and uniform system." *A Plan for the Improvement of the Internal Police of Prisons* (London, 1804), 3.

24 *PP*, 1810–11, 3: 43.

25 Ibid., 25.
26 Ibid., 33–9.
27 Semple, *Bentham's Prison*, 267–78. Romilly raised the issue of economy in his defence of Bentham in 1812. *PD*, 1812, 21: 238.
28 *PP*, 1810–11, 3: 14, 16, 78–9.
29 Ibid., 19.
30 PD 1812, xxi, 236.
31 It confirmed the historical narrative of penal reform of which it was part by offering physical reminders of what it replaced: shackles, iron rings, and heavy locks. At Millbank "an empty cell festooned with these useless chains was set aside as a museum of vanished practices." Evans, *Fabrication*, 255, 260.
32 McConville describes this expansion of government responsibility as "novel and radical." *History*, 131–4.
33 "Prisons," *Quarterly Review* 30 (1823–4), 354.
34 "I contend," H.G. Bennet wrote in 1818, "that the reformatory system is alone that which ought to be pursued." "On the Abuses Existing in Newgate," *Pamphleteer* 11 (1818): 304.
35 *Life of William Allen* (Philadelphia, 1847), 1: 264–7.
36 Francis Jeffrey, "Prison Discipline," *Edinburgh Review* 30 (1818): 463–4.
37 Ibid., 464. Jeffrey, even as he set forth his argument for the apolitical character of penal reform, could not resist taking a jab at the current administration for its neglect of prisons. The Quaker and Evangelical penal reformers had their own reasons for accepting this portrait of humanitarian reform as non-partisan. On the importance of the *Edinburgh Review*, see William Anthony Hay, *The Whig Revival, 1808–1830* (Basingstoke, 2005), 49–51.
38 Ibid., 479.
39 *Thoughts on Prison Discipline* (London, 1822), 5.
40 Sydney Smith, "State of the Prisons," *Edinburgh Review* 35 (1821): 287.
41 Sydney Smith, "Prisons," *Edinburgh Review* 36 (1822): 354.
42 Smith, "State," 290, 293, 295. C.C. Western, by contrast, in a pamphlet quoted favourably by Smith, spoke approvingly of the Bury gaol. Western too was a Whig, one who could speak highly of Buxton and Fry, even as he differed from them in his penal philosophy. C.C. Western, *Remarks upon Prison Discipline* (London, 1821), 19, 22–5, 100.
43 Ignatieff offers a vivid description of the episode and a portrait of the wider Quaker penal reform effort. It was an even more intense experience than that which Buxton and Allen promoted at the Spitalfields soup kitchen during these years. *Just Measure*, 143–67. See also *Memoirs of the Life of Elizabeth Fry* (Philadelphia, 1847), 1: 234, 284.

44 "Account of Mrs. Fry," *Royal Cornwall Gazette*, 30 January 1819; Jeffrey, "Prisons," 479–84.

45 *Life of Fry*, 1: 477–8. See my "A Powerful Sympathy: Terror, the Prison, and Humanitarian Reform in Early Nineteenth-Century Britain," *Journal of British Studies* 25 (1986): 312–34.

46 Jeffrey, "Prison," 479.

47 Smith, "Prisons," 374, 356.

48 Smith, "State," 292, 300, 297.

49 "Prisons," *Quarterly Review*, 410.

50 Ibid., 430.

51 Much the same occurred in the debate over Romilly's proposal in 1810. Both Whitbread and Wilberforce supported the motion. Yet Whitbread's sharpest words were directed not at the government but at Wilberforce, who had spoken favourably of the principle of solitude in prisons. Whitbread, speaking as a representative of the growing disenchantment with the practice, condemned solitude as inhumane. Romilly joined him on this point. *PD*, 1810, 17: 346–47, 350.

52 Holford, "Thoughts," 169.

53 Ibid., 170–1, 176. Holford complained about "the shafts of ridicule" that had been directed at him by people like Smith. George Holford, *A Short Vindication of the General Penitentiary at Millbank* (London, 1822), 11.

54 Holford, "Thoughts," 184. The *Quarterly Review* applauded Holford for his rejection of "mere employment." "Prisons," 417–20.

55 Western, *Remarks*, 26, 59–61. It was left to a reviewer for *Westminster Review*, in 1825, to complain that "the fashionable punishment of the day is that of hard labour; and there is scarcely any subject upon which a more lamentable confusion of ideas may be seen to exist." "Prisons and Prison Discipline," *Westminster Review* 3 (1825): 421, 429.

56 Gurney, "Gurney's Notes," 119.

57 Western, *Remarks*, 42.

58 *Thoughts on Prison Discipline*, 6.

59 Buxton offers us a good example of this melding of different practices. *An Inquiry Whether Crime and Misery are Produced or Prevented by our Present System of Prison Discipline (London, 1818)*, 11–16, 115.

60 Western, *Remarks*, 58–9. Significantly, he added that only "mistaken humanity, and fear of expense" stood in the way.

61 "Buxton's Inquiry into Our System of Prison Discipline," *The Philanthropist* 7 (1819): 194–5. For a discussion of the prison as a "site of utopian hopes and social fears," see Meranze, *Laboratories*, 4–9, and chapter 8. For a meditation on the paradoxes of penal reform, see Evans, *Fabrication*, 417–20.

chapter nine

When the Atlantic Went Global: A Note on Slavery and Rebellion in Fletcher Christian's Pitcairn*

EDWARD G. GRAY

It was the subject of short stories by Mark Twain and Jack London. The nineteenth-century American poet and newspaper editor William Cullen Bryant imagined its women who "for my dusky brow will braid / A bonnet like an English maid." And from its first discovery in 1808 to the end of the nineteenth century, stories of its extraordinary history and culture made their way into literally hundreds of American and British magazines and newspapers. So commonplace had it become that by 1840, the *New-York Spectator* could begin a story with the following line: "Who has not heard of Pitcairn's Island, in the Pacific Ocean – the solitary spot which Fletcher Christian, at the head of the mutineers of the *Bounty*, and their tawny wives, selected as an asylum and planted a colony?"[1]

One might well conclude that never has a smaller, more remote speck of land figured more prominently in Anglo-American consciousness. Pitcairn Island is approximately two square miles in breadth and it lies roughly halfway between Easter Island and Tahiti. It is now occasionally passed by freighters sailing from Panama to Auckland. The island lies near the passage's mid-point – between three and four thousand miles from its two end points. The closest inhabited islands are at the far south-eastern end of what is now French Polynesia (known as the Gambier Islands), approximately 330 miles to the West-North-West. During the more than forty years after it was first seen and named by the British explorer Philip Carteret (who named the island after Robert Pitcairn, the fifteen-year-old midshipman who had sighted it), Pitcairn did not exist at all. For Carteret placed the island approximately 180 miles west of its actual location. Only after 1808, when the Boston sealer *Topaz* stumbled on Pitcairn, would its true location be known.[2]

The fact that for more than four decades, the island was not where the charts placed it would have been of little moment had not the inhabitants achieved for themselves such notoriety. For the people living on the island in the year the *Topaz* arrived were not descendents of Polynesian mariners – such as one found elsewhere across the South Pacific archipelago, on islands as far east as Rapa Nui (Easter Island) and as far north as the Hawaiian Islands. They were, instead, the kin of a band of criminals, mutineers who, in 1789, had commandeered the *H.M.S. Bounty*, taken Tahitian wives, and then sought sanctuary in one of the world's remotest places. Except for a lone survivor, an elderly seafarer who changed his name from Alexander Smith to John Adams, the mutineers were all dead. What the crew of the *Topaz* found instead were the wives and children of these renegades. There were some thirty-five of them in total.

The mixed-race colony at Pitcairn has been the subject of several contemporary scholarly treatments, but little of this work has attracted the attention of students of the Revolutionary Atlantic.[3] In some sense, the reasons for this are quite obvious. The Pacific is not the Atlantic. The processes that account for Europe's Pacific empire differed sharply from those of the revolutionary Atlantic. At the time Pitcairn was colonized, European empire in the south-eastern Pacific basin amounted to little more than a tiny penal colony at Botany Bay. Although Spanish treasure galleons had been traversing the Pacific for more than two hundred years, nothing like the Atlantic triangle trade drew together the Pacific littoral. There was no trans-Pacific slave trade; and there were neither wayward colonials nor large concentrations of lettered cosmopolitans to disseminate and consume radical, revolutionary ideology. One could go on in this vain. The sheer scope of the Pacific – roughly double that of the Atlantic – made substantial European intrusions impossible for much of the early age of sail. Although the Spanish were able to move New World silver and spices, teas, porcelain, silks, and other trade goods between Acapulco and Manila, and although English navigators periodically traversed the Pacific before the latter decades of the eighteenth century, these were exceptions. The challenges of maintaining sufficient stores and fending off scurvy and other nutritional ailments during the months required to traverse the world's largest oceanic space made most trans-Pacific trade impossible. The enormous size of the treasure galleons (as much as 2000 tons, as opposed to three or four hundred tons more typical of ships in the Atlantic trade), the depth of ports at Manila and Acapulco, and the profit margins generated by Asian trade goods, account for the single principal exception. But in general, Europeans made virtually no progress in Pacific navigation until the second half of the eighteenth century. The results of this are plain: as the Seven Years' War came to an end in 1763, European empire in the Pacific looked little different than it had in 1563.[4]

This is not the place to recite the full story of Europe's turn to the Pacific, but it is worth observing that the age of Atlantic revolution corresponded almost in lockstep with that turn. Beginning with the first voyage of Captain James Cook (1768–71) and culminating in the establishment of the Botany Bay Colony in 1789 and the explosive expansion of New England's trans-Pacific trade after 1785, the Pacific basin came to be the newest frontier in European and American empire. For students of the Revolutionary Atlantic, the development is instructive in a number of ways. One might begin by simply observing that much of what happened in the Pacific in these years was driven directly by events in the European Atlantic. Cook's voyages would likely have lacked the necessary political and military support were it not for the acute sense among British policymakers that France would seek to counter its losses in the Seven Years' War with imperial gains elsewhere. Similarly, the Botany Bay colony cannot be separated from events in the Revolutionary Atlantic. Though historians of Australia's founding continue to debate the relative importance of these factors, it is quite clear that both geopolitical and domestic concerns had a role in the colony's beginning. On the one hand, France's putative victory and Britain's loss in the American War only raised the stakes for European empire in the Pacific. If France's gains were to be countered abroad, Britain would need in the Pacific the kinds of deep-water ports and stores-producing settlements that had sustained its Atlantic empire. Similarly, the overcrowding in English prisons and the proliferation of prison hulks combined with the loss of what had been the principal colonial destination of British convict labour fed the impulse to find alternative destinations for British transports.[5]

Finally, and most centrally for the purposes of this chapter, the voyage of the *H.M.S. Bounty* was a direct function of events in the revolutionary Atlantic. The *Bounty* was en route from Tahiti to the West Indies when she was seized in mutiny. The purpose of that voyage had been to bring Tahitian breadfruit saplings to the West Indies, where the abundant fruit of the mature trees could be used to feed the enslaved labour force that toiled in Britain's sugar colonies. Since British mariners had first feasted on the fruit earlier in the century, West Indies plantation owners and their lobbyists, along with a dedicated corps of imperial-minded botanists in England and the Caribbean, had seen in it a potential alternative food source for the island colonies. That such a commodity was needed became apparent during and after the American War for Independence, when markets on the former colonial mainland – supplying flour, bread, livestock, rice, and other staples to the West Indies colonies – became less accessible and after a series of devastating hurricanes confirmed the profound vulnerability of existing island food crops. The prospect that French planters in Guadalupe and Saint-Domingue would be better able to supply their plantations with produce from what was now Spanish West Florida and Louisiana presented British policymakers with the kind of commercial and strategic problem that had animated so much policy over the course of the eighteenth century. With the vital encouragement of the West India lobby and Sir Joseph Banks, president of the Royal Society and director of the king's gardens at Kew, the Crown thus ordered the Admiralty to commission a botanical expedition to transport breadfruit saplings from Polynesia to the West Indies.[6]

The larger point here is simply that as far as Great Britain was concerned, there was no separating the Atlantic from the Pacific. The two represented increasingly intertwined arenas of imperial competition as Europe's great powers jockeyed for primacy. The American War served to accelerate and solidify conduct that had begun a decade earlier with the conclusion of the Seven Years' War. To put it in somewhat different terms, it might well be said that insofar as the processes that defined Europe's Atlantic expansion in the early-modern era became global, they did so as a direct result of the American Revolutionary War. Atlantic Revolution and Pacific empire were in a very real sense indistinct.

If students of the Revolutionary Atlantic have been understandably slow to assimilate the Pacific dimensions of their subject, Pacific historians have – understandably – long recognized the global nature of eighteenth-century empire. But it must be said that even they have only just recently begun to explore the full geographic and topical scope of what we might call the "globalizing Atlantic." While scholars have amply demonstrated the imperial interrelatedness of the late eighteenth-century Atlantic and Pacific, dimensions of that interrelatedness remain to be explored. Nothing has been more emblematic of the Atlantic – indeed, no institution has done more to define the field of Atlantic studies – than American chattel slavery. Similarly, few aspects of Atlantic slavery have appeared more distinctive and more consistent with the political and social disorder that swept across the Atlantic basin at the end of the eighteenth century than slave rebellions – the most revolutionary of which occurring in Saint-Domingue in 1791. The absence of the large-scale enslavement, forced migration, and rebellion characteristic of Atlantic slavery in the eighteenth century would thus seem to represent the end of the story for the globalized Atlantic. Simply put, the defining labour system of the early modern Atlantic did not exist in the eighteenth-century Pacific.

And yet it is very clear that, contrary to what the great bulk of the scholarship might suggest, Atlantic slavery and Pacific empire were in fact intertwined. As the work of Cassandra Pybus and Emma Christopher has begun to show in great detail, the Botany Bay colony had many connections to Atlantic slavery, not the least of which was the fact that the so-called Second Fleet, which arrived in Sydney harbour in 1790 was contracted to a British firm whose primary business had been the transatlantic slave trade. For the convict passengers, the results were, predictably, not entirely unlike that of the notorious middle passage. Similarly, although the colony's governor, Captain Arthur Phillip, was opposed to slavery and had envisioned a penal colony free of slavery, the disciplinary regime of the colony very quickly imposed a contrary order. As Pybus has written, "Six months into his governorship it could not have possibly escaped him that his outpost of empire bore many of the hallmarks of a slave plantation."[7]

Following the work of Pybus and Christopher, what follows is an effort to further illuminate the relationship between patterns of slavery in the eighteenth-century Atlantic and Pacific. The story of Pitcairn is, of course, very different from that of the Botany Bay colony. But it does suggest a second vector through which aspects of the defining labour system of the revolutionary Atlantic shaped colonial experience in the newly colonized South Pacific. It also offers an opportunity to consider the arrival in the South Pacific of another aspect of Atlantic slavery: rebellion and revolt. For at the centre of the Pitcairn story was what can only be described as a slave revolt. To tell the story of Pitcairn, bound labour, and revolt is not easy. Like nearly all instances of slave rebellion in the Atlantic, the documentary record of the Pitcairn case is slight – perhaps even more slight than its Atlantic counterparts.[8] Part of the problem, as I will suggest in the first part of this paper, is that the full story of Pitcairn was enshrouded by a nineteenth-century imperial mythos. Even in the twentieth century, despite countless popular treatments in fiction and film, the full story of the Pitcairn Island colony was rarely told and little recognized. Only by understanding just how the Pitcairn story grew detached from the cruel realities of the colony's actual beginnings, can we begin to fully grasp the continuities between Atlantic empire and its Pacific counterpart in the age of Revolution.[9]

Almost as soon as news of the *Topaz*'s discovery crept across the printed page, the reading public saw a mixed-race colony that was, by all accounts, a picture of tropical harmony. Its people were neither "black" (as English and American writers typically characterized native Polynesians) nor white; they spoke the English language and believed in a Christian God. They also seemed to have assimilated the racial attitudes of their forebears. Far from self-identifying as "black," they seemed openly hostile to dark-skinned peoples. In an account by British Marine Lieutenant John Shillibeer, whose ship the *Briton* visited Pitcairn in 1814, Friday Fletcher October Christian, son of mutiny leader Fletcher Christian, who dined aboard the ship, became alarmed by the site of a West Indian servant. "The hatred of these people to the blacks is strongly rooted," Shillibeer wrote, "to illustrate which I shall here relate an occurrence which took place at breakfast. Soon after young Christian had began, a West Indian Black, who was one of the servants, entered the gunroom to attend table as usual. Christian looked at him sternly, rose, asked for his hat, and said, 'I don't like that black fellow, I must go,' and it required some little persuasion before he would again resume his seat."[10]

What most struck observers, however, was less the Anglo-European character of the Pitcairners than the simple fact that they seemed to live in perfect harmony with each other and their fecund surroundings. Drawing on the unpublished accounts of Mayhew Folger, captain of the *Topaz*, and several British naval officers whose ships had subsequently come upon the island, the editors of the London literary magazine *Quarterly Review* published an account of Pitcairn society in 1815 whose essential outlines would remain unchallenged for most of the century:

> The greatest harmony prevailed in this little society; their only quarrels, and those rarely happened, being, according to their own expression, *quarrels of the mouth*: they are honest in their dealings, which consist of bartering different articles for mutual accommodation ... But what was most gratifying of all to the visitors was the simple and unaffected manner in which they returned thanks to the Almighty for the many blessings they enjoyed. They never failed to say grace before and after meals, to pray every morning at sun-rise.

Here were no swearing, perfidious, and irreligious children of pirates and mutineers, but rather the perfectly industrious and incorrupt products of nature and Christianity. Who better, the *Quarterly* editors wondered, to extend British empire throughout Polynesia?: "The descendants of these people, by keeping up the Otaheitan language, which the present race speak fluently, might be the means of civilizing the multitudes of fine people scattered over the innumerable islands of the Great Pacific."[11]

Virtually every discussion of Pitcairn to appear in print in nineteenth-century America and Britain echoed these perceptions, adding to them further utopian traits, depending on editorial predilections. To the evangelical press, it was the intense religiosity of the islanders that captivated. Although Pitcairn was settled by mutineers, "in 1827 it is probably the spot where, of all on earth, an angel would soonest fix his residence." Indeed, it was in "seeing these secluded islanders, so completely reformed, so conscientious, so attentive to the Sabbath and word of God, so happy in the performance of religious duties, and cherishing so much of the spirit of heaven, which more than anything else, brought home to the mind of Mr. S____, the reality and importance of religion."[12] For the naive islanders seemed able to do what no amount of missionizing could accomplish among the hard-bitten rabble of the sea. "We have seen it stated," reported one evangelical paper, "that a young man, a native of Nantucket, being asked by one of those [young islanders] to give an account of his religious experience, and having nothing to say, was so struck with the circumstances of being questioned by one whom he considered a heathen, and with the conviction of being more of a heathen himself, that he was led to a serious consideration of religious truth, and in consequence became a pious and good man. Two other instances have occurred, in which officers of vessels becoming hopefully pious, attributed it to what they witnessed at Pitcairn's Island, that they were induced to examine the object of religion."[13] "I have no doubt," observed a British naval chaplain in 1852, "these people are the most religious ... in the world."[14]

In the 1850s, the American abolitionist press turned to Pitcairn as an example of universal suffrage. In a distinct news item, the *Anti-Slavery Bugle* reported "the only place we know of where women vote is Pitcairn's Island. There all of both sexes over eighteen years of age annually cast ballots for magistrate. They are a very happy people. The women love each other, and there are no quarrels."[15]

In Great Britain, where the *Bounty* voyage originated, the ubiquity of the island's story is not surprising – the mutineers were, after all, Englishmen, their ship a British-flagged vessel, and the laws they broke, British laws. But there is another perhaps less obvious reason for Pitcairn's significance in early nineteenth-century Britain. As Britons debated the validity of Malthusianism, they turned to Pitcairn as an example of another economy whose productivity was limited by its island circumstance. On the Malthusian side, William Bridges Adams observed (largely erroneously, it turns out) that "the natives of Pitcairn's Island ... have at last bred beyond the extent of food which the island was capable of supplying; and have in consequence left it."[16] On the anti-Malthusian side, the radical Thomas Doubleday saw in Pitcairn a counter to the claims that cheap, high-quality food necessarily produced misery by affording population growth. In fact, "In Pitcairn's Island we discover ... proofs of a stride in population far exceeding the most extravagant ideas of the most extravagant advocates for [the Malthusian] reduplicating geometrical ratio. But then we find this accompanied with an absence of solid food, and with constant toil and exposure to the open air, and the vicissitudes of climate." Population, in other words, can grow exponentially even in the absence of commensurate improvements in the quality and quantity of food. Like a colony, "living amidst all the vicissitudes of an outlaw, often in total want of food, and probably never well supplied, the increase of these wretched beings seems to have been extraordinary."[17] Doubleday's perspective was the less common. For the most part, the Pitcairn of the British imagination was nothing like the wretched place he depicted. It was a paradise, but it was a paradise because of its government's role in population control. As an 1849 visitor recalled, "No strangers are allowed to live on the Island; they think the population is already sufficient for the resources of the place." The wife of an American whaling captain recalled that while her husband's ship was stopped near Pitcairn, three crewmen tried to find refuge from their labours on the island, but "all the men on the Island turn'd out and look'd till they found them." For the Pitcairners "will not have anyone stop here to stay, because the Island is so small that they think as the inhabitants increase that they will have to leave some of them and find and go some whare els to live."[18] The Pitcairners themselves seemed to embrace a sort of Malthusianism: as long as they avoided unnatural population growth, their resources would be adequate and their population would remain in check.

It is worth noting that this convergence of population economics and the far-distant Pacific archipelago was not simply a random instance of scientific exemplarity. The threat of population exceeding resources was, to some, precisely the justification the British Empire needed as it continued its thrust into the Pacific Rim. Consider the following justification for empire:

> It is a truism that a community like that which the mutineers of the *Bounty* founded on Pitcairn Island, cannot, if absolutely confined within its narrow limits, permanently increase its population beyond the material means of subsistence, furnished by the narrow extent of soil, and from which alone, without foreign intercourse, supplies could be drawn. In such a position, the principles of Malthus become living truths, which no rational being can refuse to acknowledge. A population thus confined cannot multiply beyond a point, limited by the ultimate quantity of producible food. But the British Empire has no such fixed limits; and I see no possible futurity before us, when the British home dominions are to be reduced to the condition of an over-populous Pitcairn Island.[19]

In other words, island people face a common danger: population will exceed finite resources. But imperial people face no such danger. As their population grows, they can do what Britain had been doing for most of the previous three hundred years: propel that surplus population outward to the colonial periphery. If they were Britons, then presumably the Pitcairners would employ the same imperial population management theory. Much like the founders of the Massachusetts Colony or the Virginia Colony, they would counter land shortages and overpopulation by forming new colonies of their own. Such thinking may have been central to centuries of imperial policy at Whitehall and in its far distant possessions. But in Pitcairn the thinking appears to have been different. Resources and population there would be kept in balance by a combination of isolationism and benevolent government.

The intimation that government on Pitcairn was uniquely enlightened was consistent with virtually all depictions of the island. In addition to their creation of universal adult franchise and an enlightened population policy, the islanders seemed to display a unique contentedness with their government. Whether in the person of John Adams or his successors, the chief magistrates seemed to govern in a most Christian manner – never too lax, never too harsh. The first officer on a Boston ship sailing from Canton reported that upon touching at Pitcairn in 1819, he observed that none of the Islanders had any desire to remove to America, for, they told him, “we have no king, nor lord, to obey here, and every one is his own master," although "we mind what Mr. Adams tells us, because he knows best. In truth, they live together in the greatest amity and brotherly love."[20] Elsewhere, it was observed that although Adams functioned as a sort of patriarch for the islanders, "the seeds of *Republicanism* are already visible among them." Upon his demise, Adams instructed his younger progeny that "it was desirable that some one should be fixed upon as a leader ... and he had accordingly selected his only son George for this office. This was not at all relished by the young people. They replied – 'No, father: we well obey you as long as you live, but when you are dead we are all alike. George is no greater than the rest of us.'"[21] By the late 1840s, a more elaborate governing structure appeared to have evolved, but it betrayed none of the potential pathologies of a government made in nature. There was no Hobbesian absolutist, keeping order on the island; nor some kind of roughshod democracy where the base interests of the many held sway over the ideals of the few. "Their form of government is simple: they elect a magistrate every twelve months, upon which occasion every man and woman above eighteen is entitled to vote in consequence. The magistrate then chooses an assistant, and the remainder of the people choose again another, who acts as a sort of check, which is, indeed, little wanted, for there is no place in the world where such perfect unanimity and good feeling exist as in this happy island."[22]

It was as if Brook Farm or New Harmony had come into being, not by the designs of some visionary overlord, but by the passive proletarian paternalism of the natural-born patriarch, John Adams. It was no wonder that, even with the looming problems of scarcity and overpopulation, the citizens of such a benign polity should be so resistant to change. Now, the New York *Weekly Herald* reported, on 28 May 1853, that "with limited means of subsistence on the island, and an increasing population, colonization, we should imagine would be resorted to. But the natives seem to possess an ingrained repugnance to leave their native isle for the wide, wide world: although they are not ignorant of the enticements of the gold regions of California and Australia." While the rest of the world seemed to be increasing its motions, groping ever further for profit and self-fulfilment, the Pitcairners remained quiet and content. It was an ominous circumstance. After all, the islanders' primitive simplicity left them dangerously exposed to the wiles of an ever-more avaricious world – much like the original inhabitants of Eden. For "their isolated condition has not well fitted [them] for the jostle of active life, or to meet the buffets of fortune, where every man seeks only his own and not his neighbor's good."[23]

However fragile its circumstance, the isolated community of Pitcairn appeared to have found something nobody else in the modern world had found: happiness. "Probably there is no community in the world, where more real happiness is enjoyed," noted the *Western Intelligencer* of Hudson, Ohio.[24] The perception remained firmly entrenched as late as 1889, when the *Milwaukee Sentinel* could entitle a short piece on Pitcairn "A Happy Spot on Earth: No Money, No Individual Property, No Sickness, No Crime on Pitcairn Island."[25] To find Utopia on an isolated Pacific Island is, perhaps, not terribly surprising. Islands and Utopia had been synonymous at least since Sir Thomas More. As the historian John Gillis has written in his *Islands of the Mind*, "From the beginning, [the] Utopian mode of thought fastened on islands." The reason for this, Gillis suggests, is their liminality. "Islands had long been perceived as thresholds. Their status as liminal place, somewhere between land and water, made them particularly attractive to both religious and utopian thinkers."[26] In splendid isolation, then, the Pitcairners fashioned what Britons and Americans had been dreaming about for centuries: a place of perfect harmony.

We could continue down this road, exploring just what it was about the Pacific and this particular place that fed the nineteenth-century utopian longing or that made it possible for so many to conclude that antebellum Eden had arisen in this particular, remote corner of the globe. Given the limitations of space, it is perhaps best to shift to the following, much belated, intervention.

As nearly everyone who recounted its story observed, Pitcairn and its inhabitants were the product of rebellion – rebellion against one of the most vaunted institutions of the modern world: the British navy. For Americans, one can imagine the appeal of this David and Goliath story. The mutineers, unjustly treated by an effete ruler who, isolated in his quarters and unable to grasp the sufferings of ordinary and honourable men, left them no choice but violent revolt. The story lines are all quite familiar and comfortable. But the story of Pitcairn is really not the story of one single revolt. It is actually the story of at least two revolts, the second occurring several years after the mutineers initially settled the island. It turns out that the Pitcairn colony was, in addition to being the product of a mutiny against the strongest arm of the British Empire, also a rebellion against the Empire's most troubled and troubling institution: slavery.

The *Bounty* colonists (who were the second group to colonize Pitcairn)[27] settled the island in early 1790. Their party consisted of twenty-six people in total: nine mutineers, including the mutiny's leader Fletcher Christian; a Tahitian "wife" for each mutineer; and four Tahitian men and two Tubuaian men, the latter having joined the mutineers shortly after the mutiny. In addition, two of the Tahitian men brought wives of their own. By the time the *Topaz* arrived, only one of the original male colonists had survived – John Adams. The fate of the rest, not surprisingly, is somewhat murky. There are a variety of accounts, some relayed by Mayhew Folger, some by Adams himself, others gleaned from the now-lost journal of mid-shipman Edward Young, and still another related by Jenny, the Tahitian wife of mutineer and colonist Isaac Martin. The latter was interviewed by a missionary in the early 1820s after returning to Tahiti. In many details these accounts clash. But in several important ones, they are in agreement.

The first of these is that upon arrival at Pitcairn, the mutineers did what any good colonizing Briton would do: they divided the land. First to be chosen was a site for a town, safely concealed from any coastal traffic and readily defended from intruders. Here the colonists would build their dwellings. The rest of the island was then divided among the white mutineers. Exactly what this meant is not clear, but judging from patterns in other British settlements, it involved the partitioning of productive or potentially productive land. On Pitcairn, this likely included not only wooded lands and potential farmlands, but also rocky coastal terrain where birds and their eggs could be gathered. What is more significant for our present purposes, though, is precisely who was given claim to these lands: the white mutineers. The Polynesian men and women would "own" no land. As for the Polynesian men, there appear to have been no provisions whatsoever to afford them any kind of independent existence. Insofar as they would engage in any productive labour, it would be at the behest of the English mutineers. What does this mean? It could have meant that the non-white men were to be treated as wage labourers of some sort, their wages coming as a fraction of what they helped the mutineers produce. But no account suggests as much. The term most commonly used to describe these men is "servants." But servitude suggests a temporary or transient state. And the bondage with which these men were burdened was not, in the end, temporary. After all, as far as the Englishmen were concerned, once the *Bounty* was burned – which it was, shortly after the settlement was established – there was virtually no hope of leaving the island. This may not have been the Polynesians' assumption, given their sense of the navigability of the Polynesian "Sea of Islands." But judging by their treatment, it became the governing assumption of their English captors.[28]

In an 1825 interview conducted by British naval captain Frederick Beechey, an aged Adams recalled the condition of the "black" men. As communicated through Beechey, Adams said that "the island was divided into equal portions, but to the exclusion of the poor blacks, who being only friends of the seamen, were not considered as entitled to the same privilege. Obliged to lend their assistance to the others in order to procure a subsistence, they thus, from being their friends, in the course of time, became their slaves."[29] Whether we call these men slaves or not, they had clearly been relegated to a bound status. And while nothing of either the scope or historic cruelty of the Atlantic slave trade existed in the Pacific, there was a Pacific slave trade that, much like its Atlantic counterpart, was an outgrowth of European colonialism. For the most part, this has been associated with the period during and after the American Civil War, a time when sharply rising cotton prices drove cotton producers to Australasia and a sharply curtailed Atlantic slave trade drove South American slavers to Rapanui and other Pacific Islands.[30] The Pitcairn case suggests that similar patterns of enslavement were present many decades earlier. Much like the bound Polynesian men (and women) of Pitcairn, so these later slaves were initially lured aboard European and American vessels by friendly seafarers purportedly seeking companionship or trade. As the practice grew better known among islanders, slavers resorted to night raids or "Blackbirding," a name derived from dark attire donned by raiders. The captives were eventually imprisoned below deck and taken to distant plantations in Fiji, Australia, Peru, and elsewhere. In this sense, their condition is much like that of Atlantic-basin slaves: enslavement entailed not just the transformation of human beings into chattel but also what Orlando Patterson calls "natal alienation," or forced severance of ancestral social and cultural ties, and the imposition of a permanent alien status.[31]

It should be noted that in the era after abolition, the conduct of Pacific slavers appeared especially barbaric, perhaps because it so profoundly violated the Edenic reputation of Polynesia – a reputation owing much to the popular Pitcairn story. In 1871, the *New York Times* reported that the "slave kidnappers of the Pacific are, if possible, more brutal than were their fellows on the African Coast." One witness told the paper that between fifteen and twenty vessels were engaged in the nefarious trade, carrying captive Polynesians from their island homes to cotton plantations to the west. Instead of purchasing these slaves from indigenous traders, the Pacific slave traders simply captured them, usually putting a torch to their thatched huts such that "the poor, scared creatures are born down upon and handcuffed." Not surprisingly, the effect of all this brutality was to render the formerly peaceable Pacific Islanders "aggressive as all savages will when hunted like wild beasts."[32] In the case of Pitcairn, a similar process of enslavement and abuse yielded similar degrees of aggression and, ultimately, rebellion.

Shortly after the colony was settled, the Tahitian wife of seaman John Williams was fatally injured while hunting for birds' eggs. Distraught and no doubt suffering from the absence of household labour, Williams threatened to leave the island aboard one of the small boats remaining from the *Bounty*. But fearing that the loss of Williams would leave the colony without his prized metal-working skills, the other mutineers persuaded him to take one of the Tahitian men's wives, a gesture that suggests the servile status not only of the "black" men but of their wives as well. Apparently this arrangement elicited the first plans for rebellion among the slaves. But the conspiracy was discovered and, in a fashion typical of slave regimes, four of the slaves purchased their lives by agreeing to kill the two alleged lead conspirators.

The aftermath of these events was that the surviving Polynesian men faced much harsher treatment, particularly at the hands of two former able-bodied seamen, Matthew Quintal and William McCoy. Quintal is notable for being the first seaman punished aboard the *Bounty*, having received two dozen lashes for "insolence and mutinous behavior"; McCoy is notable as the island's liquor distiller. He had turned the Island's *ti* plant into a potent spirit that, in the words of the *Bounty* mutiny's most distinguished historian, the late Greg Dening, "would drive him insane and, in the last months before October 1793, incite his three companions (Quintal, Isaac Martin, also an ordinary seaman, and John Mills, the gunner's mate) to even crueler treatment of the four Tahitian men."[33] The year 1793 was *annus horribilis* for the Pitcairn settlement. Unwilling to endure further humiliation and abuse, the slaves revolted that October, killing five Englishmen – including Fletcher Christian – with axes and muskets and driving the rest into hiding. The day of the revolt was, in Beechey's gloss on Adams's account, "a day of emancipation to the blacks, who were now masters of the island."[34] But by the end of the month, infighting among the rebels and retaliation by the surviving mutineers and their wives, left the rebels dead. Now, the adult male population of the island was reduced to four – all of them mutineers, and all but Adams soon to meet their maker: McCoy died from drink; Quintal was axed to death by Edward Young; and Young died of natural causes.

Paradise born of blood and bondage. That is the early history of Pitcairn. It is perhaps not surprising that so little of this story found its way into nineteenth-century depictions of the island paradise. Somehow American and British observers could accept the notion that this particular egalitarian Christian Eden was born of a relatively bloodless mutiny. It made much less sense to imagine such a place as the product of a revolt against enslavement and bondage.

In all the newspapers and magazines surveyed for this paper I found only a single substantial instance in which slavery is acknowledged as an ingredient in Pitcairn's early history. It appears in a 1911 magazine article entitled "A Ready-Made Mendelian Laboratory in Which Human Beings are Bred." The author's interest is the degree to which Mendelian laws of biological inheritance hold for the human race. The Pitcairners, the author believed, offered the ideal laboratory for testing the theory because, unlike mixed-race peoples elsewhere in the world, the socially isolated Pitcairners bore no shame about their origins. The researcher could thus expect a clear, transparent account of the racial composition of everyone descended from the original settlers of Pitcairn. "Everywhere [else, in contrast,] the mixed bloods boast of their white origins and alas! are ashamed of their black mothers and grandmothers; thus the pedigrees which are given commonly lack the scientist's first essential, truth." Why this new scientific idealization of the Pitcairners would accompany one of the few candid references to their historical origins is unclear. But for this author, the Native "servants" who accompanied the colonists were simply slaves, for in the eyes of a British "man-of-war's men, ... a native servant was merely a slave." And "slavery proved the serpent of [the colonists'] Eden."[35]

What are we to conclude about the grave historical amnesia that for so long accompanied the Pitcairn story – at least as it was reported to the largely white, largely middle-class consumers of popular print? Is there nothing more to it than demand? For the nineteenth-century British and American publics, a story of earnest and hard-working people rebelling against oppression and reconstituting themselves as a peaceful, moral, and orderly society would have had obvious appeal. On the other hand, a story of slavery and slaughter – as opposed to one of slavery and liberation – would hardly enhance the gentle pleasures of the Victorian parlour.

But perhaps there is another way to interpret the Pitcairn story. Perhaps it reflects liberal, transatlantic ideals that shaped the nineteenth-century imperial imagination. Among those ideals was the notion that Pacific empire, even at its bloodiest, could somehow be exceptional, that it could escape the cycles of enslavement, despair, rebellion, and slaughter that characterized so much of Atlantic empire. Here at Pitcairn, after all, was a colony born of the quest for liberty and nurtured by Christian benevolence and communitarian politics. Empire in the Pacific would be, so the Pitcairn narrative demonstrated, what it had never become in the Atlantic. Even a colony born of mutinous conflict would face a future defined by egalitarianism, social harmony, and Christian charity. In other words, it was one thing to imagine that Pitcairn was a new kind of colony, removed from the processes of Atlantic history, their cruel labour systems, their bloody revolutions and rebellions, their mindless majoritarianism, their greed, and their abandonment of Christian morality. It was altogether another to face Pitcairn for what it was: a place of brutal conflict, enslavement, and violent, bloody rebellion. The Pitcairn of history was, in other words, the kind of colony that characterized most of Britain's imperial forays in the early-modern Atlantic. What could have been less consistent with the liberal imperial ideal, the governing doctrine of the "white man's burden," than this kind of imperial reality?

NOTES

* For his generous comments on an early version of this paper, the author thanks Matt D. Childs.

1 Twain, "The Great Revolution in Pitcairn" (1903); London, "The Seed of McCoy" (1909); Bryant, "A Song of Pitcairn's Island" (1832). See also the poem by Mary Russell Mitford, "Christina; or, the Maid of the South Seas" (1811). The number of times Pitcairn appears in the news is obviously not easily measured, but a search for mentions of "Pitcairn Island" in the Gale *Nineteenth-Century U.S. Newspapers* lists 257 instances. *New-York Spectator*, Thursday, 11 June 1840. And, similarly, *The New Hampshire Statesman*, Saturday, 9 July 1853, issue 1676, col. f: "The subject is one which is familiar to large numbers of the reading public; for, being of romantic character, and many of the occurrences taking place upon the seas, the story of the Bounty, the Mutineers, Pitcairn's Island, and its People, has attained

almost the same position amongst books as that of Robinson Crusoe. The narrative has been so generally read that only the most recent news from the descendants of the mutineers can be of interest."

2 It should be noted that the first American book to be published with an account of the *Topaz*'s discovery (based on the unpublished journal of *Topaz* Captain Mayhew Folger) was the Boston Sealer and merchant Captain Amasa Delano's *Narrative of Voyages and Travels, in the Northern and Southern Hemispheres* ... (Boston, 1817). Captain Delano is the basis for the fictional Captain Delano in Melville's astonishing "Benito Cereno." And Delano's description of a slave rebellion aboard the Spanish ship *Tryal* is the basis for "Benito Cereno's" strange setting aboard the Spanish ship *San Dominick*, ruled by a motley horde of rebel slaves and white sailors, its officers (aristocrats) having died or been killed, its Captain (Cereno) mad and delirious. I am indebted to Professor Günther Lottes for drawing my attention to this aspect of "Benito Cereno."

3 See, for example, Trevor Lummis, *Pitcairn Island: Life and Death in Eden* (Aldershot, 1997). The defining contemporary scholarly treatment of the mutiny and its aftermath remains Greg Dening, *Mr. Bligh's Bad Language: Passion, Power and Theatre on the Bounty* (Cambridge, 1992). But also see Caroline Alexander's masterful *The Bounty: The True Story of the Mutiny on the Bounty* (New York, 2003).

4 On the Pacific and European empire, an early seminal treatment is J.C. Beaglehole, *The Exploration of the Pacific*, 3rd ed. (Stanford, 1966). More recent treatments include Derek Howse, ed., *Background to Discovery: Pacific Exploration from Dampier to Cook* (Berkeley, 1990); Glyndwr Williams, *The Great South Sea: English Voyages and Encounters, 1570–1750* (New Haven, 1997); *The Prize of All the Oceans: The Dramatic True Story of Admiral Anson's Voyage Round the World and How He Seized the Spanish Treasure Galleon* (New York, 2000); Harry Liebersohn, *The Traveler's World: Europe to the Pacific* (Cambridge, MA, 2006); Edward G. Gray, *The Making of John Ledyard: Empire and Ambition in the Life of an Early American Traveler* (New Haven, 2007); Nicholas Thomas, *Islanders: The Pacific in the Age of Empire* (New Haven, 2010).

5 Of those scholars emphasizing geopolitical and imperial concerns, the most influential in recent years has been Alan Frost. See in particular his *Botany Bay Mirages: Illusions of Australia's Convict Beginnings* (Melbourne, 1994) and *The Global Reach of Empire: Britain's Maritime Expansion in the Indian and Pacific Oceans, 1764–1814* (Melbourne, 2003). For the "traditionalist" perspective, which interprets Australia's founding as largely

a function of Britain's domestic convict problems, see David Mackay, *A Place of Exile: The European Settlement of New South Wales* (New York, 1985) and Robert Hughes, *The Fatal Shore* (New York, 1987). Also see Mollie Gillen's critique of Frost, "The Botany Bay Decision, 1786: Convicts, Not Empire," *English Historical Review* 97 (385) (1982): 740–66 and, in response, Alan Frost and Mollie Gillen, "Botany Bay: An Imperial Venture of the 1780s," 100 (395) (1985): 309–30. I am indebted to Winfield Scott Craig for his guidance on this debate.

6 See Richard B. Sheridan, "Captain Bligh, the Breadfruit and the Botanic Gardens of Jamaica," *Journal of Caribbean History* 23 (1) (1989): 28–50. Elizabeth M. DeLoughrey, "Globalizing the Routes of Breadfruit and Other Bounties," *Journal of Colonialism and Colonial History* 8 (3) (Winter 2007), http://muse.jhu.edu/journals/journal_of_colonialism_and_colonial_history/v008/8.3deloughrey.html.

7 Christopher, "'The Slave Trade is Merciful Compared to [This]': Slave Traders, Convict Transportation, and the Abolitionists," in Christopher, Cassandra Pybus, and Marcus Rediker, eds, *Many Middle Passages: Forced Migration and the Making of the Modern World* (Berkeley, 2007), 111; and Pybus, "Bound for Botany Bay: John Martin's Voyage to Australia," ibid., 106. Also see Pybus, *Epic Journeys of Freedom: Runaway Slaves of the American Revolution and Their Global Quest for Liberty* (Boston, 2006), esp. chap. 8; and Christopher, *A Merciless Place: The Fate of Britain's Convicts after the American Revolution* (New York, 2011), esp. pp. 336–8.

8 This is not to say that stories of Atlantic rebellion defy telling. Several important recent studies include Matt D. Childs, *The 1812 Aponte Rebellion in Cuba and the Struggle against Atlantic Slavery* (Chapel Hill, 2006), Douglas R. Egerton, *Gabriel's Rebellion: The Virginia Slave Conspiracies of 1800 and 1802* (Chapel Hill, 1993), and Jill Lepore, *New York Burning: Liberty, Slavery, and Conspiracy in Eighteenth-Century Manhattan* (New York, 2005).

9 In suggesting that there are ways Atlantic slavery shaped Pacific empire, or that slavery and rebellion existed in the Pacific as well as the Atlantic, I do not mean to suggest commensurability between patterns of forced labour and resistance in the Pacific and the Atlantic – or, for that matter, elsewhere in the colonized world. Nor do I mean to suggest that patterns of forced labour and resistance within the Pacific basin can themselves be understood as commensurate. Obviously patterns in Kamchatka, the Aleutian Islands, Spanish America, and elsewhere suggest their own particularities, as do those in the many South Pacific locales where captive labour was employed. What I am suggesting, rather, is that

patterns of forced labour and rebellion evident in the British Atlantic can be seen across the eighteenth-century British imperial world, albeit widely varying in their form. To make bolder claims about the global nature of forced labour in the period under discussion is made all the more difficult by the absence of any substantial syntheses on coerced labour, slavery, and rebellion in the Pacific. While there are a number of particular studies, some of which are cited below, there are to my knowledge no large-scale attempts – akin to what scholars such as Ira Berlin, David Brion Davis, Herbert Klein, John Thornton, and others have done for the Atlantic and the Western hemisphere – to characterize the intersection of captive labour, or really any form of labour, and European empire on the Pacific littoral. The limits of current scholarship are perhaps reflected in the modest treatment of imperial labour regimes evident in two acclaimed recent syntheses. See Matt K. Matsuda, *Pacific Worlds: A History of Seas, Peoples, and Cultures* (Cambridge, 2012) and Thomas, *Islanders.*

10 Shillibeer, *A Narrative of the Briton's Voyage, to Pitcairn's Island; including an interesting sketch of the present state of the Brazils and of Spanish South America …* (London, 1818), 89.

11 The *Quarterly Review* article is reprinted in R.D. Madison, ed., *The Bounty Mutiny: William Bligh and Edward Christian* (New York, 2001), 223–6.

12 "Revivals of Religion: Revival at Sea," *The Religious Intelligencers*, 7 July 1827, p. 91.

13 *Western Intelligencer, Religious, Literary and Political* (Hudson, OH), Tuesday, 26 May 1829, issue 18, col. D.

14 *New Hampshire Statesman*, Saturday, 9 July 1853, issue 1676, col. f.

15 (New-Lisbon, OH) Saturday, 1 May 1852, issue 33. See also *Punch*, Saturday, 2 January 1869, p. 282. Also see John Keane, *The Life and Death of Democracy* (New York, 2009), 534–40.

16 *The producing man's companion: an essay on the present state of society, moral, political and physical, in England …* 2nd ed. with additions (London, 1832), 34–45.

17 Thomas Doubleday, *The true law of population shewn to be connected with the food of the people*, 2nd ed., with a postscript (London, 1843), 68.

18 *The Christian Socialist: A Journal of Association* (London, 1851), 127. Nancy Bolles to her sisters, 25 March 1851, p. 3, VFM 1655, Manuscripts Collection, G.W. Blunt White Library, Mystic Seaport Museum, Inc., Online Collections: http://library.mysticseaport.org/initiative/PageText.cfm?PageNum=1&BibID=28239.

19 Acraeus, *God's laws versus corn-laws: a letter to His Grace the Archbishop of Canterbury / from a dignitary of the English Church* (London, 1846), 35–6.
20 *Bangor Register and Penobscot Advertiser* (Bangor, ME), Thursday, 9 August 1821, issue 32, col. C.
21 *Western Intelligencer, Religious, Literary and Political* (Hudson, OH), Tuesday, 26 May 1829, issue 18, col. D.
22 *Daily National Intelligencer* (Washington, DC), Thursday, 9 September 1847, issue 10,777, col. F.
23 *Weekly Herald* (New York) Saturday, 28 May 1853, issue 22, col. F.
24 *Western Intelligencer, Religious, Literary and Political* (Hudson, OH), Tuesday, 26 May 1829, issue 18, col. D. Similarly, *Bangor Register and Penobscot Advertiser* (Bangor, ME), Thursday, 9 August 1821, issue 32; "They [the Pitcairnes] are perhaps the happiest people on the face of the globe; they know nothing bad, but live all together under the care and directions of Mr. Adams, and much credit is due to him."
25 Sunday, 26 May 1889, p. 4.
26 *Islands of the Mind: How the Human Imagination Created the Atlantic World* (New York, 2004), 76.
27 Jared Diamond, *Collapse: How Societies Choose to Fail or Succeed* (New York, 2005), chap. 3.
28 A useful discussion of the transformation of captives into slaves is Leland Donald, *Aboriginal Slavery on the Northwest Coast of America* (Berkeley, 1997), 69–73.
29 This and the other known accounts of the early history of the Pitcairn colony are reprinted in Madison, ed., *The Bounty Mutiny*. The above quote appears on p. 245. Also see the journal of Beechey's first officer, George Peard, in Barry M. Gough, ed., *To the Pacific and Arctic with Beechey: The Journal of Lieutenant George Peard of H.M.S.* Blossom, *1825–1828* (Cambridge, 1973), esp. 75–91.
30 H.E. Maude, *Slavers in Paradise: The Peruvian Slave Trade in Polynesia, 1862–64* (Stanford, 1981); Roslyn Jolly, "Piracy, Slavery, and the Imagination of Empire in Stevenson's Pacific Fiction," *Victorian Literature and Culture* 35 (1) (2007): 157–73; Gerald Horne, *The White Pacific: U.S. Imperialism and Black Slavery in the South Seas after the Civil War* (Honolulu, 2007), chap. 2; and Merze Tate and Fidele Foy, "Slavery and Racism in South Pacific Annexations," *Journal of Negro History* 50 (1) (January 1965), 1–21; Thomas, *Islanders*, 192–200.
31 Patterson, *Slavery and Social Death: A Comparative Study* (Cambridge, MA, 1982), 5–11. Also see Paul E. Lovejoy, *Transformations in Slavery: A History of Slavery in Africa* (Cambridge, 1983), esp. 2–3.

32 *New York Times,* Wednesday, 10 December 1871, p. 4. See also the account in "The Polynesian Slave Trade," ibid., Wednesday, 15 February 1873, p. 8.

33 Dening, *Mr. Bligh's Bad Language,* 319. Dening provides the fullest account of the rebellion, although the origins of his account are not always clear. See pp. 318–21. Also see Lummis, *Pitcairn Island,* chap. 5. Quote about Quintal's punishment is from Alexander, *The Bounty,* 87.

34 Madison, ed., *The Bounty Mutiny,* 248.

35 *Current Literature* 51 (1) (July 1911): 55.

Contributors

Andrew Cayton, Warner Woodring Chair in Early American History at The Ohio State University, is the author of *Love in the Time of Revolution: Transatlantic Literary Radicalism and Historical Change, 1793–1818,* and, with Fred Anderson, of *The Dominion of War: Empire and Liberty in North America, 1500–2000.*

Sarah Crabtree is an assistant professor of history at San Francisco State University. She is the author of *Holy Nation: The Quaker Itinerant Ministry in an Age of Revolution* (2015).

Anthony Galluzzo is a visiting assistant professor of English at Colby College.

Jenna Gibbs is an associate professor of history at Florida International University, where she teaches eighteenth- and nineteenth-century American and Atlantic cultural history. Her first book, *Performing the Temple of Liberty: Slavery, Theater and Popular Culture in London and Philadelphia, 1760s–1850s,* was published in 2014, and she has also published several related articles. She is currently working on her second monograph, *Evangelicalism, Slavery, and Empire: The Global Latrobe Family, 1750s–1850s.*

Edward G. Gray is professor of history and department chair at Florida State University. His book *Tom Paine's Iron Bridge: Building a United States* will be published in 2016.

Saree Makdisi is professor of English at UCLA and comparative literature at UCLA and the author of, most recently, *Reading William Blake.*

Iain McCalman is a professorial research fellow in the Department of History, University of Sydney, and co-director of the Sydney (University) Environment Institute. He is a fellow of three learned societies and former president of the Australian Academy of the Humanities. His prize-winning book *The Reef – A Passionate History* was published in 2014. He is an officer of the Order of Australia for services to history and the humanities.

Randall McGowen is professor of history at the University of Oregon and immediate past president of the Pacific Coast Conference on British Studies. He is the co-author, with Donna Andrew, of *The Perreaus and Mrs. Rudd: Forgery and Betrayal in 18th Century London*, and co-editor, with David Garland and Michael Meranze, of *American's Death Penalty: Between Past and Present.* He has written some thirty articles on aspects of crime and punishment over the long eighteenth century.

Michael Meranze is professor of history at UCLA. He is the author of *Laboratories of Virtue: Punishment, Revolution, and Authority in Philadelphia, 1760–1835*, and co-editor, with David Garland and Randall McGowen, of *American's Death Penalty: Between Past and Present.* He has written numerous articles on the relationships between culture, law, and violence.

Catherine O'Donnell is an associate professor of history at Arizona State University and author of *Men of Letters in the Early Republic: Cultivating Forums of Citizenship* (2008). She researches Catholicism in the Atlantic World and is writing a biography of Elizabeth Ann Seton.

Aris Sarafianos received his PhD from the University of Manchester. He has been awarded a number of fellowships in the United States and the United Kingdom. His publications focus on the synergies between art history and the history of biomedical sciences since the eighteenth century. He is currently assistant professor at the University of Ioannina, Greece.

Index

THE UCLA CLARK MEMORIAL LIBRARY SERIES

General Editor: Barbara Fuchs

1. *Wilde Writings: Contextual Conditions*, edited by Joseph Bristow
2. *Enchanted Ground: Reimagining John Dryden*, edited by Jayne Lewis and Maximillian E. Novak
3. *Culture and Authority in the Baroque*, edited by Massimo Ciavolella and Patrick Coleman
4. *Ritual, Routine, and Regime: Repetition in Early Modern British and European Cultures*, edited by Lorna Clymer
5. *Momigliano and Antiquarianism: Foundations of the Modern Cultural Sciences*, edited by Peter N. Miller
6. *Monarchisms in the Age of Enlightenment: Liberty, Patriotism, and the Common Good*, edited by Hans Blom, John Christian Laursen, and Luisa Simonetti
7. *Thinking Impossibilities: The Intellectual Legacy of Amos Funkenstein*, edited by Robert S. Westman and David Biale
8. *Discourses of Tolerance and Intolerance in the European Enlightenment*, edited by Hans Erich Bödeker, Clorinda Donato, and Peter Hanns Reill
9. *The Age of Projects*, edited by Maximillian E. Novak
10. *Acculturation and Its Discontents: The Italian Jewish Experience between Exclusion and Inclusion*, edited by David N. Myers, Massimo Ciavolella, Peter H. Reill, and Geoffrey Symcox
11. *Defoe's Footprints: Essays in Honour of Maximillian E. Novak*, edited by Robert M. Maniquis and Carl Fisher
12. *Women, Religion, and the Atlantic World (1600–1800)*, edited by Daniella Kostroun and Lisa Vollendorf
13. *Braudel Revisited: The Mediterranean World, 1600–1800*, edited by Gabriel Piterberg, Teofilo F. Ruiz, and Geoffrey Symcox
14. *Structures of Feeling in Seventeenth-Century Cultural Expression*, edited by Susan McClary
15. *Godwinian Moments*, edited by Robert M. Maniquis and Victoria Myers
16. *Vital Matters: Eighteenth-Century Views of Conception, Life, and Death*, edited by Helen Deutsch and Mary Terrall
17. *Redrawing the Map of Early Modern English Catholicism*, edited by Lowell Gallagher
18. *Space and Self in Early Modern European Cultures*, edited by David Warren Sabean and Malina Stefanovska
19. *Wilde Discoveries: Traditions, Histories, Archives*, edited by Joseph Bristow

20. *Jesuit Accounts of the Colonial Americas: Intercultural Transfers, Intellectual Disputes, and Textualities*, edited by Marc André Bernier, Clorinda Donato, and Hans-Jürgen Lüsebrink
21. *Skepticism and Political Thought in the Seventeenth and Eighteenth Centuries*, edited by John Christian Laursen and Gianni Paganini
22. *Representing Imperial Rivalry in the Early Modern Mediterranean*, edited by Barbara Fuchs and Emily Weissbourd
23. *Imagining the British Atlantic after the American Revolution*, edited by Michael Meranze and Saree Makdisi

www.ingramcontent.com/pod-product-compliance
Lightning Source LLC
LaVergne TN
LVHW041112090826
844660LV00061B/792/J

* 9 7 8 1 4 4 2 6 5 0 6 9 5 *